Critical Muslim 19

Nature

Editor: Ziauddin Sardar

Deputy Editors: Hassan Mahamdallie, Samia Rahman, Shanon Shah

Senior Editors: Syed Nomanul Haq, Aamer Hussein, Ehsan Masood, Ebrahim Moosa

Publisher: Michael Dwyer

Managing Editor (Hurst Publishers): Daisy Leitch

Cover Design: Fatima Jamadar

Associate Editors: Tahir Abbas, Alev Adil, Nazry Bahrawi, Merryl Wyn Davies, Abdelwahhab El-Affendi, Marilyn Hacker, Nader Hashemi, Jeremy Henzell-Thomas, Vinay Lal, Iftikhar Malik, Boyd Tonkin

International Advisory Board: Karen Armstrong, William Dalrymple, Anwar Ibrahim, Robert Irwin, Bruce Lawrence, Ashis Nandy, Ruth Padel, Bhikhu Parekh, Barnaby Rogerson, Malise Ruthven

Critical Muslim is published quarterly by C. Hurst & Co. (Publishers) Ltd. on behalf of and in conjunction with Critical Muslim Ltd. and the Muslim Institute, London. *Critical Muslim* acknowledges the support of the Aziz Foundation, London.

All correspondence to Muslim Institute, CAN Mezzanine, 49-51 East Road, London N1 6AH, United Kingdom

e-mail for editorial: editorial@criticalmuslim.com

The editors do not necessarily agree with the opinions expressed by the contributors. We reserve the right to make such editorial changes as may be necessary to make submissions to *Critical Muslim* suitable for publication.

C. Hurst & Co (Publishers) Ltd., 41 Great Russell Street, London WC1B 3PL

ISBN: 978-1-849046-749 ISSN: 2048-8475

To subscribe or place an order by credit/debit card or cheque (pounds sterling only) please contact Kathleen May at the Hurst address above or e-mail kathleen@hurstpub.co.uk

Tel: 020 7255 2201

A one year subscription, inclusive of postage (four issues), costs £50 (UK), £65 (Europe) and £75 (rest of the world).

IIIT Publications

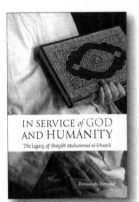

IN SERVICE OF GOD AND HUMANITY
The Legacy of Shaykh Muhammad al-Ghazali

Benaouda Bensaid

Renowned Islamic scholar al-Ghazali (d. 1996), was an outspoken critic, both of Muslim societies for their impoverished, poorly educated populations and social injustice, and of Muslims whose moral basis was fast eroding. He worked tirelessly to improve Muslim life, lay the grounds for a better elucidation of Islam, and call for a progressive, well-funded education system for all.

ISBN 978-1-56564-663-6 pb
ISBN 978-1-56564-664-3 hb
2015

THE MIRACULOUS LANGUAGE OF THE QUR'AN
Evidence of Divine Origin

Bassam Saeh

The work compares Qur'anic language to the language of pre-Islamic poetry, and the language of the Arabs past and present, to make the case that an important strand of the Qur'an's linguistic miraculousness is the fact that its Arabic was completely new.

ISBN 978-1-56564-665-0 pb
2015

Marketing Manager IIIT (USA) 500 Grove Street, Herndon, VA 20170-4735, USA
Tel: 703 471 1133 ext. 108 Fax: 703 471 3922 • E-mail: sales@iiit.org Website: www.iiit.org

Kube Publishing Ltd MMC, Ratby Lane, Markfield, Leicester, LE67 9SY, UK
Tel: 01530 249 230 Fax: 01530 249 656 • E-mail: info@kubepublishing.com
Website: www.kubepublishing.com

HALAL FOOD FOUNDATION

Halal Is Much More Than Food

The Halal Food Foundation (HFF) is a registered charity that aims to make the concept of halal more accessible and mainstream. We want people to know that halal does not just pertain to food – halal is a lifestyle.

The Foundation pursues its goals through downloadable resources, events, social networking, school visits, pursuing and funding scientific research on issues of food and health, and its monthly newsletter. We work for the community and aim at the gradual formation of a consumer association. We aim to educate and inform; and are fast becoming the first port of call on queries about halal issues. We do not talk at people, we listen to them.

If you have any queries, comments, ideas, or would just like to voice your opinion - please get in contact with us.

Halal Food Foundation

109 Fulham Palace Road,
Hammersmith, London, W6 8JA
Charity number: 1139457
Website: www.halalfoodfoundation.co.uk
E-mail: info@halalfoodfoundation.co.uk

 @HFF_UK

 Halal Food Foundation

The Barbary Figs

by

Rashid Boudjedra

Translated by
André Naffis-Sahely

Buy a copy of Rashid Boudjedra's *The Barbary Figs* at
www.hauspublishing.com or by calling +44(0)20 7838 9055
and a recieve a copy of Khaled al-Berry's memoir
Life is More Beautiful than Paradise free.

RASHID AND OMAR are cousins who find themselves side by side on a flight from Algiers to Constantine. During the hour-long journey, the pair will exhume their past, their boyhood in French Algeria during the 1940s and their teenage years fighting in the bush during the revolution. Rashid, the narrator, has always resented Omar, who despite all his worldly successes, has been on the run from the ghosts of his past, ghosts that Rashid has set himself the task of exorcising. Rashid peppers his account with chilling episodes from Algerian history, from the savageries of the French invasion in the 1830s, to the repressive regime that is in place today.

RASHID BOUDJEDRA has routinely been called one of North Africa's leading writers since his debut, *La Répudiation*, was published in 1969, earning the author the first of many fatwas. While he wrote his first six novels in French, Boudjedra switched to Arabic in 1982 and wrote another six novels in the language before returning to French in 1994. *The Barbary Figs* was awarded the Prix du Roman Arabe 2010.

CM19

July–September 2016

CONTENTS

NATURE

ARTS AND LETTERS

REVIEWS

ET CETERA

Critical Muslim

Subscribe to Critical Muslim

Now in its fifth year in print, Hurst is pleased to announce that *Critical Muslim* is also available online. Users can access the site for just £3.30 per month – or for those with a print subscription it is included as part of the package. In return, you'll get access to everything in the series (including our entire archive), and a clean, accessible reading experience for desktop computers and handheld devices — entirely free of advertising.

Full subscription

The print edition of *Critical Muslim* is published quarterly in January, April, July and October. As a subscriber to the print edition, you'll receive new issues directly to your door, as well as full access to our digital archive.

United Kingdom £50/year
Europe £65/year
Rest of the World £75/year

Digital Only

Immediate online access to *Critical Muslim*

Browse the full *Critical Muslim* archive

Cancel any time

£3.30 per month

www.criticalmuslim.io

NATURE

INTRODUCTION
OUT IN THE OPEN

Jeremy Henzell-Thomas

I need to begin with a confession and clear statement of intent. I'd like to write about nature not from a distance, neither as an object of abstract study – a disengaged academic or critical exercise – nor as an occasion for the recital of well-worn platitudes or pieties gleaned from religious texts, but as a practitioner and passionate advocate who has spent a lifetime immersed in nature of one form or another. I don't think that people are necessarily inspired to change their lives, break down barriers, activate and develop the full range of their faculties, or contribute in any active way to the hugely important enterprise of protecting the planet from environmental devastation, by being given religious texts, whether from the Qur'an, the Bible, the Torah, the Vedas, the Sutras, or any other, especially when those texts are not actually lived in any deeply experiential sense by those who repeat them for the edification of others.

For this reason, there is much in this issue that speaks of direct engagement with nature and authentic first-hand experience of the natural environment in its manifold living forms and landscapes. It can be seen through the creative imagination (in its deepest spiritual sense) of the metaphysician or mystic who can 'read' the rich tapestry of nature as the 'displayed book' of beautiful and majestic 'signs' that give overwhelming evidence of the existence and beneficent purpose of the Creator. And, as the Qur'an tells us, those signs are visible in the furthest horizons of the universe and within the soul of the human being (41:53) in his or her role as 'vicegerent' of God. It comes through in the empirical dimension encompassed by sensory experience, and the richly evocative and concrete images of the sheer splendour and riveting beauty of nature seen through the searching eye of the poet. It speaks to us through the aesthetic sensibility of the garden designer, through the work of practical environmentalism in Scotland and Palestine, and through recourse to well-researched studies which give ample evidence of the physical and psychological benefits of immersion in nature for children and adults. And we are given a preview of inspiring nature education designed to help children to create an intimate spiritual link with the natural world.

I grew up walking the coastline and sandy beaches around the Kentish seaside town where I was born, learning from a young age how to keep my balance as I strode out on the slippery, seaweed-strewn rocks to the water's edge before the tide rolled in. As a twelve-year old living for a while in Bermuda and blessed by dark night skies, I borrowed a telescope from my local public library, and spent three months meticulously mapping the heavens. I remember well the sense of awe and wonder I felt when Saturn with its rings swam into view. Later, as a starry-eyed teenager, I paced the North Downs above my school, reciting the great Nature poets of the Romantic period. To this day, the famous lines of the Lakeland poet William Wordsworth written a few miles above Tintern Abbey – and so naturally and universally 'Qur'anic' in their vision of the all-encompassing Divine Presence in the whole of creation – are still etched on my memory:

> ... And I have felt
> A presence that disturbs me with the joy
> Of elevated thoughts; a sense sublime
> Of something far more deeply interfused,
> Whose dwelling is the light of setting suns,
> And the round ocean and the living air,
> And the blue sky, and in the mind of man:
> A motion and a spirit, that impels
> All thinking things, all objects of all thought,
> And rolls through all things.

And even now, at an age where some might expect me to be thinking of hanging up my walking boots, I walk longer distances than I have ever done before: most recently the 180-mile Pembrokeshire Coast Path over twelve days (with a total ascent of 30,000 feet), and mountain tracks in the Pyrenees. When I walked the hills and crags of the Isle of Man, my father-in-law, a Manxman, used to tell me (with a deliberately playful air of mystery) to watch out for the Moddey Dhoo, a legendary black dog with long shaggy hair and eyes like coals of fire. Of course, I took this in the way it was intended, as a piece of colourful folklore, but I remember well the occasion when I dragooned a Muslim friend to venture half a mile with me into the wilds of Dartmoor. It was a bleak day, and he had the apprehensive look of a man who half-expected the hellish Hound of the Baskervilles to charge at him ravenously out of the mist and rend him limb from limb, or at the very least for him to sink without trace into a treacherous piece of boggy ground.

I cannot pretend not to be struck by how disconnected many of my British Muslim friends are from nature and the countryside. I have yet to meet more than a few who can locate where I live, and when I say that I live in Malvern, many respond with 'What part of London is that?', assuming that I must unquestionably be a city-dweller. This disconnection is confirmed by Zeshan Akhter in her essay describing the nature conservation work of Scottish National Heritage. Asserting that 'ethnic minorities are lagging behind', she goes on to explain that 'public attitude surveys in Britain consistently find that people from Asian and Muslim backgrounds have the least understanding about nature and spend the least amount of time in it undertaking any kind of activity in the countryside, parks or other types of green spaces in towns and cities.' Considered 'hard to reach', they seem largely immune to 'mainstream efforts that aim to inform the public about the environment and to encourage them to spend time outdoors'.

Several years ago, in response to an essay on walking in nature I wrote for a Muslim lifestyle magazine, I was contacted by a number of Muslim readers (and still am to this day) asking me if it was 'safe' to go rambling outdoors in the countryside. One asked me if she might be 'mugged' if she did so, to which I gently replied that she was probably more likely to be mugged on the streets of North London where she lived than in the fells of the Lake District, in a coastal nature reserve in Norfolk or Northumbria, or on a ridge in the Black Mountains in Wales. Others asked me if I knew of a 'Muslim Walking Club' which offered that comforting communitarian sense of safety and belonging. I replied that I usually walked alone, as I found that more liberating and most conducive to deep reflection. If a group was preferred, I suggested that walking was a universal human activity which did not necessitate a distinction between Muslims and non-Muslims, and to my knowledge there was no special mode or style of walking which had somehow been 'Islamised' and thus rendered 'halal', any more than there were 'Islamic' bicycles which gave one a safer or smoother ride. Halfearnestly and half-jokingly I proposed to a Muslim friend that I might start a country rambling club for Muslims, perhaps initially limited to very modest walks of ten miles or less in unchallenging terrain. He laughed and said: 'But you will never get any members. Muslims do not walk anywhere.'

Now, it's all very well for me to occupy the high ground and question Muslim reluctance to step out of the city. There is, of course, a historical explanation for this preference by migrants for close-knit urban communities and the prospects for community solidarity and economic advancement that they provided. And I'm not likely to be the victim of anti-Muslim or any other kind of anti-religious prejudice in this country because of the way I look. After all, I am not someone 'of Muslim appearance', to use the infamous phrase repeated from a Whitehall source by the BBC political editor Nick Robinson in describing the suspected murderers of the soldier Lee Rigby in Woolwich in 2013 – a phrase for which he quickly apologised. I am not of course denying that there are cultural issues, whether actual, assumed or imagined, when it comes to venturing too far beyond the confines (and perceived safety net) of a familiar heritage community. But we surely need, whatever our 'identity', to extend ourselves beyond the limitations, conditions, assumptions and fears we impose upon ourselves – or are imposed upon us by sensationalist media, group-think, peer group pressure, social conventions, or fixed ideas within communities – if we are to reap the inestimable rewards which await us through any kind of 'venturing' beyond familiar territory, whether cultural, environmental, or conceptual.

Despite the fact that Muslim communities may still be 'hard to reach' when it comes to getting them into the outdoors, there are some promising signs of change, especially amongst the younger generation. I discovered this two years ago when I was privileged to be asked to speak on the theme of 'Spirituality and the Outdoors' at an equity symposium on 'Barriers to Participation' at Haworth on the South Pennine Moors as part of the outreach programme organised by the British Mountaineering Council. This was in conjunction with MountainMuslim, an innovative organisation and website that aims to encourage and facilitate more active participation in the outdoors amongst the mainly urban Muslim communities in the UK. It was encouraging to encounter there an enthusiastic cadre of pioneering young Muslims, and most especially, intrepid young Muslim women from the surrounding industrial towns of Bradford, Keighley and Halifax, who were involved in outdoor pursuits ranging from rambling to hill walking and rock climbing, as well as health education, fitness training, and environmental activism. These young Muslims who are striking out in new ways to expand their horizons will surely be an inspiration to others.

The heart of what I tried to express there was that 'immersion in nature' should not be restricted and reduced only to the sense of arduous and challenging physical adventure (and the ultimate inflation of that in the 'conquest' of nature and the adrenaline-fuelled world of 'extreme sports') but needed to embrace the greatest adventure of all, that ongoing holistic education and self-education, at once sensory, cognitive, affective, moral and spiritual by which we discover and nurture our whole being and develop the full range of our God-given faculties. 'He has endowed you with hearing, and sight, and hearts, so that you might have cause to be grateful' (Qur'an 16:78). And I use the English word 'develop' not primarily in the sense of 'training' or 'learning' or 'acquiring skills' but in its original sense derived from Old French *des-voloper,* 'unwrap' or 'unveil'. This, too, echoes the Latin *educere,* 'educe, lead forth, draw out', the source of the intensive form *educare,* 'rear, foster'. The idea of human development as one of the unfolding of divinely endowed faculties points also to one of the most fundamental concepts in Islam, that of *fitra,* often translated as 'primordial disposition', but more simply as 'essential nature', or in Akhter's words, as 'the divine spark with which we are born'. It is that inner compass and natural orientation – the criterion (*furqan*) which enables us to perceive the truth – that accompanies our innate awareness of our divine origin and ultimate place of return. The idea that human nature or 'character' is an innate endowment is also embedded in the origin of the word 'character' itself. It comes from Greek *kharakter,* a derivative of the verb *kharassein,* to 'sharpen, engrave, cut', and hence was applied metaphorically to the particular impress or stamp which marked one thing as different from another – its 'character'. Human character is what is already 'stamped' or 'etched' upon us in accordance with the Divine Prototype or pattern, and as such it is nothing less than the repository of the sacred trust (*amanah*) accorded to the human being as *khalifah,* 'vicegerent'. In his essay on Vicegerency in this issue, Munjed Murad outlines Ibn 'Arabi's metaphysical foundation of the role of the human being as steward, custodian and protector of the earth. Here, the primary responsibility of vicegerency, realised in the form of the Perfect Human Being (*al-insan al-kamil*), is to reflect the totality of the Creator within the human soul, to act as 'Pontifical Man...the reflection of the Centre on the periphery and the echo of the Origin', or to act as the microcosm (*al-'alam al-saghir*) as the mirror of the macrocosm (*al-'alam al-kabir*). Vicegerency is thus 'the unique reflection of the synthesis and totality of the Names of God, the encompassment of all realities, the pupil to God's eye in the world'.

The primary function of the human being to 'reflect' the totality of the Names of God also requires that he or she is faithful to the Qur'anic imperative to 'reflect on' or contemplate the natural order. This is made clear in Laura Hassan's essay investigating the 'non-overlapping magisteria' of God and Nature. According to one count, she explains, 'words based on the root *kh-l-q*, 'to create', occur 248 times in the Qur'an. So prominent a theme is creation that as Izutsu puts it 'the Qur'an may be regarded in a certain sense as a grand hymn in honour of Divine creation. The cosmos, animal life, plant life, and supremely, humankind, are all subjects of the Qur'an's celebration.'

'The immediate context of all Qur'anic references to the natural order', asserts Hassan, 'is the insistent call to worship pervading the entire Qur'an. Sky, clouds, rain, seas, beasts, birds, even bees and spiders all demand the hearer's attention as evidence of God's power and benevolence. That the natural order should point its inhabitants towards God is repeatedly and persuasively stated: "Truly, in the creation of the heavens and the earth and the variation of night and day there are signs (*ayat*) for those of understanding, those who remember God standing, sitting, and lying on their sides, and who contemplate the creation of the heavens and the earth: 'Our Lord, you did not create this for nothing!'" (3:190-191).

A particular purpose of my talk on 'Spirituality and the Outdoors' at the symposium on the Pennine Moors was to connect my theme to the British context and its rich literary heritage around nature and spirituality. The area is of course a famous place in British literary culture, the setting for *Wuthering Heights*, the famous novel by Emily Brontë. The word 'Wuthering' is a provincial term describing turbulent weather, and the moors are typically depicted as wild, bleak and desolate places, full of hazardous marshes and swamps, as well as even more fearsome, hair-raising and even supernatural menaces. But as much as the moors represent threat and danger, they are also full of mystery and mystical allure. Bleak as they may be, they are a source of inspiration and relief from the prison-like atmosphere of Wuthering Heights. To Cathy and Heathcliff, the lovers in the story, the moors exist as a supernatural, liberating region without boundaries. For them, to wander on the moors is the ultimate freedom, away from incarceration in the stifling artifice of society, with all its suffocating expectations, restrictions and conventions. The book was controversial when it was published in 1847, because it challenged strict Victorian conventions of the day, including religious hypocrisy, social class fixations, and gender inequality, and although society may be very different now for many of us from what it was at that time, we need to continue to ask what barriers still exist to be broken down and how individual freedom and adventure on all levels can be hampered within any community.

And let us be clear that such barriers are not confined to any particular community, even if they may be stronger in some. Barriers are not always a matter of established social convention or traditional cultural conditioning, but may shift with the times to encompass other impediments and restrictions. When I was discussing with a friend recently my intention to travel to Norway for some mountain trekking, he told me that his teenage sons don't like going very far into the wilderness because they can't get a wifi connection. Ouch, an hour's separation from Facebook or Twitter, what torture!

The awareness of the sacred, this reverence for the manifestation of the Divine in the beauty and majesty of Nature, is accessible to us in so many ways, whether in the sublime view from the highest mountain peak in the wilderness or in the fragrant sanctuary offered by a beautiful garden in the place where we live. The outdoors is for everyone, young and old, male and female, physically active or disabled, members of faith communities or not, and whatever our ethnicity. Mountains may often be the sites of divine inspiration and revelation in many spiritual traditions, but is not paradise so often depicted as a garden? In Zen Buddhism, the maintenance of gardens is considered an elevated spiritual practice. In her essay on Islamic gardens, Emma Clark envisions these gardens as sacred art, not only as a vehicle for spiritual illumination but also as an opportunity for re-awakening our profound connection with nature – largely eroded by our predominantly urban existence.

The outdoors is not a masculine preserve dedicated solely to prodigious feats of muscularity and daring. It is not only stark exposure to the wildness of the elements and to nature 'red in tooth and claw' but also a haven for peaceful contemplation and the nourishment of the soul. It encompasses both the grand and the intimate, the starkly majestic and the ravishingly beautiful.

In his contribution to this issue, Charles Upton captures the contrast between Beauty and Power (*Jamal and Jalal*), the two categories of Divine qualities manifested in creation. 'The Beautiful and the Sublime (or Infinitely Powerful) are the two essential qualities of the natural world: the still reflective lake and the erupting volcano; the dove and the cobra.' But, as he explains so evocatively, the two qualities are also profoundly complementary:

> Without the Sublime, nature would be stagnant and cloying; without the Beautiful it would be horrendous, too much to bear. This is why a balanced relationship to the natural world – and to life itself, for that matter – requires both rigour and rapture, both war and peace, the relaxant of calm pleasure and the tonic of danger and struggle. If it's all peace, we become effete; if it's all struggle, we become barbaric. There is also Sublimity in Beauty – witness the stallion – and Beauty in Sublimity – witness the tiger. God, too, manifests as both Beauty and Sublimity, both Mercy and Rigour (or Majesty) – which is why the integral vision of nature is the primary support, outside of divinely-revealed religion, for the contemplation of God.

Within such an integral vision, it can well be argued that the correct balance needs to be restored between the worship of the incomparable and unknowable Uniqueness of God ('Utterly remote is God in His limitless glory, from anything to which men may ascribe a share in His divinity!' – Qur'an 59:23) and the loving awareness and knowledge of God's merciful Presence ('He is closer to you than your jugular vein' – Qur'an 50:16). The over-emphasis on *tanzih*, the majestic, incomparable, remote and transcendent aspect of God, can remove us from *tashbih*, the intimate and immanent aspect of God's presence in the diversity of the created world. It can incline us disproportionately to justice, severity and singularity at the expense of beauty, mercy and diversity. In its most extreme form, such imbalance gives rise to oppressive religious bigotry, intolerance, and rigid legalistic severity. After all, *His Mercy will prevail over His Wrath*, so it could even be upheld that the balance is itself loaded in the direction of *tashbih*.

The treasury of poems contributed by Paul (Abdul Wadud) Sutherland and Michael Wolfe is replete not only with pellucid images of the beauty, refinement and splendour of the natural world, but also with that 'sense sublime of something far more deeply interfused' which breaks through in flashes of awe, wonder, spiritual yearning, and utter bewilderment (*hayra*). Thus:

'...I still do hope
One day to see Your face, if just an instant.....' (Wolfe),

and Sutherland, in observing birds of prey, as one 'billowed its feathers', confesses:

'I looked long, drove slow but never understood.'

There are resonant Qur'anic allusions here, from 'wherever you turn there is the face of God' (2:115) to the verses which tells us that 'it is God whose limitless glory all creatures in the heavens and the earth extol, even the birds as they spread out their wings' (24:41). Each worships God in its own way, 'though you fail to grasp the manner of their praise' (17:44).

The experiential dimension of the human relationship with nature is also central to Daniel Dyer's contribution 'Nature for Children' which gives a taste of his forthcoming children's resource, *The 99 Names of Allah*. This aims 'to help children build a spiritual link to the natural world, making them aware that God communicates to us through nature in the most beautiful, awesome, playful, sublime, and subtle manner.' It also shows children that 'they can learn spiritual and ethical lessons from nature, that they may draw sustenance, peace, and inner calm simply by being witnesses within it, and that outside of the human soul, it is nature that is the ultimate playground for the manifestation of Allah's Names.' In highlighting the complementary aim of building ecological awareness through the resource, Dyer makes the important point that although 'mainstream secular education is at pains to educate our children on our responsibilities in the face of environmental crisis', and 'much good work is being done in schools', yet 'the nature that is generally presented to children is one divested of meaning: it is a nature held at arm's length, a superficial thing separate from us and without spiritual significance.' 'Intimate spiritual connection' through immersion and contemplation is absolutely germane to an understanding and personal realisation of nature which is not merely theoretical and abstract, and to the development of real and meaningful ecological awareness – what Dyer calls a 'spiritualised ecology'.

In detailing his 'radical political dynamics of the Prophetic model' towards 'a public theology of social activism', Nafeez Mosaddeq Ahmed has identified several core environmental principles: Sustainable Development for Social Welfare, Cosmological and Ecological Balance, Respect for Animal Life, and Environmental Conservation. To paraphrase some of his important reflections, the Qur'an conveys not only a sense of wonder at the beauty and majesty of nature, describing the natural order as a single, living, sentient system in a constant state of reflection on the Divine Reality, but also repeatedly clarifies that the entire universe, from the cosmos to all life on earth, is inter-related and in a state of natural balance that should not be altered or corrupted. Further, every life-form is described as belonging to a community, a social order, that is comparable to that of human life. Numerous verses also suggest that environmental and social corruption are a consequence of human activity that disrupts the 'due measure and proportion' and the faultless order invested in the whole of creation. The Qur'an explicitly states that 'corruption has appeared on land and in the sea as an outcome of what men's hands have wrought: and so He will let them taste some of their doings, that haply they might return' (30:41). In his note to this verse, Muhammad Asad refers to 'the growing corruption and destruction of our natural environment, so awesomely demonstrated in our time' as an outcome of 'that self-destructive – because utterly materialistic – inventiveness and frenzied activity which now threatens mankind with previously unimaginable ecological disasters.'

The only antidote to the looming ecological disasters, notes Naomi Foyle in her essay on 'Palestine and (Human) Nature', is 'a powerful but humble sense we are all one, interdependent, and dependent on all of creation'. Connecting this philosophy to 'the belief in a universal bond of sharing that connects all humanity' and 'the natural world as the ground of all sharing' expressed by the term 'Ubuntu' in Southern Africa, she affirms that for her the concept has 'a deeply spiritual dimension':

The notion of universal sharing flies in the face of the materialist conception of human nature as fundamentally driven by biological imperatives to feed, mate and reproduce our "selfish genes" and pack loyalties, and goes far beyond the concept of altruism, which evolutionary psychologists primarily understand as self-sacrifice in favour of younger generations. People inspired by universal consciousness are willing to act on behalf of others they are only very tenuously related to.

And, as Foyle points out, for 'the growing eco-Islam movement', the signal message of unity, the doctrine of Tawhid, gives expression to the fact (emphasised also by many contemporary Christian and Jewish scholars) that 'everything in the world is part of creation and is related to everything else, which makes the entire world significant, valuable, and worthy of protection.'

In line with Foyle's own description of the practice of permaculture in Palestine, Zeshan Akhter identifies one very practical way in which a vision of the sanctity of the natural order might be revived through environmental activism rooted in Islamic principles. In the light of her own work in the protection of the jewels of natural landscape and their precious flora and wildlife in Britain, she invokes the concept of *hima*, those protected areas established by the Prophet, and considered as public property or common lands, where development, habitation, or extensive grazing were proscribed. Such zones 'were reserved for forests in which cutting of trees was forbidden, grazing was restricted to certain seasons, and the whole zone was managed for the welfare of the community.' In fact, 'the community itself was responsible for its protection and conservation.' Both *hima,* and a second kind of inviolate zone, *haram*, were an integral part of the Shariah, and any historic Muslim cities, such as Fez in Morocco and Aleppo in Syria were built around them. But, as Akhter laments, 'all this is history'. Tragically, in modern times, the 'inviolable sanctuaries' of Mecca and Medina are 'the last places where we might expect to find the environment treated with respect'. Nevertheless, she is hopeful that the concepts of *hima* and *haram* may be revived in contemporary times, and identifies the Birmingham-based Islamic Foundation for Ecology and Environmental Sciences (IFEES) as one positive indication.

Just as faith traditions may provide a crucial inspirational element for activists in tackling poverty, social and economic injustice, abuse of human rights, and environmental degradation, the same goes for animal welfare and ethical consumption. Here too, respect for nature might be reclaimed from Islamic principles. For example, Ruth Helen Corbet has argued persuasively how the principle of *tayyib* (what is good) might humanely be applied so as to go beyond that of *halal* (what is permitted). One has to ask why, at Eid al-Adha, the Festival of the Sacrifice, Muslims actively collude in cruelty to animals through the mass importation of sacrificial sheep from Australia and New Zealand? Are there no Islamic standards of compassion to animals? How can one justify the horrendous conditions reportedly endured by the four million sheep and 770,000 cattle per annum transported in filthy conditions from Australia alone, packed onto ships 100,000 at a time, subject to trampling, disease, starvation, trauma and heat stroke during their month long journey, and a high percentage of deaths in transit?

Of course, it is easy to point to the 'hypocrisy' of Westerners who condemn ritual slaughter and yet consume vast quantities of meat derived from industrialised, mass slaughter while evading any personal responsibility for taking the life of an animal. True as that may be, it does not shed much light on what has become a pressing controversy amongst Muslims themselves. We cannot keep wagging our fingers at the assumed hypocrisy of others any more than we can keep shouting 'Islamophobia' as a means of stifling self-criticism. Every individual and every community have to deal with whatever is in their own bag.

And how convincing today is the argument that mass sacrifice originally provided many valuable services to the Muslim community? Did it not inculcate, for example, a sense of sacrifice and compassion in the giver, who had to give up an animal, an important source of livelihood in times gone by? Did it not also serve a worthy social purpose in providing meat, one of the few protein-rich foods in early Islam, to the poor, who ate it only on the occasion of the two Eids? Indeed, but how relevant are these circumstances for many Muslims in today's world?

Shahid Ali Muttaqi questions the necessity of performing the traditional Eid al-Adha sacrifice, maintaining that ritual slaughter in Islam is merely customary, and derives from the norms and conditions of pre-Islamic Arab society, and not from Islam. Pre-Islamic blood sacrifice, by which pagan Arabs sought to propitiate a pantheon of Gods and attain favour and material gain, is specifically qualified in the Qur'an: 'It is not their meat, nor their blood, that reach God; it is only your *taqwa* (consciousness of God) that reaches Him' (22:37). The Jews also sought to appease the One True God by blood sacrifice and burnt offerings, and it is worth noting that the word 'holocaust' comes from Greek *holos* (whole) and *kaustos* (burnt) and originally meant 'a sacrifice consumed by fire'. Even the Christian community felt Jesus to be the last sacrifice, the final lamb, in a tradition of animal sacrifice through which one's sins were absolved by the blood of another. Muttaqi points out that the notion of 'vicarious atonement for sin' is nowhere to be found in the Qur'an. Neither is the idea of propitiation or gaining favour or material gain through the sacrifice of a life. All that is demanded as a sacrifice is one's personal willingness to submit one's ego and individual will to Allah. Is not self-surrender, after all the essential meaning of *islam?*

Foyle's recognition of the new dynamism within exemplars of 'eco-jihad' confirms the heartening promise of change I observed amongst the enthusiastic cadre of pioneering young Muslims engaging with nature on the Pennine Moors. By the same token, it is important to reiterate the point that although disconnection from nature is still pronounced in urban Muslim communities, we should be aware that it is a growing problem in every section of society. In fact, I would fervently claim that the spiritual crisis of our times is most clearly reflected in our relationship with Nature.

In his influential book, *Last Child in the Woods*, Richard Louv identifies what he describes as 'the staggering divide between children and the outdoors' which he aptly labels as 'Nature Deficit Disorder' (NDD). He directly links the disconnection from nature in the lives of today's wired generation to some of the most disturbing childhood trends, such as the rise in obesity, attention disorders, and depression. In her contribution to this issue, Lali Zaibun-Nisa refers to the strategies recommended by Louv for reconnecting people (children especially) with nature, including 'direct contact in the form of wilderness immersion practices such as forest schooling, and indirect contact in the form of increased visual access to the natural world'. She goes on to refer to well-researched studies cited in Louv's later book *The Nature Principle: Reconnecting with Life in a Virtual Age* which detail the positive impact of these strategies: for children, marked improvement in their psychological health, including a reduction in the symptoms of Attention Deficit Hyperactivity Disorder (ADHD); increased attention span; improvement in test scores, scholastic ability and motivation;

enhanced self-esteem; and even improved conflict-resolution and cooperation skills.

Zaibun-Nisa goes on to describe how 'for adults too the gains are immense, both psychologically and physically: a reduction in the symptoms of mental health conditions and recovery for otherwise intractable conditions; an enhanced ability to cope with stress; faster recovery from illness and injury; better pain management in conditions such as heart disease; enhanced immune resistance; and improved mood and self-esteem.'

Further research, reported in the journal *Nature* last year in an article entitled 'The Myopia Boom', has identified an increase in time outdoors as a major factor in reversing the short-sightedness which is reaching epidemic proportions in East Asia. Sixty years ago, the article reveals, 10–20 per cent of the Chinese population was short-sighted, but, today this has risen to an astounding 90 per cent amongst teenagers and young adults. In Seoul, a whopping 96.5 per cent of nineteen-year-old men are short-sighted. 'Other parts of the world have also seen a dramatic increase in the condition, which now affects around half of young adults in the United States and Europe – double the prevalence of half a century ago. By some estimates, one-third of the world's population – 2.5 billion people – could be affected by short-sightedness by the end of this decade.'

Old ideas about the causes of the disorder tended to associate it with the 'bookish child', and it is true that its striking modern escalation mirrors a trend for children in many countries to spend more time reading, studying or – more recently – glued to computer and smartphone screens. This is particularly the case in East Asian countries, where the high value placed on educational performance (increasingly reflected in high global school rankings) is driving children to spend longer in school and on their studies. An OECD report last year showed that the average fifteen-year-old in Shanghai now spends fourteen hours per week on homework, compared with five hours in the United Kingdom and six hours in the United States.

That said, the most recent research is challenging the 'bookishness' theory, and is instead coalescing around a new notion: that spending too long indoors is the real problem. 'We're really trying to give this message now that children need to spend more time outside,' says Kathryn Rose, head of orthoptics at the University of Technology, Sydney. Three or more hours of daily outdoor time is now recommended, and this is already the norm for children in Australia, where only around 30 per cent of seventeen-year-olds are myopic. These three hours 'need to be under light levels of at least 10,000 lux, which is about the level experienced by someone under a shady tree, wearing sunglasses, on a bright summer's day.' In stark contrast, a well-lit office or classroom is twenty times dimmer, at usually no more than 500 lux. Sadly, a new report in March this year entitled *Play in Balance* (as part of the 'Dirt is Good' campaign) on the lack of time spent outdoors by children in the UK, has revealed that three quarters of British children aged between six and twelve spend less time playing outside than the sixty minutes a day recommended for prison inmates. 'Let's be clear', asserts an article *in The Times* entitled 'Why nature is better than Netflix', 'they weren't asked how often they climbed mountains or trekked into unadulterated forest. Just how often they played in a local park, a garden … anywhere in the fresh air'. Nearly eight out of ten parents admit that their children often refuse to play without some form of technology or 'screen-time' being involved, and this can pose an obvious barrier to spending more time outdoors. A similar number report that their child prefers to play virtual sports on a screen inside rather than playing 'real' sports outside.

I've been careful to question the false assumption that outdoor pursuits have to be adrenaline-fuelled, time-pressured exploits or extreme sports testing the limits of human daring and endurance if they are to offer a real sense of achievement and personal fulfilment. This does not actually contradict the value of those awesome physical and mental feats that may be needed for great exploits of exploration any more than it devalues the many examples of physical privation, austerity and asceticism within the wilderness as elements of spiritual training and practice in many spiritual traditions. It was, after all, the regular retreat, seclusion and fasting of the Prophet Muhammad in a mountain cave near Mecca, which prepared him to receive the first revelations of the Qur'an. In Hinduism, the third of the four traditional stages or *ashrama* of life is the stage when one's own children have grown up, and one renounces all material pleasures, retires from social and professional life, and goes to the forest as a hermit to live a simple life of spiritual devotions. And then there is the tradition of Christian hermits and ascetics in the wilderness, including the desert Fathers, and monasteries on mountain-tops and other hard-to-reach places. Some Tibetan Mahayana

Buddhist monks took asceticism to the limit by meditating on mountain tops in sub-zero temperatures. There is even a yoga called the 'yoga of the psychic heat' practised by these monks which reputedly enabled them to generate their own heat from within so that they could engage in such austerities without freezing to death.

It's also clear that many of the virtues of character developed through adventurous exploits in the outdoors may well have great value for the development of spirituality. For example, the virtue of perseverance, endeavour and patient endurance (*sabr* in Islamic tradition), the virtue of intrepidity and courage, the virtue of decisive intention and aspiration (*himmah*), and the chivalric virtue of heroic generosity (*futuwwah*) which puts others before oneself. I remember with great affection an incident recorded in a television programme about the Coast to Coast Walk when the presenter Julia Bradbury encounters a walker somewhere in the Yorkshire Dales about half way through the 190-mile trek. He was an eighty-three-year-old American undertaking the hike for the seventh year in succession. He said, 'If I should collapse, I only hope that I do not block the path.' We can see here the beautiful virtue of resignation and natural spiritual courtesy, a completely self-effacing respect for others. We tread here on the path of what is described in Islamic tradition as *adab,* a level of exemplary courtesy and decency which is a fundamental aspect of excellence of human character. In spiritual traditions, excellence is not simply about mastery, achievement and success, but always includes a moral and spiritual dimension.

There is robust research which has shown that students who participate in adventure programmes do indeed show long-term improvement in their problem-solving abilities, leadership skills, social skills and independence. But, perhaps above all, young people benefit enormously from simple immersion in the spaciousness and tranquillity of nature without any necessary goal-directed activity. One of the recognised problems I have seen in schools and within families is too much emphasis on controlled and organised activities, and not enough on creative play, which by its very nature has no definable objective. Walking with a child on the beach does not have to involve the specific quantitative educational objective of collecting, identifying and naming ten different kinds of shell or pebble. Education in nature is not essentially about ticking boxes; it is a holistic and qualitative state of freedom and immersion through which we let the full range of our faculties unfold in a natural way.

A rather common lack of independent thinking and imagination is only too evident in the popularity of 'bucket list' books like *100 Things to Do before you Die,* or *100 Places to Visit before you Die,* which perpetrate the absurdly conformist fallacy that you're falling behind if you haven't conquered iconic hotspots like Mount Snowdon, or met the ultimate challenge of climbing Mount Everest without oxygen, or walked on a tightrope from one hot air balloon to another at 10,000 feet and taking a selfie doing it. There are regular pictures in the newspapers on August bank holiday of hundreds of people queuing on their way up Snowdon and at least thirty crowded on the summit, many trying to take pictures of themselves. Similar pictures taken on Mount Everest regularly depict climbers crowded together as they queue for up to two and a half hours on their way up to the summit.

A young man who had discovered the joys of walking recently announced to me that he had decided to do the 'Three Peaks Challenge', climbing the three highest peaks in Scotland, England and Wales (that is, Ben Nevis, Scafell Pike and Snowdon) in twenty-four hours, even though he has not yet climbed one of them. Of course, I expressed my approval of such a venture, not wanting to dampen his enthusiasm, but part of me yearned to say to him: why don't you climb just one of them and just sit on the top in silent contemplation and awe, reflecting on the beauty and majesty of the view, and forgetting about the time pressure to rush to the next peak? Why not deeply consider and ponder what the exquisite and awesome signs of nature tell us about the beneficence of the Creator, the wonders of the created universe, and your place within it? Why not contemplate in stillness the perfection and sublimity of the natural order, as expressed not only so pervasively in the Qur'an, but also in so many fine words in the English cultural tradition, such as those of the eighteenth century English theologian and mystic William Law: 'this world', he wrote, 'with all its stars, elements, and creatures, is come out of the invisible world; it has not the smallest thing or the smallest quality of anything but what is come forth from thence'. Mahmoud Shabistari (1288–1340), mystic poet of Iran, wrote:

know that the whole world is a mirror; in each atom are found a hundred blazing suns. If you split the centre of a single drop of water, a hundred pure oceans spring forth. If you examine each particle of dust, a thousand Adams can be seen.

And that is exactly the message of our own poet William Blake when he wrote:

> To see a World in a Grain of Sand
> And a Heaven in a Wild Flower,
> Hold Infinity in the palm of your hand
> And Eternity in an hour.

Finally, let me say that in my experience there is an inverse relationship between time and space. We live in such a frenetic and hyperactive contemporary culture, subject to declining attention span and under constant pressure to do more and more in less and less time, and one of the best ways to escape the tyranny of time pressure is to get into space. When you walk in nature, the expansiveness of space somehow dissolves time and enables you to be fully present in the moment. That physical spaciousness is like a reflection of the limitless and timeless space within our own being, at the very centre of ourselves, within our heart.

I wish for you all the expansion of that inner space in the great outdoors.

CONCEPTS AND SYMBOLS

Charles Upton

1.

The central doctrine of Islam is *al-tawhid,* Unity. God is One; there is no god but God. And the Unity of God is reflected in the universe, in the unity of nature's laws, as well as in the uniqueness of each object in nature. To construct circles is to make a geometrical diagram of *al-tawhid.*

The Arabic word for 'heart', *qalb,* is derived from the root QLB or QBL, which embraces a number of concepts having to do with 'turning'. In Sufi metaphysics the Heart is the centre of the psyche, the point at which it is intersected by the vertical ray of the Spirit *(ruh).* This symbolic image has obvious affinities with the act of constructing a circle using a compass and a sheet of paper. The Heart is who we really are in the sight of God; it is the central point of our full and authentic humanity. Whoever wants to rise along the vertical path of the Spirit, the *axis mundi,* first has to have reached the Centre, the Heart, which is another way of saying that we can't relate to God with only a part of ourselves. A line drawn from any point on the circumference of a circle so as to intersect a line passing vertically through the circle's centre can never be one with the infinite elevation which the vertical line symbolises. It must intersect the vertical line at some point short of infinity. Furthermore, it only 'represents' its own point-of-origin on the circumference; it can in no way stand for the circle as a whole. But the centre of the circle does stand for the whole circle, since it is the point from which the circle expands, and to which it returns. And only the central point of the circle is available to the ray of infinite elevation which symbolises the relationship between the human form and God. It is said that God holds the Heart between His fingers, and turns it however He will. This is a way of saying that the Heart is the reality through which we can see how all the changes-of-state we experience in passing time have the same Point-of-Origin; that change on the horizontal plane is an expression of permanence on the vertical one; that the *waqt,* the present moment of spiritual time, is the manifestation of God's eternity in the created world. And just as God *turns* the Heart however He will, so the Heart is the point through which and by which the human soul *returns* to God on the spiritual Path; it is the spiritual Kaaba, the *qiblah* toward which we turn.

2.

Beauty and Power (*Jamal and Jalal*) are the two categories of Divine qualities manifested in creation: sometimes blended in varying proportions as in the beauty of a swiftly running stallion or the power of a rushing waterfall. The Beautiful and the Sublime (or Infinitely Powerful) are the two essential qualities of the natural world: the still reflective lake and the erupting volcano; the dove and the cobra. Created Beauty is an expression of the Names of God which fall under the category of Beauty (*al-Jamil*); Sublimity is an expression of those Names which fall under Majesty (*al-Jalal*). Without the Sublime, nature would be stagnant and cloying; without the Beautiful it would be horrendous, too much to bear. This is why a balanced relationship to the natural world – and to life itself, for that matter – requires both rigor and rapture, both war and peace, the relaxant of calm pleasure and the tonic of danger and struggle. If it's all peace, we become effete; if it's all struggle, we become barbaric. There is also Sublimity in Beauty – witness the stallion – and Beauty in Sublimity – witness the tiger. God, too, manifests as both Beauty and Sublimity, both Mercy and Rigour or Majesty – which is why the integral vision of nature is the primary support, outside of divinely-revealed religion, for the contemplation of God.

3.

When Muhammad cast the idols out of the Kaaba, he was not only reminding his people that it was their duty to worship Allah, not the natural forces which are Allah's creation; he was also casting the idols of self-worship out of the temple of the human heart.

It was the Prophet's mission to remind the Arabs, and all later Muslims, that there is more to reality than what your five senses can tell you: [God] said, Did I not say unto you, verily, I alone know the hidden reality of the heavens and the earth? [2:34]. In this revelation, the ancient religion of Abraham was being renewed. And thus we gave Abraham insight into [God's] mighty dominion over the heavens and the earth – and to the end that he might become one of those who are inwardly sure. Then, when the night overshadowed him with its darkness, he beheld a star: he exclaimed, 'This is my Sustainer!'– but when it went down, he said, 'I love not the things that go down.' Then, when he beheld the moon rising, he said 'This is my Sustainer!'– but when it went down, he said, 'Indeed, if my Sustainer guide me not, I will certainly be one of the people who go astray!' Then, when he beheld the sun rising, he said, 'This is my Sustainer! This is the greatest [of all]!'– but when it [too] went down, he exclaimed: 'O my people! Far be it from me to ascribe divinity, as you do, to aught beside God' [6:75-78].

We think of nature as something outside of us which also contains us, instead of realising that the Spirit of nature – God in his Names Al-Khaliq (The Creator), Al-Bari (the Producer), Al-Musawwir (the Fashioner), the Life-Giver (Al-Muyhi), and Al-Hafiz (the All-Preserver) – is within us as well as all around us, that He holds both us and the universe we are a part of between His two hands. He shows us His signs on the horizons and in our souls; He is Al-Shahid, the Witness over everything.

4.

Earth has always helped humanity remember Eden. The English word Paradise comes from a Persian word meaning 'walled garden'; the Qur'an describes Paradise as an area of gardens beneath which rivers flow (i.e. a world of visible forms whose secret springs of life are in the Unseen). When witnessed in the Light of God, the earth is the very image of these gardens, her green trees and grasses the colour of Paradise, which is also the colour of Islam, of life and abundance.

God made the universe to remind of Him. *I was a hidden treasure and loved to be known; I created the universe so that I could be known (hadith qudsi).* And he made the human heart capable of knowing Him, just as the ear hears sounds or the eye sees light.

We have God's two books to learn from: the universe, and the Holy Qur'an. *And in your own nature, and in [that of] all the animals He scatters [over the earth] there are messages for people who are endowed with inner certainty* [45:4].

Every Muslim has a duty to seek knowledge: of nature, of God, of other people, and of himself. *He who knows himself, knows his Lord.* This is why the Prophet (peace and blessings be upon him) said: *O Lord, increase me in knowledge*; and *Seek knowledge, even as far as China*; and *O Lord, show me things as they really are.*

5.

When trying to tell the difference between things by naming them, we tend to rely on our eyes: we attach a particular name to a particular object we see. But to get a sense of the original Unity that exists *before* we start naming things, one thing we can do is pay more attention to what we *hear* than what we see. When we name things, we merely attach words to them; when God names things, He brings them into existence. If we stop speaking and talking to ourselves for once, and listen instead to the sounds of the world, it is as if we were listening to the sound of God's original act of creation.

Listening softens the gaze. And if we listen deeply enough – if, that is, we stop talking to ourselves completely enough – then the Eye of the Heart may open, and let us see into the heart of things.

The world is God's first Book, in which every form is a letter or sentence. But the world is also an echo of God's spoken Word, in which every sound is a reverberation of the original word *Kun,* 'Be!', by which He brings all things into existence. The sense of sight is related to our ability to tell things apart by naming them. The visual forms of objects appear as established facts; they seem to exist in their own right. In the face of their matter-of-fact existence, we tend to forget that, in reality, all things are signs of God.

The sense of hearing is different. It is related more to God's continuous act of creating the universe than to the catalogue of what He has already created. This is why, in Islam, the written and spoken word is emphasised over the image, and why making images of the natural world is discouraged, and why making an image of God is forbidden: because an image is always in danger of turning into an idol. Whenever we take something literally, as if it existed in its own right rather than being an act of God, we have made an idol out of it. If we see the universe as made up of *things,* we are tempted to identify with those things, to desire and possess them; and the first step toward possessing something is to define it, to give it a name. *That which you serve, apart from Him, is nothing but names yourselves have named* [12:40]. But if we see the universe as made up of *acts of God,* acts which we can no more predict, or control, or grasp with our greedy hands than the next gust of wind or the next cry of a bird, then this kind of idolatry becomes impossible to us. All we can do is wait, in attentive silence, for God's next gift. His next warning. His next command. Instead of always trying to name and define things, why not keep silent, and listen to how *God* is pleased to name and define things? Why not let *Him* teach *us* their shapes and definitions? *He taught Adam the names, all of them* [2:31]. After all, it is He, not us, who creates them.

Sound is bigger than us; it surrounds us and washes over us. We can deliberately look in a particular direction, but we can't deliberately *listen* in a particular direction. Sounds simply come to us, unpredictably, uncontrollably, from beyond what we know. This is why *hearing* is related to *obedience* – instead of judging and discriminating, we simply 'hear and obey' [2:285]. To *hear* is to *heed*. With our eyes we investigate, we spy things out – but the knowledge that flows into our ears is something that is impressed upon us, not something we can grasp or locate on our own initiative.

The will of God comes into our experience through the dimension of time. We become sensitive to the will of God by paying attention to the changes that are always going on – and one of the best ways to do this is simply by listening instead of looking. If we listen deeply enough we can hear the subtle changes in the quality of passing time, like changes in the weather, or in the quality of light, or the mood we and our friends are in. If we listen deeply enough to the sounds of the world, we may almost hear the silent pressure of God's creative power – the word *Kun* – by which He brings all things into existence. *When He decrees a thing, He but says to it 'Be,' and it is* [19:35].

In listening to the sounds of the world, you simply sit and attend to all the sounds within your range – birds, wind in the trees, flowing water, traffic sounds, human voices – and hear them as the voice of Allah, the vibration of the primal creative Source of the Universe, finally reaching your ears.

When you listen to the sounds of the world, you begin to see yourself as part of the world around you, a universe created by God before you were born, immensely bigger than you in space, immensely older than you in time. And you also come to understand that God's act of creating the world never ended; it is still going on. If he were to stop saying *Kun!* (Be!) for one instant, the universe and everything in it would fall into oblivion. This is one way of coming to a deeper understanding of what it means that *God is Creator, Producer, Fashioner, Lord of all Worlds.* Although this kind of deep listening can be practised anywhere, among the best places to do it are by a stream or waterfall, or on the shore of the ocean, or in a wooded area, during a gentle wind. (Or if at night, among the frogs and the crickets.)

The practice of paying attention to the natural world is a discipline in itself; it requires us to suppress our formless agitation, our obsessive planning and strategising, as well as the images produced in our mind by fear and desire. We must never forget that heedlessness is only cured by discipline; we must also never forget that Paradise is a Garden, of which the natural world is the clearest of signs. *As for those who have attained to righteousness – what of those who have attained to righteousness? They, too, will find themselves amidst fruit-laden trees, and acacias flower-clad, and shade extended, and waters gushing and fruit abounding, never failing and never out of reach* [56:27-33].

When we go out into the natural world, into that part of the planet which is neither destroyed nor cultivated by human action – the part that 'arises of itself', not by our own efforts and plans and agendas, but by the will of God – we meet a different part of ourselves. When you are in a natural, living environment, an environment that possesses life, like you do, but does not possess serious heavy ego, then you can begin to feel how your body is a part of nature, part of God's creation, one more living organism among the bugs and plants and birds...*there is no beast that walks on earth and no bird that flies on its two wings which is not [God's] creature like yourselves: no single thing have We neglected in Our decree* [6:38].

6.

The Qur'an mentions something called 'the Trust' which God offered ... *unto the heavens and the earth and the hills, but they shrank from bearing it and were afraid of it. And man assumed it* [33:72]. What exactly is this *'Trust'*?

The Trust is our ability, which is also our duty, to see the forms of the world around us, both natural and man-made, as signs of the Creator. The angels can witness God's presence without having to deal with the many distractions our five human senses confront us with. The animals are immersed in the world of the senses; they have no way of standing apart from it. Only we human beings have the power to sense God's presence and submit to His will, while at the same time living in, and dealing with, a material world. In other words, humanity is the bridge or *barzakh* (isthmus) between God and the created universe. We are God's *khalifa* on earth, his delegated representative. And because we are *khalifa,* we have a privileged relationship to knowledge. The animals are fixed, by God's will, in their basic views of reality; we call this 'instinct'. Humanity alone is capable of growing in knowledge by moving from view to view.

This ability to change and enhance our view of reality is the reason why humanity has been able to develop art, culture, science and technology. But if this ability remains separate from our capacity to sense the presence of God – which is also our God-given duty, since it is part of the Trust – then it becomes destructive. We end up using our uniquely human ability to manipulate the environment in the service of desires which are still basically on an animal level. This sort of desire is appropriate for animals, of course, since they don't possess civilisation and advanced technology. But if dogs or pigs, for example, had access to nuclear weapons, this would definitely not be a desirable state of affairs. Our ability to fulfil our desires has grown over the centuries; our ability to *change what we desire,* or *sacrifice a given desire entirely,* apparently has not. Rationality helps us to satisfy our desires, but faith gives us the power to change or sacrifice them. And faith is the basis of the Trust. If we do not fulfil this Trust, then we are not yet, or no longer, fully human; rather we are animals without the protection of a single unchanging pattern of perception, chaotic animals who are always shifting from pattern to pattern without being able to control ourselves, who are addicted to 'trying things out' and so end up destroying much of the world we might have loved.

Part of the Trust is the human capacity to know the names of things, their inner essences. *And He imparted unto Adam the names of all things* [2:31]. *This is a kind of knowledge even the angels do not possess. He brought them within the ken of the angels and said: 'Declare unto me the names of these [things]... They replied... 'No knowledge have we save that which Thou hast imparted unto us... Said He, 'O Adam convey unto them the names of these [things]'* [2:31-33]. It is because God taught Adam all the names, names which even the angels did not know, that it is often said that the human form, alone in all creation, is capable of reflecting all the Names of God; it is precisely this which makes us so destructive when we fail to live up to this form, or when we betray it.

To name something is to distinguish it from its background, to see it as a separate entity. When God taught Adam all the names, He gave the human race the unequalled ability to discriminate between things, largely through the gift of human language. Yet God is not many; He is One. His Names are not separate entities; they are names of Him alone. The forms of the universe are not separate 'gods' which exist in their own right, but signs of the One God. This means that our heightened ability to tell the difference between things is a two-edged sword. If we practise discrimination while remembering God, then we are fulfilling the Trust. But if we forget God in our desire to analyse, dissect and control the world around us, then we have become idolaters....

One of the arts of appreciating nature is developing our knowledge of the names and characteristics of things; the other, companion art is knowing how to keep quiet and pay attention, both within and without. Speech is knowledge of the many; silence is knowledge of the One. Only if we forget, for a while, what we already know, will we be able to learn something we don't yet know. (And it is exactly the same in relation to God: we can know *about* Him through His Names, but we cannot know God Himself in His Essence; and yet – if we are silent enough and vigilant enough – God Himself may make His presence known to us.)

7.

Our soul needs a sense of place. We often experience soul in nature because the direct experience of the sun, trees, grass, flowers, and the earth is so nourishing to our soul...When I am truly present in nature I feel a sense of awe and reverence from just witnessing the beauty of it all... Thomas Moore advocates a 'soul-ecology' where we respect the soul in nature that is based on a 'felt relationship'. He argues that the root meaning of ecology is seeing the Earth as 'home'. We are moved to take care of earth as we would our own home when we feel a deep affection for it.

Moore goes on to suggest that the problem of what he refers to as our homelessness is rooted in our abstraction from the earth. Because we have lost the felt relationship to the Earth most human beings have become inwardly homeless on the planet. The Zuni Indians of New Mexico see their home as 'a particular place and the entire world'; Muslims, if they have retained their sense of the sacred, see Mecca and Jerusalem in the same way.

Earth education demands that things and events be looked at within larger patterns and relationships. David Orr suggests that many of our personal and societal problems stem from seeing the world in a fragmented and disconnected way. Building freeways, shopping malls, parking lots at a non-stop pace without consideration of the real need and impact on ecology is a product of the compartmentalised way of seeing and behaving.

These things are threads of a whole cloth. The fact that we see them as disconnected events or fail to see them at all is, I believe, evidence of a considerable failure that we have yet to acknowledge as an educational failure. It is a failure to educate people to think broadly, to perceive systems and patterns and to live as whole persons.

John Ralston Saul in his 1995 Massey Lectures, *The Unconscious Civilization,* points out the failure to make important connections in our society. In one ecological example, he states:

The world-wide depletion of fish stocks is a recent example. The number of fish caught between 1950 and 1989 multiplied by five. The fishing fleet went from 585,000 boats in 1970 to 1.2 million boats in 1990 and on to 3.5 million today. No one thought about the long or even the medium-term maintenance of stocks; not the fishermen, not the boat builders, not the fish wholesalers, who found new uses for their product, including fertiliser and chicken feed; not the financiers. It wasn't their job. Their job was to worry about their own interests.

As we awaken to the Earth and its processes, we free ourselves from this modern blindness and start to look at life interdependently; we see how *all that is in the heavens and all that is on earth extols the limitless glory of God* [62:1]. We then can discern the effects of industrialisation in the air we breathe and the water we drink, not to mention the harm to the ozone layer and the ongoing process of global warming. A strictly rationalist approach to life denies this broader perspective. A soulful approach not only enables but demands such a perspective because soul is immersed in connections; it lets us witness Allah's creation through the Eye of the Heart.

8.

To learn how to see nature as a carpet woven of symbols or signs of God, you must, in a sense, become profoundly naive – guileless, sincere and simple-minded. You must learn, again, to trust your direct experience of things, like you did when you were a child. Symbolic consciousness reminds us how to see the world as it actually appears, and how to let that appearance instruct us. It was not without purpose that God placed us in a world of mountains and plains and forests and deserts and oceans, with the sun, moon, and stars above us, with winds and clouds and rain, the day following the night and the night the day. It was not without purpose that he gave us the kind of bodies we have, and the kind of senses that allow us to perceive the world around us in exactly the way He has willed us to perceive it.

In order to really see the natural world as a living symbol of its Creator, we must 'cleanse the doors of perception'. But we also need to sense how, as we contemplate the universe, we are also *being contemplated;* as we sit quietly, watching the natural world, Someone Else is watching us. In the words of Muhammad, peace and blessings be upon him: *Pray to God as if you saw Him: because even if you don't see Him, He sees you.*

VISIONS OF MAN AND NATURE

James E. Montgomery

Let us explore how the natural world is figured in several Arabic texts by looking at some key moments.

Moment One, al-Andalus, ca. 544-5 / 1150: The Story of Ḥayy ibn Yaqẓān (Alive Son of Awake), the boy reared by a gazelle on an equatorial island as imagined by Ibn Ṭufayl

The setting is the Isle of Wāqwāq south of the equator in the Indian Ocean. Men and women are born on the island but without father or mother. Women are born from a special tree. Here the four elements are in complete balance. The light in which the island is bathed produces an ambient atmosphere which is a perfect prerequisite for spontaneous generation. It is thus that an archetype of the noble savage, Ḥayy ibn Yaqẓān, literally 'Alive the Son of Awake', is born. Or is it? For the narrator of Ibn Ṭufayl's philosophical conundrum presents us with a second birth story. As an infant, Ḥayy was put to sea in a casket by his noble mother who feared for his life, just as the mother of the baby Moses did. The narrator does not tell us how to reconcile these two stories. Indeed, the point they are intended to make is not clarified either. Is it that we are invited to choose between religious credulity and scientific causality, between faith and science?

The creator of this experiment, Ibn Ṭufayl poses us many, many more puzzles of this ilk. His narrator tells the story of how Ḥayy is nurtured and reared by a gazelle and, as he grows to manhood, penetrates the secrets of natural science (his first act is to dissect his dead gazelle mother), develops and practises ethics (he cares for plants and protects vulnerable animals, eats only what he can forage), explores physics and then abstracts metaphysics. His final achievement on this journey is communion with the divine, leaving the supralunar world behind.

Upon his descent back to terrestrial form in the cave, Ḥayy learns how to bring about this separation of body and soul, almost at will. His solitary life is soon to end, however, for Absāl, an interloper from the mainland, visits the island and finds Ḥayy engaged in his ascetic and meditational practices. It is in the company of Absāl that Ḥayy acquires language and learns that there are many more people like Absāl. He agrees to travel with him to the inhabited world and to share his knowledge with others. He finds humans, however, to be frustrating creatures, unable to rise above their everyday concerns, and in despair abandons human society to return to his island.

Tales such as this speak beyond their time and place. *Ḥayy ibn Yaqzān* captured the imaginations successively of the Renaissance humanist Pico della Mirandola (d. 1494), of the British empirical philosopher John Locke (d. 1704), of the English novelist Daniel Defoe (d. 1731) and possibly even of the Dutch rationalist Benedict Spinoza (d. 1677). Each of these scholars read *Ḥayy ibn Yaqzān* as a philosophical programme, as a manifesto of autodidacticism – of what the human mind is able to achieve through the unaided and untrammelled application of reason.

Imagined places give birth to imagined tales, in a manner not dissimilar to the spontaneous generation we have just heard about on the Isle of Wāqwāq. Let us begin in al-Andalus, the landmass of the Iberian Peninsula as conquered and inhabited by the Muslims from the third/eighth to the tenth/fifteenth century. Al-Andalus is itself an imagined space, a site of nostalgia, and, according to many moderns, a beacon of *convivencia*, an oasis of multicultural coexistence where the Abrahamic religions lived side by side in harmony. It is hardly surprising, then, that some scholars trace the etymology of the name *al-Andalus* to the lost city of Atlantis of which Plato wrote, for both are figments, shards of myth. The end of al-Andalus is marked by the discovery of the New World, a hitherto undreamed of place, by Christopher Columbus in 1492.

But these tales also live in their time and place and retain echoes of where they are born. Al-Andalus was a site of natural experiment, fabled for its material abundance, its agriculture and advances in botany, and its magnificent gardens set in and around palaces of breath-taking scale, complexity and beauty. The Alhambra in Granada is a late, but wonderful, example of this Andalusi vision. Andalusi poets such as Ibn Khafājah (d. 533/1139) were also adept at composing poems in celebration of their natural paradise.

Al-Andalus throughout its long history was intimately connected with the Maghreb, North Africa. During the sixth/twelfth century, a powerful Berber reform movement, the Almohads, were in the ascendancy. Their name in Arabic is *al-muwaḥḥidūn*, those who profess the unity of God – a brand of purified and chastened monotheism, so pristine in fact that to profess it meant in many ways to discard the particularities of religious identities. It was a universal and universalising monotheism, a system which did not cherish belief informed by an unquestioning acceptance of dogma based on prior authority. So there is an Almohad aspect to Ibn Ṭufayl's tale, for, by growing up without any parents or elders or teachers, the narrator suggests, Ḥayy is not trammelled by the acceptance of any prior dogma at all and is thus able to connect with the light of reason which God has implanted in each and every human being and so attains a level of spiritual enlightenment none but prophets have achieved.

Ibn Ṭufayl, who died in 581/1185–6, was a prominent courtier, probably a member of the cadre of intellectuals and scholars maintained by Almohad rulers. He was an older contemporary of the great Ibn Rushd (Averroes) (d. 595/1198). He presumably had an all-round education: in Qur'anic studies; grammar and lexicography, belles-lettres and poetry; medicine; and possibly even the law. He may have worked as the ruler's personal censor, reviewing the works commissioned by the ruler.

His profession as censor certainly fits with the enigmatic and puzzling style he uses for his story. Most readers of the work are seduced into seeing its message as one of outright triumph. It is indeed a tale of triumph, but a compromised triumph, for Ḥayy is incapable of communicating what he has learned to other men and Absāl succeeds by imitating Ḥayy's example before Ḥayy can speak and *as* he learns how to speak. Ineffable knowledge is necessarily incommunicable. The acquisition of language signals the inability to express the experience of the divine. Thus, Ḥayy cannot really communicate what he knows and returns to his almost solitary life of ascetic devotions on the Isle of Wāqwāq.

We are left to exercise our own powers of reason in order to evaluate Ḥayy's fate. His return to his island paradise reveals nature and corporeality to be ambiguous – it is both how Ḥayy is empowered to discover and commune with God, and how he is hindered from perpetual communion with the divine.

Moment Two, Baghdad ca. 338 / 950: The Debate Between Man and the Animals at the Court of the King of the Jinn by the Brethren of Purity (Ikhwān al-Ṣafāʾ)

My second moment also occurs in an imaginary setting but it is not a setting that is an imagined physical space. I mean the philosophical coterie of the Brethren of Purity. This group of philosophically minded thinkers are in a very real sense the direct descendants of Plotinus and his followers in Rome during the second century AD. As Plotinus and his fellow seekers of the truth lived lives of contemplation, yearning to found the ideal city of Platonopolis, so the Brethren of Purity explored the secrets of nature and God's creation in each other's company. The community which they sought to found was not a physical but a psychic city, a city of souls, for they shared with many other Muslim intellectuals of the classical eras a belief that through ethical cultivation and virtuous living, together with philosophical reasoning, their souls could somehow transcend their bodies and coexist with the souls of other like-minded humans in a manner which left materialism behind.

These enigmatic writers set out to write an encyclopaedic collection of fifty-two epistles, in which all learning, wisdom and correct bodily regimens would be set forth. So strong was their rejection of their physical selves, so keen their desire to efface their corporeal individualism and to realise psychic community through the annihilation of identity, that we do not know their identities with any real certainty or even when the epistles were written, despite the phenomenal popularity their writings enjoyed (and continue to enjoy) in the Muslim world. This prioritisation of the communal over the individual must also have been central to how they wrote, for the uniform style of the epistles suggests that they are the product of group composition.

Epistle Twenty-Two is *The Case of the Animals versus Man Before the King of the Jinn*. (The translation of the Arabic title of the work is: *On the Classes of Animals, their Wondrous Physiques and Unusual Behaviour*). Once again we find ourselves on an idyllic island in the Indian Ocean near the equator: the kingdom of Bīwarāsp the Wise, the King of the Jinn. (In Islamic folklore, the jinn, genies of the European imagination, are beings of fire who are often malevolent to man; in the Qur'an, we learn that some of the Jinn are Muslims, some unbelievers).

The Brethren tell us briefly of the history of human civilisation. Exiled from the Garden, Adam procreated and his descendants spread throughout the earth. For as long as humans were outnumbered by the animals, they lived in far-away places, in fear. They lived as vegetarian gatherers and foragers but did not molest or interfere in the animal kingdom. With towns and cities came the domestication of the animal kingdom. Domestication led to the enslavement and enforced labour of the beasts, much to the chagrin of the non-human animals. The animals who remained wild now inhabit the far-away places where once men lived in fear. But unlike the animals who did not molest these reclusive humans, the humans went beyond the domestication of non-human animals to hunting and trapping them out of a conviction that non-human animals were their slaves. So things continue, even after the arrival of Prophet Muhammad and his conversion of many of the Jinn.

We are told that Bīwarāsp and his people live in edenic bliss until a ship carrying merchants reaches his shores. The humans from the ship settle and build towns in this paradise regained. They impose their will on the non-human animals, beasts and cattle who, prior to the ship's arrival, inhabited the island in a state of natural splendour and harmony. In sum, humans are caught in a cycle of repression and unthinking hostility to the animal kingdom. This time, however, the animals send a delegation to Bīwarāsp and protest that the humans wrongly consider the animals to be their runaway slaves. Bīwarāsp, a wise and just king, invites seventy humans to come to his court to defend their position against the plaint of the animals.

A long and brilliant debate ensues between the animals, human and non-human, in which a dazzling array of positions are presented. At each turn, the non-human animal delegates defeat the arguments of their human opponents. In order to comprehend why the Brethren use the fabular device of giving voice to the animals in order to compose the zoological section of their encyclopaedia, why they excoriate humankind for their atrocious mistreatment of the natural world, and why they eventually conclude the debate as they do, we need to think about their Neoplatonic universe.

The Brethren's starting point is God's overwhelming grace and mercy. He is a providential creator who has so fashioned His creation as to ensure that every creature has what it needs in order to exist for its allotted span in a universe of perfect harmony and regularity. Stars and planets are set in hierarchically arranged spheres, and the course of these spheres is set by the angels who are both Neoplatonic intellects and Platonic Forms. God's beneficence emanates down through the spheres and angelic intellects. The regular rhythms of the universe are thus made possible by His providence but also exhibit His providence. Each link in this cosmic chain is charged with an obligation from God: that it must pass His bounty down to the level below it. This regularity and providential harmony is evident also in the supralunar world, that is the world of nature. God gives to each and every creature all that it needs and in return each and every natural being, set in the environment that God has decreed for it, acts in accordance with God's allotted gifts.

To man alone, however, God has granted an immortal soul, 'a ray of light shed by the Divine,' as ibn Tufayl's translator L E Goodman puts it, and this means that man alone will be resurrected and judged – only he can win paradise and thus only he is accountable for his actions. In order for man to win redemption and remain true to God's gift of an immortal soul, he is given the ability to make choices. Man alone in the universe as the Brethren constructed it is equipped with the faculty of choice, a faculty not even given by God to the angels.

Only man out of all of God's creation is not content to remain within the boundaries God has set for him. He has forgotten what the non-humans are only too cognisant of: that his achievements in science, tradecraft, industry, and ingenuity, would be impossible were it not for God's beneficent providence. Man has waxed arrogant and denied God's grace. He has failed to comprehend that, for all its regularity, the universe is not eternal, because its continued operation is another manifestation of providence. Man's achievements and capabilities are surpassed by similar capabilities in the non-human world, be it the social organisation of ants, the skilful fabrications of bees, the vision of birds, the compassionate behaviour of the griffin.

What man must learn from the other animals is that, although man has been singled out by God, and although the cosmos is anthropocentric, it is anthropocentric in a special sense. It is anthropocentric insofar as it exists to enable man to secure salvation and thus fulfil God's gifts to him; but it is not anthropocentric insofar as it does not exist for him to do with as he pleases.

According to the Brethren, the non-humans are natural monotheists: 'the highest piety, as the animals show by their own lives, is but a celebration of God's mercies and a quest for His compassion'. Goodman argues persuasively that for the Brethren, 'animals are not subjects', but have a 'virtual subjecthood' that recognises their 'moral standing'. The Brethren give animals the power of speech, Goodman posits, because of their 'intrinsic worth.'

Man is thus enjoined to emulate the non-humans and fully to grasp that God's decree is inexorable, that all things must pass, and that only God is perfect. The wisest choice a man can make is to seek refuge in God. In order to do this, he must recognise the teleology of non-human subjecthood, designed, at least as far as man is concerned, to allow the opportunity for him to perceive that choices are part of a system that is not articulated solipsistically. Such a perception is the crux of human obligation.

In what is both a surprising turn of events (because the non-humans are the real victors in the debate) and an inevitable conclusion (because the Brethren are unwilling to sacrifice the presence of the divine soul in man), victory is in the end given to the humans – but only just. Victory is awarded to the humans for the very thing which lifts them above the level of human and non-human: their ability to attain the status of 'friend of God' – i.e. the human capacity to leave the condition of humanness behind:

> Please realise that these men who are the friends of God, the purest and best of all of His creation, behave honourably and pleasingly, with deeds that are pious, learning that is multifarious, insight deific, character angelic, lifestyles just and beatific, behaviour wondrously majestic.

But as we saw with the tale of Ḥayy, the crux of the matter is ineffable:

> No one can describe their essential attributes adequately, and tongues grow
> weary when eloquent speakers try to list them. Over the ages many may have
> spoken of them in public gatherings, long homilies may have been devoted to
> the explanation of their exemplary lives and goodly ethos, but still their true
> nature has not yet been comprehended.

Thus, victory in the debate goes to the human, not because he is superior
to nature and to the eloquent representatives of the non-human kingdom
– quite the opposite, he abuses the position of responsibility God has given
him, his stewardship of the natural world is, as the non-humans establish,
tyrannical, and in the debate he is bested at every turn by the
representatives of the animal kingdom. Man is victorious because he can
achieve the incommunicable, he can realise the ineffable.

So, in what is a paradox typical of the Brethren's thought, humans must
exercise their God-given gift of choice in order to emulate the angels who
are not blessed with the gift of choice. Choice must be used judiciously,
wisely and piously, in order to be eradicated in utter, unquestioning
obedience. This is why the Brethren state right at the beginning of their
epistle that 'when virtuous and good, man is a noble angel, the best of
creation.' In order to fulfil our humanity, we must transcend what defines
us and marks us out as genuinely human – we must embrace the ineffable.

Moment Three, Arabia c. 620: Man and the Natural World in the Qur'an

It is hardly surprising that the first human to speak at the court of the
King of the Jinn builds his defence of humankind on verses from the
Qur'an. It is worth quoting this speech at some length, as it provides
many of the major aspects of the revelation which outline man's position
in the natural world:

> An orator, one of the descendants of al-ʿAbbās, stood up and delivered this
> speech from the pulpit: Praised be God, Lord of the Worlds, goal of those who
> are God-conscious, enemy of only those who do wrong. God bless our master
> Muhammad, Last of the Prophets, Imam of the Envoys, Dispenser of
> Intercession on Judgement Day. Praised be God 'who created man from
> water'(25:54). He created his wife from him, and spread their seed, men and

women, far and wide, honouring their offspring, carrying them by land and sea, and nourishing them with good things. As Almighty God says, 'He created cattle for you, for they bring warmth, and give many benefits. You can eat of them. They delight you when you drive them to pasture and lead them home at the end of the day. They carry heavy loads for you to lands you would struggle and suffer to reach' (16:5-7). The Almighty also says, 'You are carried on them and on ships' (40:80), and, 'Some cattle are beasts of burden, some are for slaughter' (6:142). Praised be God who says, 'horses, mules and donkeys for you to ride and take pride in. You cannot know all that He creates' (16:8), and 'for you to sit astride their backs and be mindful of your Lord's bounty when you are astride their backs' (43:13). There are many verses in the Qur'an, the Torah and the Gospels that show that animals were created for us and on account of us. They are our slaves, we their masters. I ask God's forgiveness for us all.

As Goodman and McGregor note, there are other key passages in the Qur'an which the orator does not adduce, such as 16:14-16:

He it is who subdued the sea, that you might eat moist flesh from it and bring forth from it jewellery to wear, and see ships cleaving it, that you may seek His bounty and mayhap be thankful. He pitched towering mountains on the earth, lest it shake you; rivers and passes that you may find your way, and landmarks – for by the stars are they guided.

At first sight, the evidence seems compelling. We could easily be forgiven for concluding with the orator in his defence of humankind that the whole created world is put at man's disposal for his benefit. The Qur'an appears to present creation as anthropocentric. Man is put in a position of pre-eminence and privilege. The mountains are created to stop earthquakes, which are a Qur'anic portent of the Last Day, the end of the world. Rivers and mountain roads allow man passage across insurmountable regions. The stars revolve in the night sky to help man find his way in safety. Cattle were created to provide transportation and food and skins to keep warm.

So how can the non-humans have a case before the King of the Jinn? Are they not simply being obstreperous, perverse and obstructive? Let us pay close attention to two aspects of the verses quoted by the 'Abbasid orator, verses which are almost drowned out in the hubbub:

horses, mules and donkeys for you to ride and take pride in. You cannot know all that He creates (16:8);

for you to sit astride their backs and be mindful of your Lord's bounty when you are astride their backs (43:13)

In short, these verses contain two important Qur'anic messages: (1) man's knowledge of things is limited compared to God's – His design may contain more than man is aware; and (2) man is enjoined to ponder, reflect upon and consider what God has given him in the form of these natural blessings. God puts the natural world at man's disposal to be enjoyed and used responsibly in keeping with the humility we feel in respect of His omniscience and the gratitude due to Him for His kindnesses.

Despite this encouragement and guidance, the orator concludes his series of quotations with a declaration that the non-human world is in thraldom to man.

The Brethren of Purity devote the remainder of their epistle to challenging this as an unwarranted inference to draw from the verses of the Qur'an.

The Qur'an has much to say about animals, human and non-human. In terms of non-human animals, the focus in the Qur'an is on the animals that its first audience would observe most frequently. This is most evident in the prominence of the insect world: spiders, flies, locusts, bees and ants abound. Perhaps the most conspicuous non-human animal is the camel, but the Qur'an reminds us that in God's universe jinn and angels are non-human animals. Furthermore, God repeatedly draws attention to all the aspects of His creation that man is not party to, so the universe may even be populated by unknown and unspecified creatures. We are also reminded of the animal languages that God occasionally makes it possible for human animals to comprehend. The natural, non-human world of the Qur'an is a numinous mystery. The human world, however, is all too often deaf to this numinousness.

Paradoxically, the Qur'an presents creation as both theocentric and anthropocentric. It is theocentric because, in the words of Sarra Tlili, 'any being that worships and obeys God obtains God's pleasure and is rewarded in the hereafter.' She also notes that 'non-human animals ... are answerable to God, not to human beings' and argues that 'privileged status is

contingent upon moral and religious uprightness, not species membership.'
She draws attention to how the Qur'an 'presents non-human animals as
psychologically complex beings' situated in a cosmos that is 'highly
interactive with its Creator: It makes choices, experiences emotions, takes
divine commands, prays, and hymns the praises of God.'

But it remains anthropocentric in that the Qur'an is addressed to
mankind, both good humans (i.e. those who are God-conscious, those who
are grateful to Him for His bounty and so have embraced Islam) and bad
humans, the wilful, woeful wrong-doers who have rejected God in their
ingratitude. Tlili reminds us that the Qur'an 'does challenge humans' self-
perceptions and brings to light many of the features that it considers moral
and spiritual flaws.' But not all human animals in the Qur'an are flawed.
All humans need constant reminders of God's grace, of course, but some
humans are so depraved and corrupt that they need constant
admonishment, in God's limitless mercy. In the Qur'an, the natural world,
while existing to obey and worship God, is designed somehow or other to
alleviate the burden of the good members of mankind. It is hard, Tlili's
persuasive arguments notwithstanding, to resist the conclusion that God's
creation and its non-human animals are figured in the Qur'an as a gift to
recompense the faithful for their displays of faith in this life. But that of
course should not be taken to mean that everything is placed in man's
power exclusively for his sake or that the sake of any non-human animal is
defined, delimited or determined by man's sake. It is an error of teleology
to assume that this is so.

In fact, it is a double teleological error. It misrepresents the purpose for
which non-humans and the natural world were created – to worship God
through uncompromising obedience and thus draw man's attention to
God's overwhelming kindness to him by committing such things to his
stewardship. And it misrepresents the purpose for which man was created
– to celebrate God's generosity through the appreciation of His blessings.
Creation is thus anthropocentric, albeit in only a limited way – for it is
actually theocentric. Man is not the end of the chain but another link
fashioned by God. Man's brutal treatment of non-human animals and abuse
of the animal kingdom is a perversion of God's plan for man and for His
creation. As His special creature, before whom God asked the angels to
kneel down in supplication, man should aspire to emulate God insofar as

he is able. God is kind to man. Man should show gratitude to God for his gifts by being kind to other creatures in turn and in so doing 'join a harmonious cosmic order of submission to the decrees of their Creator.' It is thus that man will be rewarded in this life and the next.

Moment Four, Arabia ca. 600: The Zoomorphism of the Outlaw Poet al-Shanfarā

The era before the revelation of the Qur'an to Prophet Muhammad is known in Arabic as the *Jāhiliyyah*: the Age of Ignorance, i.e. of the Revelation; or the Age of Savage Barbarism. For many in the classical era, a potent sign of the divine origin of the Qur'an was the forbidding, hostile and savage landscape into which it was revealed. Not only was the terrain inhospitable – desert upon desert of barren waste, with few settlements and townships. The people who inhabited that terrain were equally savage and inhospitable: lawless Bedouin nomads who were devoted to their ideals of vendetta and waged continuous warfare on each other as they crossed the deserts in their seasonal transhumance, from watering-hole to pasture land.

This savage barbarity was celebrated in mighty odes of a daunting complexity and forbidding diction. These odes sing of conquest, of masculine triumph over women, foe and nature, defiant challenges to the implacable desert.

The poets of these odes were thought to be gifted each with their own *shayṭān*, the word which we today know in English as 'Satan' – a familiar demon who whispered to them intimations of the unseen world. They were wild warriors, charged with singing the achievements of their tribe but they also lived on the margin of the tribe whose praises they sang, because they were both of this world and not of this world.

Of all the wild warriors, few were wilder than the *ṣa'ālīk*, the 'brigand' poets, outlawed by their tribes for conduct which could not be tolerated of even a peripheral presence. One brigand poet, Ta'abbaṭa Sharrā, whose name means 'he picked up wickedness and carried it under his arm,' taken by the tradition to be an allusion to his easy familiarity with noxious snakes, sings of how he encounters a *ghūl*, a shape-shifting ghoul, in the desert:

Who will tell the braves of Clan Fahm   my tale?
At Raḥā Bitān   I came face to face with a ghoul
darting through a barren desert   flat as a sheet of vellum
'Back off!' I warned her,   'we're both exhausted, always on the move'
but she lunged in attack   I parried with polished Yemeni steel
my aim was true   down she fell, flat, on face and hands.
'Hit me once more!' 'Stay still. My resolve is true!'
I lay on top of her all night   waiting for dawn to see
what had attacked me   eyes in a cat's grim skull
split tongue   an aborted camel's misshapen legs
head of dog hair   rags
like an old cloak   or a tattered waterskin

Of all the wild brigands, few were wilder than al-Shanfarā, the wild
man of the tribe of Azd. Ostracised by his tribe, the outlaw poet becomes
zoomorphised. In his relentless defiance of his society, he successively
surpasses the hardiness of the wolf and the speed of the sand-grouse to
become a mountain ibex. Here is the climax of his famous poem known
as the *Lāmiyyat al-'Arab*, the poem of the desert Arabs rhyming in the
letter '*lām*':

Dog-days   mirages melt
vipers slither   on terracotta sand
I face the sun   bare but for a few rags and
a mane of wild hair   messy knots that blow in the wind
caked in a year's grime   lice-ridden
tangled   unchrismed

A desert torn by winds   shield flat
empty   no sign of humans
I climbed the mountains   at its farthest lip
I stand and squat   the lord of all I survey
amid the dark fleecy ibexes   like girls in long flowing robes
my shelter   from the midday blaze

Safe in my fastness   I am a buck

white-legged   massive-horned

By the end of his poem, the outcast poet, so long uncivilised and so far
from the company of other humans, has transformed himself into an ibex.
Zoomorphism has effaced humanity – though like the non-humans in the
epistle of the Brethren, al-Shanfarā retains the power of speech.

The brigand poets are in a sense not so different from Ibn Ṭufayl's wild
man, Ḥayy ibn Yaqẓān, on the Isle of Wāqwāq. To be sure, the
Neoplatonism of Ibn Ṭufayl takes Ḥayy into the presence of the divine. But
both Ḥayy and al-Shanfarā exult in the wonder of nature, unlike the men
before the King of the Jinn who mistreat God's creatures and inflict pain
upon them.

Moment Five-Basra, 244/858: The Book of Living by Abū ʿUthmān al-Jāḥiẓ

Iraq in the ninth century was where one of the most startling cultural
events of the pre-modern world unfolded: the translation into Arabic on a
phenomenal scale of works in Greek, Syriac, Pahlavi and Sanskrit. The
ninth century intellectual elite of Iraq had access to more of the writings
of Greek antiquity than we enjoy today. They spent roughly the equivalent
of the annual scientific research budget of a first-world country on
locating, establishing and editing the manuscripts, translating them into
Arabic and retranslating them if the original translations proved deficient.

Al-Jāḥiẓ was an omnivorous reader of this material. A theologian and
writer, he died in Basra in Iraq in 868, imprisoned in his own body by a
stroke. His bold synthesis of the meaning of existence and his difficult style
of writing marked him out for posterity as a wild man and thus he became
proverbial for his ugliness.

His magnum opus is one of the most remarkable books to have survived
in Arabic: a detailed, extensive, and at times breath-taking survey of the
natural world. This tumultuous and seemingly anarchic seven-volume
treatise is known as *The Book of Living*. In it al-Jāḥiẓ intended to explore
God's creation and to reveal the multifaceted design which it contained.
For al-Jāḥiẓ, creation was a semiotic system, a site filled with a cornucopia
of signs and indications which God had tasked man with reading correctly.

Many of these signs, according to al-Jāḥiẓ, were located in the non-human animals God had created to share the world with man.

Here are two passages from the book that showcase the author's verve and bravura. In the first passage, Polemon, the first speaker, is the author of an important text from Greek antiquity known as the *Physiognomy* and the second speaker Māsarjawayh is a Christian Arab physician. The third speaker is, of course, al-Jāḥiẓ himself:

Polemon said: 'Understand that pigeons and other birds do not respond well to being loosed from great distances. Their sense of direction depends on their training and on whether they have been habituated to a particular place. The first step is for the bird to be taken up and out onto a roof top, and for a marker which it recognises to be set up. It should not fly beyond where it dwells. Food should be thrown to it on the roof, morning and evening, close by the marker set up for it, in order for it to become familiar with the spot and accustomed to returning there. Let the fancier attend to what the marker is made out of. It must never be black or anything which looks black when viewed from a distance. The bigger the marker, the better it is as a sign. He should never let the pigeon fly at the same time as its mate. He should pluck the feathers of one and let the other loose in flight. Both should be brought out onto the roof at the same time. The one with its feathers intact should be loosed in flight for it will yearn for its mate and, when it knows the place, it will circle and return, having become familiar with the spot. When the feathers of the other bird have grown back, this bird should be treated in the same way. It is even better to bring them both out onto the roof with clipped wings, so that they can become familiar with the spot. Then one of them should be loosed in flight before its fellow, and the second should be treated in the same way the first had been.'

How similar these words are to what Māsarjawayh said. In his book he gave an account of the nature of all types of milk and drinking them as medication. When he had finished his account, he said: 'Thus I have given you an account of the condition of these types of milk *qua* milk, but attend to the patients for whom you prescribe milk to drink. In the first instance, you, the patient, need to purge your stomach and you need to consult someone who knows how much milk your disorder requires, and how the class to which your disorder belongs relates to the class to which the milk belongs.'

This is similar to what a carpenter once said in my house. I had employed him to hang a large, expensive door, so I said to him, 'It is a difficult thing to hang a door well. Scarcely one in a hundred carpenters has the knack. Someone may have an excellent reputation for being skilled in constructing ceilings and domes but not be fully proficient at hanging a door properly. Yet ordinary people generally think that ceilings and domes are harder. There are parallels for this. For example, a servant or a maid may be adept at roasting a whole kid or a new born goat, but not at roasting a side of meat. Those who have no knowledge suppose that it is easier to roast a part than the whole.' 'You did a good thing to let me know that you were examining my work,' he replied, 'for now that I know what you know it will prevent me from doing a botched job.' He hung the door and did an excellent job. But I did not have a ring in the house for the front of the door, for when I wanted to lock it, so I said, 'I do not want to detain you until my servant can get to the market and back. So bore me a hole for the pin to go in.' When he had bored the hole and received his payment he went to leave and then turned back and said, 'I have drilled the hole properly. But attend to the carpenter who will fit the pin for you – if he misses with just one blow he will split the door. And that would be a shame for a crack will spoil the door!' Then I understood that he knew his craft inside out.

This was a society which valued personal testimony and eye-witness, in which every day, mundane events demanded the attention of the man of reasoning intellect. In the passage, I especially like the way the ancient Greek heritage, medical knowledge and ordinary, personal experience are ranked side by side and provide a running commentary on each other.

Personal testimony and eye-witness are central to the practice of experimentation. Consider the following account of a scientific experiment:

Now, the reason why our companions know about the intoxication of animals is as follows. When Muḥammad b. ʿAlī b. Sulaymān al-Hāshimī had fed alcohol to ʿAlluwayh (whom everyone knows as 'The Dog of the Kitchen'), then to al-Duhmān, to the imbibers of Basra, and to anyone who visited Basra – in fact to all the hard drinkers who came within his reach – he decided to feed alcohol to camels, Bactrian and Arab, to ungulates, buffaloes and cows, and to horses, thoroughbreds and jades. When he had finished with every animal which had a large frame and a capacious stomach, he moved on to sheep and gazelles. Next he moved on to vultures, dogs and weasels. Then a snake-charmer visited them and they secured his services. He had a trick – he knew of how to open the mouths of snakes and to pour liquid right into their stomachs using stalks and nose-syringes. He would use what was appropriate for each thing. He was hardly human – material things complied with him and other men did his bidding. Thus it was that they were able to observe these differences in all those different classes of animals.

The Arabic title of the work that these passages are included in is *Kitāb al-Ḥayawān*. This is usually rendered as *The Book of Animals*. As we begin to appreciate the centrality of man to al-Jāḥiẓ's vision for the book, more and more scholars are beginning to refer to it as *The Book of Living Beings* or *Living Things*. I hear a deep echo of the word *ḥayawān* in the Qur'an, 29: 64, a verse in which the word carries the meaning of 'living': 'This life down here is but frivolity and dalliance. The next dwelling – it is living (*ḥayawān*), if only they knew.' And in fact al-Jāḥiẓ himself alludes to this meaning:

> If someone says, 'So and so has produced a book on the classes of living things (*ḥayawān*) but does not include the angels and the jinn, though that is normally how people use the word,' there is another occurrence of the word 'living' (*ḥayawān*) – the words of the Great and Glorious God in His Book: 'The next dwelling – it is living.'

I think al-Jāḥiẓ must have meant his title to evoke this unique Qur'anic use of the word.

Al-Jāḥiẓ was a bibliomaniac, a master of the dialectical method of thinking about God and reality (material and moral) known as *kalām*. He was also a prominent intellectual, a spokesman for influential members of the political and cultural elite, and a writer who lived, counselled and wrote in Iraq during the first century of the ʿAbbasid caliphate.

He came to prominence during the reign of Caliph al-Maʾmūn (r. 198-218/813-833), famous for its promotion of the Arabic translations of Greek philosophical and scientific learning, and died shortly after the caliphate of al-Mutawakkil (r. 232-247/847-861). In the intervening years he advised, argued and rubbed shoulders with the major power brokers and leading religious and intellectual figures of his day, from the caliphs and the brutal vizier (but accomplished epistolographer) Muḥammad b. ʿAbd al-Malik al-Zayyāt, to the forbidding Chief Judge Aḥmad Ibn Abī Duʾād and the cultured courtier al-Fatḥ b. Khāqān, from the brilliant dialectician al-Naẓẓām and the Neoplatonising philosopher al-Kindī to the pious scholar Aḥmad b. Ḥanbal.

At one time or another al-Jāḥiẓ acted as counsellor and adviser to these masters of the political universe, often expressing views with which they did not agree. And at one time or another he crossed swords in debate and argument with the architects of the Islamic religious, theological, philosophical and cultural canon. He did not agree with most of them. His many, tumultuous writings engage with these figures, their ideas, theories and policies and thus afford an invaluable but much neglected chronicle of the anxieties, values and beliefs of this cosmopolitan elite.

'Abbasid society was swamped with a proliferation of new types of knowledge, most of it, as we have seen, coming from translations of Greek and Indian science and philosophy, and was challenged by new ways of disseminating and devouring the knowledge to which it was already so deeply attached. Books became a cultural obsession.

The introduction of papermaking techniques into second century Iraq heralded a third century technological revolution in the refinement of rag-paper and the production of books written on rag-paper rather than leather or parchment (although there was a period of overlap in which all three media continued to be used). It quickly became no longer acceptable simply and without justification or premeditation to rely on predominantly oral forms of disseminating knowledge.

Al-Jāḥiẓ was at the vanguard of this 'knowledge revolution', an insatiable reader and writer of books who would hire out bookshops overnight in order to consume its stock of volumes without being disturbed. Indeed, in one late source he is said to have died on one such occasion, when, a frail and elderly man suffering from paralysis, he was crushed by a collapsing pile of books. The popularity of this story in modern scholarship attests to the power of its appeal.

The Book of Living was written over more than a decade that was marked for al-Jāḥiẓ by personal catastrophe (a debilitating stroke) and political danger (the death of two patrons). Work on it was begun before 232/847. The latest events it refers to are in 244/858. This was a decade which witnessed a turning away from kalām theology when the Caliph al-Mutawakkil banned debate and so endangered the dialectical method for ascertaining the truth which al-Jāḥiẓ considered central to the ordering, stability and preservation of his society. He wrote *The Book of Living* in response to these concerns.

The enterprise began as an attempt to fulfil a moral imperative – the need to thank God for His creation by producing a comprehensive inventory of it. The production of such an inventory involved the proper application of the special gift which God had given to man: the reasoning intellect.

To this end al-Jāḥiẓ sought to codify his inventory in the form of a totalising book. Yet the process was paradoxical: in order to write it, al-Jāḥiẓ had somehow to become the ideal writer. This meant that he had effectively to mimic God by aspiring to omniscience, while fully aware that he could never be such an ideal writer. He must have wondered whether his book could ever be complete, yet his notion of moral obligation (*taklīf*) required that he undertake the task. He produced possibly the longest, and probably the most complex, book written in Arabic at the time. But it seems that the struggle for completeness resulted in the work being unfinished.

Not all of his contemporaries agreed or approved of the enterprise. *The Book of Living* was subjected to a withering criticism that extended beyond *The Book of Living* itself to engulf most of his public writings and become a categorical rejection of the benefits which the book as an artefact brought to society. Al-Jāḥiẓ reverts throughout *The Book of Living* to this criticism. The initial 200 pages of the first volume (in its modern edited version) engage specifically with the attack.

Al-Jāḥiẓ designed his book to save society from the competitive strife in which argument and debate had engulfed it. Debate could now be internalised in the soul of the reader. This was made possible because books encouraged solitary reading and interior debate. How could someone think that a book could save society? Al-Jāḥiẓ's answer lay in an appreciation of God's design in the universe. The third century abounded in books on the subject. The theological premise of the *Book of Living* is that God has put in man a primary appreciation of His design. Al-Jāḥiẓ's book explores this primary appreciation of design and so directs its appeal at the monotheists in his audience. By participating in the process of becoming his ideal readers, this audience will be led to recognise that creation can only fully and properly, however imperfectly, be appreciated through al-Jāḥiẓ's (Islamic) account of design.

But for al-Jāḥiẓ this task of reading the semiotic system of creation was not straightforward. In fact, viewed from an Enlightenment perspective we might perhaps be tempted to describe his grand labour as a failure. If we did, however, we would be as guilty of misrepresentation as are the men at the court of the King of the Jinn. This is because al-Jāḥiẓ set out to explore exactly what it means for man to be placed at the centre of creation—for the sake of man, and for the sake of the other creatures with whom he shares this world. Like the Brethren of Purity, he believed that everything created has a purpose, but that its purpose is not always apparent, or even discernible upon careful consideration and examination. In other words, al-Jāḥiẓ heeds the injunctions from the Qur'an which I discussed previously: (1) man's knowledge of things is limited compared to God's – His design may contain more than man is aware; (2) man is enjoined to ponder, reflect upon and consider what God has given him in the form of these natural blessings.

This *Book of Living*, this textual survey of creation, is based extensively on the early Arabic translation of Aristotle's biological writings. It investigates the limitations of language and scientific taxonomy in classifying the natural world. Al-Jāḥiẓ sets up lists and categories and then subsequently collapses them and leaves them hanging with little explicit guidance on how we his readers are to reconstruct them or on whether we are to abandon them. His interest is almost exclusively in the hybrid, the inter-category, the creature which can belong to more than one category. The eunuch is one of his favourite examples, for the eunuch is both male and not-male because it has been deprived of the ability to procreate, to do what characterises a male human being as male. The ambiguity of his status after castration raises important problems for the laws which in Islam govern how men and women should mix.

In a sense then this difficult and impenetrable book mimics the impenetrability of God's plan as it is demonstrated by His creation of the natural world and the animal kingdom. And so once again, we are back at the unknowability of things and the ineffability of the divine. Al-Jāḥiẓ's commitment to the moral obligation he believed God had put man under through God's gift of the reasoning intellect (ʿaql) and his primary vehicle for expressing his gratitude to God (eloquence) was so strong that he would never have had recourse to an embracing of the ineffable. After all, he refused to have recourse to silence when his powers of speech were strongly impaired by his stroke. He may certainly have struggled to find the means adequately to communicate his appreciation of God's design, and he would never have for one moment have presumed to think that his communication of it could ever be comprehensive or exhaustive, for God was ultimately unknowable and beyond man's comprehension. But struggle he did and I, for one, am grateful to him for his uncompromising efforts, because this struggle has given us *The Book of Living*, one of the truly great books of the human spirit.

Epilogue: J.M. Coetzee, Elizabeth Costello and The Lives of Animals

In 1997-98 the Nobel-prize winning novelist J.M. Coetzee delivered the Tanner Lectures at Princeton University. However, he did not deliver two ordinary lectures, for this most elusive of writers delivered two lectures which tell the story of how a famous Australian novelist, Elizabeth Costello, delivers two lectures at Appleton College, an occasion that, of course, mirrors the event hosted by Princeton.

Originally published as *The Lives of Animals*, the lectures are 'The Philosophers and the Animals'; 'The Poets and the Animals.' Perhaps I should not refer to two lectures because the visit is narrated through the eyes of Costello's son John Bernard, an Assistant Professor of Physics and Astronomy at Appleton, and he is delayed by a meeting and so we miss the delivery of the second lecture, 'The Poets and the Animals.' Instead, we attend the question and answer session that follows the lecture. And in John's company, we also attend the staged dialogue between Costello and Thomas O'Hearne, Appleton's Professor of Philosophy.

Just as Costello's lectures elicit a plethora of words in response, so Coetzee's lectures elicited responses in *The Lives of Animals* – a series of four 'Reflections,' by Marjorie Garber, Peter Singer, Wendy Doniger and Barbara Smuts. The volume also contains an introduction by Amy Gutmann. In turn, the book elicited a second book of responses: *Philosophy and Animal Life*, with contributions from Cary Wolfe, Cora Diamond, Stanley Cavell, John McDowell and Ian Hacking. And clearly Costello's lectures did not leave Coetzee untouched, for he subsequently included them as Lessons Three and Four in his novel *Elizabeth Costello*. (For that matter Costello clearly would not leave Coetzee alone, for she suddenly appears in the sickroom of Paul Rayment, the protagonist of Coetzee's 2005 novel *Slow Man*, who must try to adapt to life after losing a leg in a road traffic accident.)

As I re-read Coetzee/Costello in the context of writing this article on man and nature, I was struck by Costello's articulate struggle with words. She is not short of words, yet seems incapable adequately of expressing the lived consequences for her of her horror and revulsion at the lives animals are forced to live in modern societies. At the end of 'The Poets and the Animals,' as she is being driven to the airport by her son, she declares:

> I no longer know where I am … Calm down I tell myself, you are making a mountain out of a molehill. This is life. Everyone else comes to terms with it, why can't you? *Why can't you?*

The italics express a muffled scream. When her son looks at her he sees her 'tearful face.'

Elizabeth is rarely hesitant to express herself. Like al-Jāḥiẓ, she refuses to seek recourse to silence and is eloquent (in writing and apparently also in talking, if not in delivering her lecture). In 'The Philosophers and the Animals,' she mounts a sustained critique of the hegemony of reason (and attendant concepts like consciousness and self-awareness) which she dismisses as merely a tendency in human thought, one among many (p. 67), for reason has consigned all beings that do not exhibit or express its like to a second-class status (p. 78). According to Elizabeth, fiction allows us to enter the minds of others, whether those others are real or imaginary persons, and therefore fiction, and not philosophy, allows us to think our way into 'the existence of a bat' (p. 80). So when pressed to enunciate the point of her talk, to state her principles, she urges the audience to 'listen to what your heart says' (p. 82). At the end of the dinner hosted by the President of Appleton College in her honour, Elizabeth declares, 'I don't know what I think … I wonder what thinking is, what understanding is. Do we really understand the universe better than animals do?' (p. 90). (Of course, this is the very thing Elizabeth refused to do earlier: to offer a statement of principle.)

However, the existential crisis Elizabeth finds herself caught up in is not a struggle for words but a struggle for communication. For though she is not lost for the words to express the horror she feels and thinks, she fails to communicate this horror to others. This is the reason why everyone she meets finds her difficult, if not impossible, to get on with, including her son John. She is unable to get her fellow human animals to share her reality. And in this respect, she fails where the poets she discusses in her second lecture succeed.

The topic of 'The Poets and the Animals,' the second lecture, is a discussion of three poems: *The Panther* by Rainer Maria Rilke, and *The Jaguar* and *Second Glance at a Jaguar* by Ted Hughes. These poems, according to Elizabeth, invite us to inhabit the body of the panther or the jaguar (p. 98). They are 'the record of the engagement' with the animal, though when transmogrified into words, whatever feelings this engagement engenders are abstracted 'for ever from the animal' (p. 98).

In a statement that resonates very powerfully for me and has much to say about how I have endeavoured to read the five texts from the classical Arabic textual tradition, Coetzee's Costello, who is not uncritical of Ted Hughes, notes how:

> when we read the jaguar poem, when we recollect it afterwards in tranquillity, we are for a brief while the jaguar. He ripples within us, he takes over our body, he is us.

Let me end, then, with a poem from the Arabic tradition that in my opinion does just what Costello says happens when she reads Hughes's *Jaguar*. The Arabic poem is one of the *ṭardiyyāt*, the hunting poems, a genre of poetry that enjoyed great vogue from the third/eighth to the fourth/tenth centuries. The poem is to be found in the *dīwān*, the collected poetry, of al-Ḥasan ibn Hāni', better known as Abū Nuwās (d. c. 200/813-814). It describes a horse of elemental power that takes over our body.

Rays lit up the sky
Black night struck camp –
Proof it was day.
I brought out Colt – a stallion of brute power and pedigree.
Fire's energy coursed
Through his tight-twist, taut-rope joints
He was sent to earth by night clouds guided by a rising star
Showered with their gifts

Blessed by clouds black with rain
In constant downpours.
He drank from their bounty. Limbs grew strong.

We approached. The ass neighed in alarm.
Colt stirred with lust.
The ass sprinted from al-Ṭuwā's holy trees.
I said to my slave, an expert hunter:
'Mount! Colt makes me anxious.'
His light frame settled on Colt's back.
He fired him. Colt's eyes swam with water.
He hunted a hardloin male –
A thrust that made its jaws spew
Thick belly blood mixed with spit
The bitter food of death
Delivered by doom's lightning bolt
Neck iridescent, voltaic.

INVESTIGATING GOD, INVESTIGATING NATURE

Laura Hassan

In 1997, Stephen Gould coined the term 'Non-Overlapping Magisteria' (NOMA) to label the conviction that science, dealing in the realm of 'facts', and religion, dealing (as he suggests) in the realm of 'values' should be carefully distinguished as fields of enquiry. This cleaving of the investigation of nature and its phenomena from the study of the Divinity is, for many theists, problematic. The casual reader of the Qur'an quickly understands why this is true for many Muslims, so insistent it is on celebrating the natural world as the supreme manifestation of the sovereignty and mercy of God.

One recent Muslim reaction to the notion that religion and science do not mix has been the attempt to show the inherent compatibility of the Qur'an with all that modern science has to offer. This trend, termed 'scientific exegesis' is, however, incapable of countering the firm trajectory of modern science in its resolute dissolution of the relationship between the realms.

Considering how Muslim *mutakallimūn* of the classical and post-classical periods related to nature and its study within their works of *kalām* offers an alternative perspective to what Gould considers the 'standard position' on the boundaries between 'science' and 'religion'. We will find that physical theory, that is, the investigation of matter, features within a global enquiry into all reality and that for the theist, since reality includes the Divine, there need be – can be – no neat divisions of magisteria.

So let's begin with the Qur'an's basic conception of nature's status, and then consider how this is interpreted across several centuries of theological reflection. The aim is to demonstrate how the investigation of nature in Muslim history concurred with what we might consider 'theology proper', offering an alternative to Gould's understanding of the science-religion interface.

The Qur'anic imperative to its hearers to reflect on the natural order is clear. According to one count, words based on the root *kh-l-q*, 'to create', occur 248 times. So prominent a theme is creation that as Izutsu puts it 'the Qur'an may be regarded in a certain sense as a grand hymn in honour of Divine creation.' The cosmos, animal life, plant life, and supremely, humankind, are all subjects of the Qur'an's celebration. Some Qur'anic references to creation touch on the processes by which phenomena in nature occur. For instance, Sura 30 v 48 reads: 'God is He Who sends the winds, so they raise clouds, and spread them along the sky as He wills, and then break them into fragments, until you see rain drops come forth from their midst! Then when He has made them fall on whom of His slaves as He will, lo! they rejoice!' The stages of human reproduction are the Qur'an's favoured example of a step-by-step process by which something wonderful comes to be.

The immediate context of all Qur'anic references to the natural order is the insistent call to worship pervading the entire Qur'an. Sky, clouds, rain, seas, beasts, birds, even bees and spiders all demand the hearer's attention as evidence of God's power and benevolence. That the natural order should point its inhabitants towards God is repeatedly and persuasively stated: 'Truly, in the creation of the heavens and the earth and the variation of night and day there are signs (*āyāt*) for those of understanding, those who remember God standing, sitting, and lying on their sides, and who contemplate the creation of the heavens and the earth: "Our Lord, you did not create this for nothing!" (3:190-191).'

The Qur'an's celebration of nature is, then, (unsurprisingly) really a celebration of the One outside of nature. The intricacies and order of life as we know it, and in particular the manner in which the natural order accommodates mankind, demand not an appreciation of nature in itself as much as an attitude of humble reverence toward its Creator – a God with a special interest in mankind. Rahman termed this Qur'anic notion the 'non-ultimacy' of nature. Creation is, in the Qur'anic worldview, the natural counterpart to the Qur'an itself, both signs pointing beyond themselves to their author.

How does the call to reflect on God's supremacy as revealed in the natural order inform nature's study? On the one hand, nature is to be celebrated. The Qur'an itself apparently provides some data about physical processes, which would seem to encourage investigation of the natural world. On the other, nature in itself is not the object of reverence. This precludes natural theories which do not accommodate a supernatural agent. Rahman views certain natural philosophies as undermining the Qur'an's message: 'For many naturalists', he writes, 'the universe is not a sign pointing beyond itself, but is the ultimate reality.' He believes that for such individuals, the stability of nature and its apparent self sufficiency provide a 'snug haven' within which to avoid moral accountability.

Science, the study of nature, is, then, in one sense invited by the Qur'an, and yet it is clear how the same can be construed as a threat to the Qur'anic worldview. So what is the appropriate approach to scientific investigation for the thinker committed to the Qu'ranic vision of nature's status?

I have already mentioned the trend for scientific exegesis of the Qur'an (known as *tafsīr 'ilmī*). In response to the dominance of modern scientific theories, some have sought to prove the Qur'an's compatibility with such knowledge. Maurice Bucaille's well-known 'The Bible, the Qur'an and Modern Science' is a proof-text for this trend, compiling Qur'anic references to the natural order and explaining how they are true to modern science (to give a famous example, Qur'anic references, such as Sūra 96 v 2, to the human embryo as an *'alaq,* 'clinging thing', are hailed for their accuracy in relation to the process of implantation). Numerous editions have been circulated by those who view such exegesis as a timely and strategic tool for apologetics and evangelism. The impulse is to demonstrate the reliability of the scripture and therefore God's supremacy over modern learning.

This is not, of course, a natural philosophy in its own right. It involves no independent investigation of nature, relying instead on modern science and an occasionally tortuous reading of the Qur'an. This in fact makes modern science, and not the Qur'an, ultimate, by suggesting that the reliability of the latter is premised on its compatibility with the former. Sardar, Mir and others have criticised this trend for its reductionism. It is apologetic at best, and at worst, involves a decontextualising hermeneutic which compromises the more obvious intent of the passages in question. This kind of exegesis may reflect a certain insecurity on the part of some Muslims faced with the way in which modern science is sometimes so confidently promoted as an alternative to theism, as if the two were mutually exclusive.

Historical *kalām* approaches to scientific study offer an alternative. Classical *kalām* theologians took interest in nature within a far more comprehensive framework for investigation of all reality which did not distinguish the 'scientific' from the 'theological'. It is to this tradition which I now turn, picking out some moments in the history of *kalām* pertinent to its approach to the investigation of the natural world. The theologians in question were responding to the tension maintained within the Qur'an between nature's non-ultimacy on the one hand and its inherent interest on the other. Several lessons can be learnt from some simple observations on their resolutions of this tension.

Lesson 1, The Mu'tazila: Scientific investigation can form a legitimate part of a comprehensive investigation of reality also including study of the Divinity

I begin with the Mu'tazila, the Islamic world's first practitioners of rational, dialectical theology, known primarily in Western scholarship for their emphasis on divine justice and free will (and normally contrasted with the other dominant school of rational theology, the Ash'arīs, characterised by their emphasis on God's absolute freedom of action and the denial of genuine human agency). My task is complicated by the lack of extant sources for the earliest history of *kalām*. Ideally, we should access those *kalām* sources in which cosmology, physics, and so on, first appeared. This is as impossible as establishing with certainty the origins of *kalām*. Our earliest sources (aside from al-Ash'arīs' doxography, *Maqālāt al-Islāmiyyīn*) are a number of works from the sixth/tenth century, each with its own procedure and priorities. Taken together, the sources attest that physical theoretical investigation is already by this time integral to the project of Mu'tazilism.

The earliest surviving Mu'tazilī source, ibn al-Khayyāṭ's (d. 912) *Kitāb al-Intiṣār*, is a defence of school positions against the renegade Mu'tazilī turned sceptic ibn al-Rawandī (d. c. 910). Although the agenda is set by ibn al-Rawandī's critique, here already it is clear that physical theory is integral to Muʿtazilism. For instance, according to ibn al-Khayyāṭ, al-Naẓẓām's (d. c. 845) response to the eternalists (al-dahariyya) relies on premises known through observation of nature, including the finitude of material bodies, and the impossibility of eternal motion. Whilst here the physical theoretical premise that motion must have a beginning serves the theological end of proving the world's origination in time (and in turn, its need for a creator), physical theory also appears independently. For instance, ibn al-Khayyāṭ clarifies al-Naẓẓām's theory on fire, namely that it constitutes the mixture of the two bodies heat and light, both of which possess the accident endurance (baqāʾ), such that fire does not come to exist anew moment by moment. The nature of sound is another exemplary topic the debate over which has no underlying theological import.

At one point in his response to ibn al-Rawandī, ibn al-Khayyāṭ refers to laṭīf al-kalām, the 'subtle questions'. This recalls a common distinction between jalīl al-kalām and laṭīf al-kalām, the former concerning major doctrinal issues such as the existence of God and his attributes, the latter, physical theoretical, epistemological, anthropological and other beliefs. Ibn al-Khayyāṭ comments that the Muʿtazila have the best insights into the latter because they are 'the masters of kalām and the people of knowledge and insight into the subtle questions of kalām, having mastered its manifest questions'. Elsewhere he suggests that their mastery of subjects other than theology proper is what distinguishes the Muʿtazila from others. These comments show that the Muʿtazila considered their own theology marked out by the breadth of its discussions, scientific theory included.

The first three volumes of ʿAbd al-Jabbār's (d. 1025) Kitāb al-Mughnī fī abwāb al-tawḥīd wa-l-ʿadl, the first extant systematic treatise of Muʿtazilī theology, which undoubtedly contain his discussions of body, substance and accident, are unfortunately as yet unpublished. A shorter work, a commentary on his own Kitāb al-Uṣūl al-Khamsa, is, however, another important source for classical Muʿtazilism. As the title suggests, the focus of this work is key theological doctrines. Thus, physical theory appears in the service of theology proper. Three brief examples will illustrate exactly how science functions here.

In proving the doctrine that God is not body (which is part of the kalam understanding of God's transcendental greatness), ʿAbd al-Jabbār treats definitions of body. This involves statement of his own physical theoretical belief that the smallest number of atomic parts constitutive of body is eight, a theory formed in the context of intra-Muʿtazilī debates. In the doctrinal context of establishing that the human agent is incapable of creating body, ʿAbd al-Jabbār's argument entails defence of the physical theory of the existence of the void. Similarly, ʿAbd al-Jabbār's theory of motion, namely his doctrine that bodies possess accidents of spatial occupation (*akwān*) is proven within the doctrinal context of establishing the world's creation *ex nihilo* by a Creator God. Though, in themselves, questions related to body, space and motion are physical theoretical, the intent of the discussions in this work is clearly not scientific in that the inherent interest is in the nature of God, and not of the material world. Yet it is remarkable how integral scientific questions are to the investigation of God.

Though Muʿtazilism is most generally known for its distinctive theological positions as evidenced by works like *Kitāb al-Uṣūl al-Khamsa* and its commentary, other lesser-studied extant works tell of the towering significance of natural philosophical doctrine for the Muʿtazila. Ibn Mattawayh's (d. c. 1010) *Tadhkira fī aḥkām al-jawāhir wa'l-aʿrāḍ* is an extensive compendium devoted exclusively to the properties of substance and accident. The work begins with a categorisation of objects of knowledge (*maʿlumāt*) and proceeds to exclude the eternal (*al-qadīm*, that is, the deity), from its investigations. What remains is everything else: this work is envisioned as a comprehensive investigation of created reality.

This includes physical theoretical topics, but also anthropology, psychology, epistemology and ethics. What is remarkable is the seamlessness with which the author navigates between diverse realms. A large part of the first volume is devoted to the discussion of substance. This involves what we would describe as scientific investigations: the constituents of body, the nature of spatial occupation, the phenomenon of fire, the divisibility of matter, and so on. The discussion of accidents occupies the remainder of the first volume and the entirety of the second. Within this remit fall topics from investigation of the phenomenon of colour and its perception, of pleasure and pain, of motion, to the definition of 'human' and related anthropological topics, epistemological questions, through to psychological topics such as the nature of laughter and crying. Occasionally, questions arise which we would consider theological: that bodies can only come into existence by the power of God, that it is within the human agent's power to create sound, and that accidents of colour can only be created by God.

A comparable work is al-Nīsābūrī's (fl. first half eleventh century), *al-Masā'il fī al-khilāf bayn al-baṣriyyīn wa'l-baghdādiyyīn*. In his introduction to this work, its author sets out his project of investigating 'the issues over which dispute arose between our Master Abū Hāshim and the Baghdādī [Mu'tazila]' and providing resolutions to 'those who oppose him'. Remarkably, although al-Nīsābūrī does not tell us that he will narrow the scope of his defence of Abū Hāshim any further, the work deals exclusively with topics relating to substance and accident, following broadly the same schema as ibn Mattawayh's *Tadkhira*, which is to say that properly 'theological' topics (the existence, essence and attributes of God, the definition of faith, reward and punishment, and so on) are not treated at all.

What can these diverse works, united under the banner of Mu'tazilism, tell us about how early *kalām* theologians understood the relationship between investigation of nature and of God?

Immediately remarkable is the presence of theories concerning the nature of matter, space, and motion across the investigations of these theologians. Theological doctrines for which the Mu'tazila are renowned, such as their theory of human agency, rely upon natural philosophical premises. Ibn al-Khayyāṭ's response to al-Rawandī utilises physical theory in theological matters. In 'Abd al-Jabbār's commentary on his theological treatise, theories on the natural world provide the framework within which it is established that God is superior to and other than His world. The natural world is not a focus of attention in its own right, and yet science is integral to the theological project.

The inverse is also true, as attested in the *Tadkhira*: though the focus is on investigation of the natural world, the way in which that world relates to the deity is not ignored where it arises. In introducing his treatise, ibn Mattawayh states that His project excludes discussion of the Divinity only because His superiority to his created world is so great that it is not fitting to treat both within the same work. However, this seems a piety aimed to justify the work's focus on the natural world and on humankind. It obscures the presence of theological topics where they arise within the investigation of reality.

This integration of 'scientific' and 'theological' investigation is, I would argue, part of the broader philosophical project of the Mu'tazila. For all our tendency to focus on the theological distinctiveness of the Mu'tazila, it is clear from works like the *Tadkhira* that these theologians took an interest in the nature of reality as a whole. The framework provided by the doctrine of accidents allowed for a comprehensive and integrated philosophical investigation. This is because the notion that all non-substantial existents other than God are accidents unites the investigation of physical theoretical questions relating, for example, to the nature of space, motion and the composition of body (in reference to accidents of spatial occupation) with the issue of what it is to be human (in reference to the accident 'life'), the question of how one acquires knowledge (in reference to the accident 'knowledge'), and the nature and limits of human agency (the accident in question being 'power').

The prominence of investigation of nature in Mu'tazilī *kalām* has, perhaps, been obscured in modern scholarship. The fact that two of the small number of extant Mu'tazilī works are devoted in such large part to the investigation of natural philosophical questions tells of its importance for classical Mu'tazilism. That al-Nīsābūrī does not feel the need to specify that his treatise on intra-Mu'tazilī debates will not cover the main ground of theological doctrine but focus on natural philosophical and other domains also suggests that such topics were at least as important to theologians of this period as strictly theological questions.

The tendency of Western scholarship to focus on theological doctrine was observed by Van Ess in his study of Islamic atomism. He attributed it to the historical and sociological emphasis of the study of Islamic theology in the West, arguing that since atomism was not exciting sociologically, it fell by the wayside. There may be other reasons why the natural philosophical bent of Mu'tazilism have been under-represented. Since the Ash'arīs and Mu'tazila shared the cosmological framework of atomism, and since, broadly speaking, their disagreements were over major issues within theology proper, it is unsurprising that key Mu'tazilī doctrines like the createdness of the Qur'an and the nature of human agency loom large in our characterisation of the school.

More pertinent to my interests here, modern western scholars may also have brought their own expectations of theology to bear on their approach to the study of Mu'tazilī thought. The dawn of modern science was characterised by its assertion of the boundaries between physical theory and theological doctrine. Perhaps scholars have gone about their study of Mu'tazilism with the selection bias of their times, in search of its religious doctrine to the neglect of its investigation of nature. Yet it is clear that for the Mu'tazila, these could not be cleft from one another. What we learn from the Mu'tazila is, then, that scientific theorising need not be alienated from theological thought when a comprehensive philosophical project is undertaken.

Lesson 2, the Ash'arīs: Holding a particular metaphysical belief does not invalidate associated physical theories

If I am right that the early history of *kalām* shows that investigation of the natural world is neither incompatible with nor other than theology, is there anything in the history of *kalām* to suggest that science and theology really don't mix?

Ash'arī occasionalism has led to the school's characterisation as anti-empirical and anti-rational. Surely it represents everything that Gould claims is wrong about the mingling of science and religion (or 'fact' and 'value')? The belief that it is God who intervenes to set cotton alight each time a flame is set to it appears to contravene the notion that observation of the natural world reveals its workings. The occasionalist doctrine is, indeed, the most extreme understanding of the Qur'anic doctrine of the non-ultimacy of nature. God's supremacy is understood to constitute his constant intervention in every aspect of his world.

Certainly, the occasionalist theologian's position entails the denial of 'nature' as a disembodied entity possessed of independent causal efficacy and its own 'laws'. However, to dismiss Ash'arism as the height of anti-scientific, non-rational theology, and thence to dismiss its physical theoretical contribution offhand, is to hold a narrow-minded vision of what science actually is. It is plainly true that Ash'arī theology possesses – indeed that it heavily relies upon – a conceptual framework which is essentially scientific. Ash'arism's distinctive metaphysical positions do *not* nullify its theory of matter.

Let us consider that theory of matter for a moment. Atomism, the theory that all bodies in the world around us are composed of a finite number of discrete particles, is a physical theory that has appeared in various versions across a number of traditions, including ancient Indian and Greek Democritean and Epicurean philosophy, and which was the common natural philosophy of both schools of *kalām* theology.

Sharing this physical theory, the Ash'arīs, like the Mu'tazila, understood bodies to be constituted of individual parcels of matter (*al-juz'* or *al-jawhar al-fard*) held together by an accident of aggregation (*ta'līf*). They also described motion (*ḥaraka*) and rest (*sukūn*) as accidents without endurance. Time was conceived of as a series of discrete moments analogous to the indivisible units of matter. Indeed, all physical phenomena could be accounted for in terms of the two categories atom and accident (*'arḍ*). For instance, the weight of a body is explained by the quantity of its atomic particles alone, and not with reference to any external gravitational force. The position of physical bodies is attributable to the accidents of spatial occupation (*akwān*) inhering within it. Even corporeity itself is accidental to matter, each atom possessing its own accident of aggregation, there existing no unity distinct from the sum of its aggregated parts.

One cannot deny that the *kalām* theory of matter is a scientific theory of merit. It is remarkable that early atomists, Epicurean, Democritean, Indian and Islamic, in fact came close to our modern knowledge of matter's composition of discrete quanta before they ever had the tools to prove their theories true. Atomism is a legitimate physical theory, and in a time before experimental science was normative, certainly a valid explanation of the material structure of the physical world.

As well as being a scientific theory in its own right, atomism, as Sabra has argued, provided the theologians with an ontological framework within which to present a comprehensive vision of all reality, including the metaphysical. This is already true of the Mu'tazila, who introduced this theory of matter into the Islamic world. A version of the proof from accidents for the temporal origination of the world is present in 'Abd al-Jabbār's commentary on his *Kitāb al-Uṣūl al-Khamsa*. This proof relies on premises taken from the physical theory of atoms and accidents (including, for instance, the premise that bodies cannot exist devoid of accidents). Atomism also provides the Mu'tazila with a framework for their theory of human action. It is used to explain the relationship between God, human capacity, and resultant human actions. God is understood as the creator of accidents of capacity (*qudra*) within the human person which are used for acts for which their actor, the human agent, is morally responsible.

Though the Ash'arīs share an ontological and physical theoretical framework with the Mu'tazila, it is put to very different ends. Over issues of common belief, such as the existence of God, little distinguishes the schools in their use of the atomist theory. But the Ash'arīs disagree with their opponents over the creation of human action, and also over the presence or otherwise of any kind of natural causation. According to the Ash'arīs, God creates every single accident at every atomic moment, such that he is constantly and in every place responsible for the continual sustainment of creation. An example of how this dispute with the Mu'tazila finds its context within the atomist framework is debates over which accidents have endurance (*baqā'*), and which do not. For the classical Ash'arīs, no accidents endure, whilst for certain Mu'tazila, there are accidents, such as accidents of colour, which are not perpetually recreated but exist from one atomic moment to the next until removed.

Despite a common physical theory, the Mu'tazila and Ash'arīs differ over key metaphysical issues. The significance of this is that, at one level, much of the *science* of both is the same. Their different metaphysical philosophies about how the material world relates to God impact little on their understanding of the nature of matter itself. It is tempting to see Ash'arī atomism, with its emphasis on the non-continuity of nature, as a physical theory borne out of the desire to preserve God's constant intervention in nature. And yet the theory does not 'belong' to the Ash'arīs at all. The belief that matter is constituted of indivisible particles is theologically neutral (as evidenced by its presence within diverse thought systems across the centuries) despite the theological ends to which it is put.

Of course, one may object to the Ash'arī explanation for how physical processes unfold. This aspect of their natural philosophy, so heavily reliant on supernatural explanations, is alien to the dominant mentality of modern science. And yet this does not render their entire understanding of the physical world anti scientific or invalid. In fact, the feeling that Ash'arism is anti-scientific stems in part from modern sensibilities about the nature of science. Modern science has been characterised (in contradistinction to medieval science, more normally described as natural philosophy) by the deliberate refusal to explain physical phenomena with reference to supernatural forces (termed 'methodological naturalism'). Since Ash'arism does indeed represent the height of supernatural scientific explanation, some modern minds reject it outright as non-scientific. Labelling the Ash'arī version of the *kalām* theory of matter and motion 'anti-scientific' says more, perhaps, about the worldview within which modern science is conducted than it does about the physical theories in question. The Ash'arīs offer a particular outlook on God's relation to the world and on the meaning of nature's non-ultimacy, alongside a developed theory of matter which is worthy of the title 'natural philosophy'. We may disagree with the explanations given for causal processes, yet it would be a mistake to write off all Ash'arī discussions of the physical world on this basis alone.

Al-Juwaynī's *al-Shāmil fī uṣūl al-dīn* can be considered the peak of classical Ash'arism and exemplifies the place of scientific discussion within Ash'arī *kalām*. Within the section entitled 'proving the world's temporal origination', al-Juwaynī treats matter's indivisibility, the existence of accidents, their inherence in substance, their non-endurance, and a number of other physical theoretical topics. Later in the work, al-Juwaynī treats a number of physical theoretical questions, such as the nature of spatial occupation, as standalone topics devoid of direct theological interest. The space given to these questions within the *Shāmil* indicates that the natural philosophical element of *kalām* theology never died out. Ash'arī theologians were not uninterested in the natural world nor anti-scientific in outlook. Nor did their interest in nature serve exclusively theological ends. Ash'arī occasionalism did not preclude an interest in and legitimate theorising about the natural world and its workings.

It is often (though not in Gould's case) atheist scientists who are most concerned that religion and science should be strictly separated. One can, rather cynically, observe, however, that a theory of matter upheld and developed by the theologians most profoundly committed to preserving God's constant intervention in all reality, is one that comes close to what modern science has established about the nature of matter. We learn, then, from the Ash'arīs that a scientist's metaphysical beliefs do not automatically render his theories about the constitution of the natural world unscientific or invalid, whether we happen to agree with them or not.

Lesson 3, Ibn Sina: The Qur'anic worldview does not yield a homogenous natural philosophy

Kalām and *falsafa* have so often been seen as rival traditions the former of which eventually 'won', cancelling out the philosophical tradition in the Islamic world for good. The old trope of al-Ghazālī's decisive death blow to philosophy has been bandied about too often. The traditions' respective approaches to science have been one focal point of this picture of the relationship between the traditions. It is true that on many issues, ibn Sīnā's Physics is alien to that of the indigenous tradition of *kalām*. Key issues include his belief in the infinite divisibility of matter, his theory of secondary causation, and his cosmological position that the world has eternally existed. Each of these beliefs was classically a site of deep difference between proponents of *kalām* and *falsafa*. Indeed, in the Physics of his *Shifā*, ibn Sīnā gives the most sustained refutation of atomism known within the Islamic tradition.

However, I would argue (and it is being increasingly understood) that ibn Sīnā's philosophy is in fact a Muslim theology in its own right. Indeed it is for this reason that it came to influence traditional *kalām* so decisively. I therefore consider ibn Sīnā's approach to the physical world within this survey.

Despite his developed theory of natural causation, ibn Sīnā also holds to the non-ultimacy of nature. His theory of four causes allows him to name God both the final and efficient cause of all things whilst still allowing for natural causal processes. According to his doctrine of emanation, everything proceeds by way of necessitation from the existence of God such that he is the remote efficient cause of all things though each also has a proximate efficient cause, such as (to use his own example) the sinew in moving the limbs. Since all things have as their goal God's perfection, he is also the final cause of everything. The doctrine that God is the efficient and final cause of all things is supported and integrated into an elegant vision of reality by ibn Sīnā's famous ontological distinction between the modes of existence 'necessary by virtue of itself' and 'possible by virtue of itself'. This permits him to ascribe maximal glory to a God upon whom every other being and process in all existence depends.

It is clear how this doctrine answers the Qur'anic call to make God ultimate and superior to the natural world and everything in it. This is despite his doctrine of the world's eternity and of the necessity by which natural processes unfold. Ibn Sīnā offers another vision of Islamic divine transcendentalism, an alternative to the dogged insistence on creation *ex nihilo* common to all theologians before him, and to the occasionalism of the Ash'arīs. In his understanding, God's ultimacy is wholly expressed in the very mode of his existence. His relation to the natural world is one of existential superiority. This he sees as superior to the *kalām* vision of God's superiority over the world in time. Despite our impression that such an alternative was received frostily by the *kalām* tradition, it is in fact true to say that he profoundly influenced that tradition – a fact that is only in recent years coming to be properly investigated and understood, thanks largely to pioneering studies by scholars such as Gutas, Shihadeh and Eichner. Indeed, in the thought of post-classical Ash'arī theologians like Fakhr al-Dīn al-Rāzī and Sayf al-Dīn al-Āmidī (whose works are the subject of my own research), the metaphysical doctrine of the dual modes of existence is absolutely fundamental to conceptions of the God-world relationship.

The doctrine I have just described is an amalgamation of natural philosophy (Ibn Sīnā's theory of secondary causation) and philosophical-theology, or metaphysics. This warrants comment on ibn Sīnā's conception of the relationship between the two. Ibn Sīnā's doctrine that God is the ultimate efficient and final cause is not a matter for Physics, since ibn Sīnā carefully distinguishes between the respective subjects of Physics (the body in that it is subject to motion) and Metaphysics (the existent *qua* existent) and sees God's existence and essence as proven within the Metaphysics. In fact, ibn Sīnā views the existence of the four causes as a matter to be proven within the Metaphysics. The natural philosopher is concerned with the essences and states of those causes. That is to say that he holds that Physics is established on premises proven in the superior science of Metaphysics. In practice, this means that ibn Sīnā's discussions of causality in his Physics and Metaphysics are closely related. So despite ibn Sīnā's careful delineation of the subject matter and realms of natural and metaphysical philosophy, he is unable to extricate the one from the other. This is, of course, because reality itself is not divisible into such neat and non-overlapping realms.

We learn from ibn Sīnā, then, as from the Mu'tazila that investigation of the natural world and of God go hand in hand as part of a comprehensive and integrative quest to understand reality. What we also learn from ibn Sīnā's alternative vision of the relationship between God and the natural world is that a Qur'anically-inspired natural philosophy can take many forms. The Qur'anic worldview, when it comes to bear on a thinker's understanding of the natural world, need not yield an homogenous science. Scientific theories which are poles apart (such as matter's composition of discrete particles on the one hand and the notion that an infinitely divisible substratum of matter underlies all bodies on the other) were both developed by Muslim intellectuals.

Historically, then, the Qur'anic worldview has not yielded a single vision of the constitution and workings of the natural world. This is important because it counteracts a suspicion on the part of some modern scientists that religious values, when involved in scientific theorising, are inherently associated with particular conceptions of the natural world (I have in mind Creationism). In fact, committed religious scientists vary in their understanding of nature and its relationship to God, and clearly always have.

Conclusions: Science and Theology as Overlapping Magesteria

I have so far deliberately used the terms 'natural philosophy' and 'science' interchangeably. Reeves has recently counselled a return to the term 'Natural Philosophy' to describe the activities of modern science. He shows that the process of deriving scientific knowledge from observation always involves choice of theory, and that the philosophical understanding of natural phenomena is therefore not equivalent to the results of the technical control exerted in experimentation. Theological and philosophical perspectives and worldviews exert nuanced and complex influences on the interpretive choices made. Indeed, Kuhn's influential depiction of the process of scientific theorising as a process of 'puzzle-solving' involving a web of commitments on the part of the theoriser suggests the impact of a variety of factors on a scientist's interpretation of data.

Yet the prevalent notion of science (typified by Gould's claim that science deals in the realm of 'fact' alone) does not reflect such nuances; 'Unfortunately', as Reeves puts it, 'at least since the nineteenth century, there has been in Western culture a strong scientism that has not always appreciated the ambiguities of theory construction and evaluation.' However, as Reeves demonstrates, individuals considered pioneers of modern experimental science, figureheads of the scientific revolution of the seventeenth and eighteenth centuries are more correctly described as natural philosophers in recognition of both the theological impetuses and explanations for many of their investigations (they were not methodological naturalists), and their desire to provide a comprehensive explanation for reality (Galileo and Faraday are examples). It is only much more recently, Reeves argues, that supernaturalism has been deliberately excluded from the realm of scientific investigation – and yet, worldviews inextricably continue to influence scientific theory.

The Islamic theologians are certainly characterisable as natural philosophers. In Muʿtazilī thought in particular, science and theology are not only overlapping magisteria, they are part of a united philosophical project aimed at explaining all reality. Furthermore, as we learn from the Ashʿarīs, even the most extreme cases of supernaturalism do not necessarily invalidate associated theories of matter, space and motion. Isaac Newton's (d. 1727) groundbreaking discovery of gravitational force, described in mathematical terms, was not invalidated by the fact that he ascribed the force to a powerful God (despite his being criticised by Leibniz as having made the action of gravity a perpetual miracle). Each scientific theory must thus be taken on its own merits, without undue bias based on the religious and metaphysical position of its proponents.

Sayyed Hossein Nasr has described modern science as 'a science based on the forgetfulness of God'. The Journal of Islam and Science (now 'Islamic Sciences') was founded out of the desire of thinkers like Nasr and Iqbal to promote a modern tradition of science which is not only theistic, but Qurʾanic, in its worldview. As the latter has put it, this would be a science which takes the natural order as an $\bar{a}ya$ (sign) pointing towards, and not away from, a deity, a science with a worldview in which (as Nasr put it) 'God reigns supreme, where one is aware of the purposefulness of His creation, where all causes are ultimately related to Him'.

And yet, from ibn Sīnā, we learn that a Qurʾanic worldview does not produce a homogeneous understanding of the constitution and workings of the natural world. Ibn Sīnā was no less a Muslim than al-Ashʿarī, yet their conceptions of the natural world are poles apart, their interpretations of the Qur'anic notion that the world is not ultimate wholly unlike one another. Belief in the Qur'anic God need not, should not, entail just one vision of the workings of nature. Indeed it seems to me that the methods of scientific exegesis discussed earlier are so fatally flawed because Qur'anic depictions of nature are often so pictorial as to *permit* more than one interpretation of its workings.

Perhaps more desirable than the development of an independent and homogeneous modern tradition of Islamic science is for the scientific community at large to develop greater transparency about the process of theory choice. In such a context, individual Muslim scientists could be open about their own worldview and its basis in their understanding of the Qur'an. This would permit a dialogue between Muslim and other scientists, and also between Muslim scientists about the real relationship between Islamic religion and scientific theory and discovery.

GEOPOETICS CALL

Mohammed Hashas

American Indians, whose great heritage of how to be in touch with the Universe we moderns miss in many ways, gave it the right name: 'Mother Earth.' They considered themselves part and parcel of Nature around them, and took of it only what they needed to survive. They cared about it as a mother. They cared about *being* in nature and were not obsessed with *appropriating* it. The Bedouins of Arabia also experience elevating moments in being walkers and wanderers in the vast spaces of the Desert. It is no wonder some Europeans fall in love with the Desert and romanticise the Orient for this reason. Some, like Charles M. Doughty (d. 1926), would travel to the Levant with Hajj Caravans to write two volumes of *Travels in Arabia Deserta* (1888), not only to revive the English language but also to revive the spirit of his religion as well. The pre-modern world lived in nature and with nature. Even the most devastating moments of wars could not do so much damage to nature as much as it did to human beings because the weaponry used was traditional and especially close to nature. Horses and elephants are elements close to nature, and they do not damage it (that much); warriors could see each other and know that numbers and their physique matter; physical fight was a strong component of warfare, since it was honorific to win physically first. The point here is not to glorify physical war but to make a point in relation to the distance human beings are making towards each other and towards nature. Modern warfare does not depend so much on personal physical prowess and honour gained through chivalry. The modern warfare terribly damages nature, besides damage to man himself. The chemical weaponry used, manipulated through computers and 'invisible' aircraft from far distances, is ravaging not only the ethics of war, if and only if entered in defence, but also ravaging from distance nature and its sources for generations to come. The chemical weapons and uranium radiation that is absorbed by earth, waters, and inhaled and consumed by man has future impacts on human health, wealth distribution, and natural catastrophes that leave entire populations in disadvantaged positions. Nature has become a 'thing' to be used and abused in many parts of the modern world.

The Iranian-American philosopher Seyyed Hussein Nasr says this: 'for modern man nature has become like a prostitute – to be benefited from without any sense of obligation and responsibility toward her.' That is why cries for a 'global ethic' have been raised since at least the 1993 Parliament of the World's Religions second conference in Chicago, after its first one in 1883. Its declaration 'Towards a Global Ethic: An Initial Declaration', drafted by the renowned Swiss Catholic theologian Hans Küng (b. 1928) has become a reference in the field of environmental ethics, though it has received some critique. The Moroccan philosopher of ethics Taha Abderrahmane argues that the declaration remains abstract and unable to bring what empowers world religions in giving value to such a declaration; he sees that it is practice, besides faith, that makes agency of believers positive in the world, and he applies the same to such important declarations that do not emphasise religious practice, and keep the declaration void of the spirit of work (i.e. practice). For him, like many other fields, nature cannot be protected with a global ethic that is not practical, and this praxis is based first of all on individual practice. Good intents are good, but practised good intentions are much better. The fact of speaking of ethics instead of their applicability is what also drives scholars to critique political engagements like the United Nations Climate Change Conferences, the last of which was held in Paris (COP21), 30 November–12 December 2015. The Egyptian-Canadian theologian Jasser Auda says that religion – in his words 'ethical religion' – can play a substantial role in protecting the environment, if religious leaders and communities get involved, because their messages are still influential on human behaviour, unlike state politics that are more and more interested in 'growth rates' at the economic levels, and 'social responsibility' only as a charitable or additional act and not a deep ethical component of human conduct.

Taha Abderrahmane dismisses the Cartesian premise of 'man is the master of nature' as mere fiction, 'this premise is no more than a metaphor that falls within the realm of beautiful fiction.' Man did not create nature; he does not own it, so he cannot master it. Its mysteries do not stop from enthralling the modern man at times, and at revolting against him at others owing to human waste, contamination and over-technologisation. The perception he holds on this is that of an ethical being with nature that requires a treatment of gratitude, 'Nature is the mother to man, not his slave [...] and the mother can never be a slave to her infant.' This is a critique to the part of modernity that is exhaustive of Nature and man's vast space of liberty, imagination and creativity. This version of modernity that is European in the first place is being exported worldwide, so the critique is not only coming from Europe itself but is especially coming from outside Europe, since the damage is felt outside more than inside.

Descartes' Europe has given birth also to a critique of modernity's excessive mastery of nature, the growing loss of contact with Earth, and its impact on cosmic sensation that enriches human life on various levels. This critique, and at the same time a project for renewal, is geopoetics, led by the Scottish-French poet-philosopher Kenneth White (b. 1936). This project is post-religious, post-ideological, and at the heart of which is renewing contact with Earth (Nature) for human cultivation of genuine and multicultural being that lives immensely with Nature as part of the human self. Below is a presentation of the beginnings of geopoetics, its horizons, as well as its interdisciplinary fundamental features. It synthesises the place of geography, poetics, culture, thinking, and science in the project of geopoetics. The introductory and closing paragraphs, however, highlight the aim behind introducing such a project: Nature that is underlined here as fundamental to human existential being is being ravaged, and with it the loss of a primordial source of being human is being sadly witnessed through modern excessive abuse of its sources. Internal human growth can happen only when contact with the universe at large is intelligent and caring.

Culture, Place, World

The emergence of Kenneth White's geopoetics as a new movement of thought goes back to the 1960s, but the use of the term did not start till the end of the 70s 'when he was walking along the north bank of the St Lawrence River into Labrador [Canada].' Geopoetics is the culmination of ideas White nurtured early in his life, especially due to his openness to a variety of academic disciplines like geology, geography, literature, philosophy, as well as his mastery of a number of languages (like English, French, German, Latin).

Geopoetics could have started somewhere else where quietude and natural sceneries are plenty, but the climate seemed better in Europe, mainly in France and Scotland, for some revision and renewal in thought, for a felt crisis in philosophy, distrust in science and religion, and personal dissatisfaction with some aspects of the modern age. White believes that Western thought, and the world influenced by it, is the victim of what he calls 'Motorways of Western Civilisation', the cause of the malaise he tries to overcome, or in the least rejuvenate, through geopoetics. These 'Motorways' are illustrated both in an essay entitled 'An Outline of Geopoetics' in his *The Wanderer and His Charts* (2004) and in *Geopoetics: Place, Culture, World* (2003), to which reference will be made 'so as to see where exactly we now stand.'

The first stage in the 'Western Motorway' is the Classical Age that is summarised and dominated by Plato and Aristotle. The first is known by his metaphysics and idealism (the ideal world), away from the real world. To White, this philosopher is 'a person interested in something beyond 'mundane' concerns: the Good, the True, the Beautiful,' which implies that he should not build ivory towers and forget to 'get his feet on the ground, and get back to 'the real world.' The second, Aristotle, is known by his Classification, which 'most of our knowledge is based on.' White does not oppose this system in its entirety, but just when it is used to divide the studied things/phenomena into separate parts, the study of each alone leads to distortions or unsatisfactory scrutiny of the parts as a whole; the problem for White is when parts are studied while conclusions about the whole are forgotten, a phenomenon which 'narrows' the mind, and make it 'flow' over the study of real and living life.

Stage two in the Motorway is typified by Christianity which would build vertical towers in preparation for a transcendental life in heaven. The 'obsession' by the Original Sin and the Second Coming of the crucified Christ is another main hindrance that made the Christian world 'agonisedly demoralised,' as he describes it in *The Wandered*. With the Renaissance, which makes the third stage, the Classical Age heritage would re-appear after its disappearance during the dark Middle Ages of Christianity. Such a re-birth of a tradition would be embodied in mythological creatures (gods, goddesses, naiads, dryads) that took the forests and mountains as spaces of interest, which would in turn raise the importance of science and nature. However, such a re-birth of interest in science and nature would, according to White, be influenced by Aristotelian classifications and the New World turned to be 'a blow-up caricature of some parts of the Old.' For example, when a new island is discovered, it takes the name of its discoverer or the name of a king, while it should be given the name that suits its geography and geopoeticity. With Cartesianism, that makes the fourth stage of the Motorway, Modernity age begins and with which 'nature becomes more and more objectified,' and 'considered exclusively as raw matter to be exploited.' That is, nature became an object, while man the master, the subject, that would soon be either 'robotised' and 'wrapped up in some clinical, scientific, astronautic, military uniform,' or turn into a frustrated object in psychoanalysis clinics. As a reaction against the abuse of nature and science came the Romantics who make stage five in this chain of Motorways. With Romanticism, the call for a return to Nature became the focal point. The aim was to arrive at some 'wholeness of thinking and being' that goes beyond classification and 'compartmentalisation of thought,' though in so many ways sentimentally, as *The Wanderer* explains.

The Historicism of Hegel takes the sixth stage in Kenneth White's thermometer. Wilhelm Friedrich Hegel advanced the idea that history has an orientation, and that this orientation is *Weltgeist,* 'the spirit of the world.' Put differently, with Hegel, history 'has a purpose', and it leads 'somewhere,' a theory which marks the birth of 'the ideology of progress.' The endeavours of different Western communities to keep up with the idea of progress through differing economic and political ideologies, which could be summed up in the idea of markets as the source of development and progress where values are measured by how beneficial they are, and not by how far they push man to a better presence in the world. Such a presence is far from being achieved in the Contemporary Situation, stage seven. Hollowness, helter-skelter, discontent, mediocracy (instead of democracy) are the traits that characterise the Contemporary Situation. The literature and art of this era/stage are a good illustration of the situation. They are shallow and have no value imbedded in them, as White further illustrates in an article entitled 'Pathways to an Open World' in an edited volume *Islam and the West — for a Better World* (2007).

After having enumerated the seven stages of the Western Motorway, White finds himself at a point where this question raises itself: 'Where to then?' One of the possible answers is that which is written, as Blurb to *House of Tides* (2000), by *Le Figaro littéraire*: 'Kenneth White lifts the mind from so much stale discourse and raises intelligence to a rare level, or *The Sunday Times*: 'it seems we are looking for a new prophet. It could be that White is the very man.' For the *Belles-Lettres* magazine, in Geneva, geopoetics seems the remedy to the modern age malaise and 'cultural illness':

> White's movement, both deeply sensitive and highly intelligent, may well be heralding in a new world-epoch. At a time when a certain mediocrity is reaching planetary propositions, one of us has stood up, turned his back and, possessed of real knowledge, moves off. Coming back, he reveals a method of thought and a way of being in the world which announces an art of life. (Blurb to *Geopoetics*)

Kenneth White's geopoetics envisions a world in which the human being comes to good terms with the Universe. White started using the term after long years of intellectual and physical nomadism worldwide. At first he used the term 'biocosmopoetis' which stands for the energy of life (bios) that poetry should be rekindled with, as well as the movement that gives this energy a form, weight, and coherence (cosmos), as is described in Emmanuel Dall'Aglio's *Kenneth White: du nomadisme à la géopoétique* (1997). In *Le Plateau de l'albatros* he says:

> The project of geopoetics is neither a cultural variety, nor a literary school, nor a poetry considered like a personal art; it is a movement that concerns itself with how man founds his existence on earth; it is not a question of building a system, but of accomplishing, step by step, an exploration, an investigation, by being situated as a start somewhere between poetry, philosophy, and science.

The intentions are not to establish a literary or philosophic school. The quest is beyond that. Geopoetics 'is concerned, fundamentally, with a relationship to the earth and with the opening of a world' — as the definition in *The Wanderer* reads. However, a deconstruction of the word into — at least — its two components may clarify the concept: geo-poetics.

Because geopoetics is not intended for a particular culture but for world cultures, it takes the earth as the basis, the 'central motif' that all cultures

(North, South, East, West) could share, thus the presence in 'geo' in geopoetics. Regarding poetics, it does not mean a particular use of language; rather, it is a language that stands by its own; he intends the word poetics the way others use the word mathematics, i.e. as a language. Geopoetics is a genuine language of Earth.

With geopoetics, the essential question is cultural. For White, culture could be understood from two points of view: first, in the context of the individual, it stands for 'the way human beings conceive of, work at, and direct themselves. Culture implies some conception of the human being. Within this scope of culture, White suggests that man should be a 'poetic inhabitant of the Earth,' which comes through work embodied in cultivation, for 'there is no culture without work' as outlined in *Geopoetics*. Here, cultivation of the individual is analogous with the cultivation of land; without cultivation, no crop grows, and thus no man's mind flourishes. Culture within the second collective scope is defined according to what is essential to this collective group. And since geopoetics 'cultural work-field' concerns itself with a world-culture, it seeks to find what could be the central concern , or an archipelago as White says, that is able to be shared by all, North, South, East and West. This makes what he calls in *Une Stratégie paradoxale — éssais de résistance culturelle* (1998) 'an intercultural and transcultural movement.' The mutual ground (space, geography) that could embrace different cultures around a central motive is the very Earth on which we live, henceforth the presence of 'geo' in geopoetics. With this geopoetic conception of culture in mind, the culture(s) spoken about in newspapers, TV, and markets is a miniature and in fact a distortion of the real meaning of culture. While real culture means cultivation and work, the commonly known culture now stands for more consumerism, 'infantilism,' and 'intellectual platitude' than any more open work. What White wants is a 'cosmosculture' instead of a 'show culture,' as described in *Une Stratégie paradoxale*.

The world White proposes 'emerges from the contact between the human being and cosmos, represented by the Earth,' which implies that the cosmos is larger than Earth, and that the sensation of Earth is what makes being in the cosmos sound and interesting. The contact he speaks about in *The Wanderer* is:

intelligent, sensitive, subtle, you have a world in the full and positive sense: a satisfying context, an interesting and life-enhancing place. When the contact is unintelligent, insensitive, heavy-handed and clumsy, what you have instead of a world is a diminished context, if not a precinct of horror.

Differently put, contact with Earth enlightens man's existence, and instinctively teaches him sane ways of living. However, when such a contact is absent, changing society cannot occur as prophesied or desired to the extent that it (the change) can be backwards. A world where this sought-for contact is missing is no longer a world, '*un monde*,' an open and vast space for genuine being, but is an '*immonde*,' originally meaning disgusting and repulsive in French, or *mundus in* English, meaning platitudinous and uninteresting. White thinks that it is time man returned to the aesthetic connotation of the word 'cosmos' which etymologically meant 'a beautiful, harmonious totality' (*Kosmos* in Greek). To be able to lead change towards this beautiful and harmonious world, one needs to be cultivated, and it is here that culture intervenes. For him, a world is a place, a space that one cultivates, and so as to be up to that world-cultivation one has to cultivate oneself because there is no real culture without work. By work is meant the sharpening of man's senses for a better recognition of space, and for a better presence in the world, a process which behooves an intellectual energy. This knowledge of space is provided by knowledge of geography, geology and ecology. White's geopoetics is all-encompassing. White's 'open world' is oriented neither commercially, politically, ideologically, locally, provincially, nationally, nor purely secularly. Rather, it is universally oriented; it takes world-culture as its quest, which the intellectual nomad is supposed to figure out. Such a work is both mental and linguistic, hence the importance of poetry, or delight in sensation, in geopoetics.

Poetry, Philosophy, Science

Poetry, philosophy, and science undergo a denotative metamorphosis with geopoetics. Poetry is most of the time linked to melodious and highly polished language written in a rhythmic form that pleases the ear, especially if sung. This kind of poetry is now rampant; very many poems are written to be published on newspapers or to be sung in video clips. Nonetheless, it may remain superficial if it is not the fruit of an intellectual effort and true sensation of the world. Fake poetry in general has succumbed to personal and socio-personal ideas, far from being grounded on a vast space. It is a poetry without world, devoid of poetics, a verbose rhetoric, in contradistinction to poetry that has a world, 'the poem of earth' which 'is still to be written,' as the American poet Wallace Stevens (d. 1955) writes, quoted in *Geopoetics*. White's cry is clear, 'We are badly in need of poetry that has a world' as underlined in *On Scottish Ground – Selected Essays* (1998).

Poetry accordingly does not mean carefully chosen words; it is, however, a reflection of 'a poetic listening to nature,' using the words of the Chemist Nobel Laureate Ilya Prigogine (d. 2003), cited in *Une Apocalypse tranquille* (1985). In *Open World (2002)* White writes in the Foreword that what he is interested in is 'world poetry':

> In the poem, without going back to myth, metaphysics or religion, I tried to get out beyond personal poetry and social poetry and linguistic poetry, into what I called 'world poetry,' poetry concerned with *world*, that is, what emerges from the contact between the human mind and the matter-energy of the universe.

With this definition White moves on to his own 'image' of poetry after having tried 'institutions' and 'doors' of poetry, but none satisfied him. To his new image of poetry he invites the poets of the world:

> I've been in and out of institutions
> banged a few doors
>
> in and out of lives and loves
> come way with a few scars
>
> I've gone deeper into poetry
> the space where the mind clears –
>
> now I'm walking in my own image
> follow me who dares.

Poetry is a solace for White; it is his own 'world' when the outside world exasperates him: 'the world is a provocation to me. Over against it, I evoke my own world, which is a more real world. Poetry is affirmation of reality.

No more, no less.' These are White's words when he was still twenty-seven years old, as Tony McManus' *The Radical Field: Kenneth White and Geopoetics* (2007) puts it chronologically. White's 'world poetry' harbingers what he calls 'new poeticity' by means of which thought becomes poetry. Here we enter the realm of mind.

True poetry is that which involves thinking, though it may be written in very simple words. In *L'Esprit nomade* (1987) White writes that 'poetry should thus be open to thinking; but so as not to be an insane puzzle, thinking must be founded on poetry.' In other words, poetry without thinking is nonsense, and vice versa. This reciprocal tendency towards one another is what geopoetics is trying to trace. White is working out the possibility of bringing the three major disciplines together: science (represented by geography, ecology, geology, and the exact sciences), poetry (represented by language), and philosophy (represented by thought and meditation). For the world-culture project, classification should be trespassed, and the presence of the three elements/disciplines seems a requisite. It is as if the world needed the classical types of 'polymaths', poets who were also philosophers, mathematicians, doctors, theologians, etc. Early in 1982, in *La Figure du dehors*, White quoted the English poet John Dryden (d. 1700) to stress this idea of overlapping between these sciences: 'man should be versed in various sciences, and should possess a reasonable, philosophic, and to some extent a mathematical mind so as to be an excellent and accomplished poet.' With openness to other sciences the poet is also supposed to be a lover of the world, a mondomaniac who follows his desire of the world, because it is owing to the poet's school that we learn the courage of intelligence and the audacity of being oneself, as White believes – quoting the Romanian philosopher Emil Michel Cioran (d. 1995). Geopoetics tries to go beyond the ordinary definition of poetry as a literary genre. Poetry targets the poetics of existence. Poetry can be seen then as a way of life, a mode of thinking that helps the poet and man in general to establish himself on Earth as a wise being, as a 'poet thinker,' and when this happens poetry takes more importance than philosophy.

From the Whitian perspective, 'poetic thought' is more open than the logic of philosophy. White starts this argument from where some of his European 'companions' stopped, namely, Friedrich Nietzsche, Arthur Rimbaud, Vincent Van Gogh, and Martin Heidegger. *En passage* here, White

admires these figures' evaluation of Western philosophy which has been
through a radical crisis, with questions being raised as to its limits and
perspectives since the end of the nineteenth century. Heidegger was among
the first moderns to raise the issue so as to find ways into regions philosophy
has not explored. As to the three other philosophers, they all live in
solitude, and two of them (Nietzsche and Rimbaud) go mad. They felt
alienated in a moribund civilisation. White, then, takes these 'companions'
to help him form the 'quicker procedure' that is 'required,' leaving behind
the many 'criticist discourse[s]' that one finds here, there, and everywhere
when reading about culture and civilisation. At a time when 'a quicker
procedure is required,' White confirms in *La Figure du dehors*, that good
criticism should open up a new world:

> That criticism is necessary in this context is something I go with. But criticist
> discourse tends to become a process in itself, integrated into the system [of
> thought]. The result is a vast accumulation of studies and statistics that give the
> impression of being valid and to-date, but get nobody anywhere and tend to
> simply clutter up the space of manoeuvring.

One way of opening up this new road is through the discrimination White
makes between poetry and philosophy, basing his choice of words on
Nietzsche's. To leave the classical motorways of philosophy, Nietzsche
proposed a particular type of philosopher, i.e. 'the artist philosopher,' or
what White names the 'poet-thinker,' 'thinker-poet.' The link White makes
between philosophy, thought and poetry emanates from his belief that
'poetic thought is more dynamic than philosophy.' By implication this means
that the poetics White aspires to live mixes both thought, reason, and
language, a language open to spaces that have largely been left out when
official philosophy emerged. What White aims at here is to transgress the
Greek thought, Plato and Aristotle's, which divides reality into two: the
world of being, and the world of becoming. The former is the realm of
ideas, of all that is immutable and eternal, and is also the region of
philosophy, a logic of identity, and science, whereas the latter is seen as the
world of multiplicity, of all that is unstable, inconsistent, and transient. The
second type of thinking is far from being philosophic or scientific; it is
cunning rather than knowledge. Like the poet and philosopher Eratosthenes
(276 BCE–194 BCE), who made fun of the Greeks for having divided the

world into the civilised folk of the Greeks and the uncivilised Barbarians, White too disagrees with their conception of reality, and thinks of the 'traveller-poet,' or 'the poet-thinker,' as the most suitable to combine the two realities they esteem as very separate. Accordingly, the poet recovers his position as an intellectual being, able to think and come in good contact with his society and space. He is no longer the poet the Greeks expelled from the city for fear of his imaginative powers and his possible influence on the weaker sides of the mind.

The imaginative capacities the poet is endowed with are, according to the French poet René Daumal (d. 1944) whom White quotes, either black or white, and they produce black or white poetry, and they both try to communicate what is essential, though differently. The former utilises much imagination and lives a world of fantasies, prestige, pleasures, chivalrous achievements, and opens many worlds lighted by unreal sun. The latter, on the contrary, prefers living a bitter reality instead of imaginative and prestigious lives. White poetry opens just one world and satiates it with the real, non-prestigious sun. It is a kind of work that requires yoga exercises, with much mental concentration. Kenneth White is looking for white poetry.

On Scottish Ground (1998) contains a dense essay on poetry and its import to geopoetics. It is entitled 'Into the White World.' From the first lines of the article White puts forwards his argument, 'poetry speaks ultimately of the white world, [...] poetry signifies the transcendence of the individual conscience and the introduction to a world (a cosmos, a beautiful whole in movement).' This means that neither poetry nor the white world still exist in abundance. They are the project of geopoetics. In simple terms, 'white-world poetry' is 'real poetry' that is yet to be walked to:

> Real poetry, and the life it implies, begins a few thousand miles, as the gull flies, as the wind blows, away from this 'civilised' compound. Nietzsche, at Sils-Maria [in Switzerland], lived '6,000 feet above men and time.' The Chinese say (or used to say) that to know what real poetry is you have to meet a man distant from you by 3,000 miles.

The aspirations towards 'real poetry,' 'world poetry,' that White wants to write and the new and open world he tries to reach are enticed by the *eros*, the 'desire' that pushes the self to purification and that tends towards the liberation of the mind and finally drives towards real self. The *eros* heads with the self towards the summit, the 'difficult area,' where it joins the logos, 'the cosmic unity' that governs all. The nostalgia of the *eros* to fuse the self with the whole, with the unity of the logos, stands for the fusion of desire and reason. This fusion occasions the power of the real poets who know what a white world means and how poetry should sound. That is why their poetic ideas start by a rejection of the [civilised] world. Such poets appear like mad men among the ordinary men who cannot understand nor feel what it is like on the 'summit,' there where the *eros* and *logos* fuse(d); the poet, for White, is a madman (marked first by extravagant energy, then with a large logic) in this sense. Since the objective world of the poet is a quest, he lives in a 'pseudo-world,' an unobtainable space, or what White calls 'chaos-cosmos,' 'chaosmos.' It is also in this sense that real poets are said to be more than mere philosophers since their energy is not simply what is commonly known as logic but the logos which transcends it, henceforth the power of 'the poet-philosopher' or 'poet-thinker' over the philosopher or even the scientist as will be noted below.

Though the poet may appear an uncivilised being whose intelligence develops according to primordial norms, he does not deny science because of 'scientific' exactitudes. If he stands against science, it is because he knows that where it leads is not that 'difficult area' that looks upon the white world. The poet rejects the sciences that shut the ears and close the eyes to the sounds of the earth and the cosmos. The sciences that dumb the senses are not within the orbit of the poet, nor that of geopoetics, despite the fact that the latter has much in common with science. Throughout his 'essay-books,' a category of free philosophical writings, White showers his reader with a variety of figures and books belonging to a wide range of sciences, to demonstrate that being a practitioner of geopoetics is not departmental but interdisciplinary: archeology, geography, geology, botany, biology, ecology, ornithology, sociology, psychoanalysis, physics, mathematics, architecture, etc. The spirit of classical polymaths comes back to capture the complexity of life.

White, in *L'Esprit nomade,* notes Jean-Francois Lyotard's declaration that 'scientific knowledge is not all knowledge' to come up with his own conclusion: thinking, at its limits, ends in poetry. So, since science is a way of thinking it is very likely to turn into poetry; that is, it can share a lot with poetic thinking. White's project is to build links and establish an alliance between the two (as he does with culture, geography, poetry, and philosophy) so as to arrive at that image of, say, poet-scientist, who does his work in the laboratory but is at the same time open to nature, the universe, the source of any sane/poetic thinking. Olivier Delbard, in *Les Lieux de Kenneth White* (1999), refers to White's quote of Heidegger's famous statement 'science does not think' to talk about the modern more systematic, applied and exact sciences, without disavowing the achievements of, for example, the methodical works of Descartes and Newton whose theories still influence the modern scientific developments. Delbard also quotes White: 'an encounter between science and poetry seems again possible, a new culture seems under formation which will be the concern of poets and artists as much as it will be that of scientists.' This is also poetically signed in 'Walking the Coast' in *Open World* with two lines that we interpret to have the same signification: 'the way of true science / which is poetry's commencement.' Also in *Open World*, White presents poetry, and not science, as the key to 'order' and 'harmony' in the world and to any study of the elements of nature:

> for the question is always how
>   out of all the chances and changes
>   to select
> the features of real significance
>   so as to make
>   of the welter
>   a world that will last
> and how to order
>   the signs and the symbols
>   so they will continue
>   to form new patterns
>   developing into
> new harmonic holes
>   so to keep life alive
> in complexity
>   and complicity
>   with all of being –
> there is only poetry.

In 'An Outline of Geopoetics,' the last essay in *The Wanderer*, White goes through some names in different scientific fields to explain how in the last few decades scientists have realised that science alone is not everything the world needs. He says that the term 'poetics' is most often included in the recent scientific publications. He refers to Albert Einstein in physics, to the Chilean biologist Humberto Maturana (b. 1928) and his student Francisco Varela (d. 2001) who both introduced autopoiesis to biology, to the French philologist Gustave Guillaume (d. 1960) in linguistics, and especially to one of 'the first ancestors of geopoetics,' the German naturalist Alexandre von Humboldt (d. 1859), who says that 'science, poetry and philosophy are not fundamentally separate,' and that 'they can come together in the mind of one who has achieved a state of unity.' Part of 'Walking the Coast' in *Open World* gives the example of the 'alliance' that could take place between the poet and the scientist through similar perceptions of the same natural phenomenon (contrasts, order, disorder, change) of the world they share:

> [...] *when a physicist*
>   far out in his field
>   *says* the starting-point
>   for the realm of unknowns
>   is a
>   'universe of contrasts
>   grouped into
>   complexes of relations
>   with aspects of
>   order and disorder
>   including
>   change and tendency'
> *I say that's it*
>   that's my territory
>   that's the world I'm living through
>   and trying to work out. (My italics)

The openness of geopoetics to the multitudinous aspects of science, be they social or exact sciences, makes it an interdisciplinary/transdisciplinary complex field of work from which its perspectives could take other pathways. The variety of essays in *Une Stratégie paradoxale — Essais de resistance culturelle* (1998) — shows how open the project is. The work touches upon fields like politics, education, culture, arts, sociology, and biology. In 'Art,

Music, Poetry,' in *Geopoetics*, White widens the arena of 'poetics' in geopoetics to reach the sciences and arts:

> While including poetry, it [poetics] also has a larger application. It applies not only to poetry as literary form, but also to art and music, and can be extended beyond these domains into science and even social practice.

Michèle Duclos says that when White was invited in 1994 by Transdisciplinary Encounters magazine and its director the physician Basarab Nicolesco, the founder of The International Center for Transdisciplinary Research (CIRET), located in Paris and founded in 1987, he had the occasion to voice the transdisciplinarity of his project: 'geopoetics is naturally (basically) transdisciplinary,' and 'is ready to associate itself assiduously, while always maintaining its geopoetic specific preoccupations, with any movement and manifestation going in this sense: internationalism, transnationalism, transdisciplinarity.' In describing the 'White Seminar' Kenneth White delivered at the Sorbonne in the early 1990s, George Amar says that they (the students at attendance) did not have a particular curriculum to study, 'we roam: we learn that it is the best way to start to explore a territory.' He delineates the process as a kind of intellectual navigation whose captain is White and his 'intellectual judo' practices. This shows the interdisciplinary aura that envelops (and develops) the project.

Intellectual and Geographic

The cultivation of a new spirit of being in the world requires both physical and intellectual nomadism, to reach out to new inspiring landscapes and mindscapes, or what he calls 'fields of energy' in search of '*la vie principielle*.' White is a practitioner of geopoetics, a nomad, as *Open World* reads:

> I started off
> by growing up
> like everybody else.
>
> Then I took
> a bend to the south
> an inclination east

a prolongation north
and a sharp turn west.

The intellectual nomad should be endowed with the spirit of 'outgoerism' or 'outgoingness,' as he calls them, the ability to merge landscapes and mindscapes together, with a language that should not be culturally biased nor superficial. Such a language should reflect a profound closeness to space, to earth, to world, moving from cosmos, pushed by *eros*, and reaching the original *logos*.

Since geopoetics aims at a more universal grounding of a world culture, away from the historic-cultural and socio-political differences, ideologies, revolutions, and religions that have created more gaps between man and man, and more distance between man and the world he lives in, White has opened the scope of his project to world spaces, geographies, and cultures. Starting from Europe, and mainly from his native land Scotland and later on from his host country France, White moves on earth, walks the world, sees nature, and seizes, (say 'sucks the marrow of life,' as his companion Henry Thoreau says) the breezes of the wind, shine of the sun, light of the moon, and most importantly vastness and openness of the world. From Scotland, France, Germany, White journeys to other European places first as a wanderer, an intellectual nomad, and then as a lecturer – in Holland, Poland, Sweden, Portugal, Spain, Corsica, Italy, to name but these. In these 'trans-European trips' he always has some companions to share his moments of meditation, thinking, and cultural (re-)grounding, companions like Rimbaud, Nietzsche, Van Gogh, Holderlin, Heidegger, Artaud, and Segalen.

With the same verve he heads to America, mainly to where he could still see and live with the Indians and Eskimos in Labrador in Canada, one of his most loved geographies. He also passes by the lands where some of his American friends, Emerson, Walt Whitman and Henry Thoreau, lodged, in addition to his many trips (eleven till 2004) to The Isles of America (Martinique, Guadeloupe, and the Saintes). From America he heads to the East, the Orient, another inspiring world space where Buddhism, Zen, and Taoism dominate, and where haiku and yoga are practised, physically and mentally. In the Orient, new companions are encountered, like Wei, Hakuin, and especially Bashŏ and Sesshu. About the Orient he says, in Duclos' *Le Poète cosmographe*, 'Once we pass through the Orient, we have a fresh look at the Occident [...]. The result of the Orient journey is that the geography of being and thinking change. Asia [...] is the vagina of nations.', was much referred to in White's early narratives like *Les Limbes incandescents* (1976), and *Lettres de Gourgounel* (1986). With his waybooks and poetry that followed his travels to Asia since 1975 (at the age of thirty-nine), Asia lands gained more focus and poured much of his ink. White also journeys to Africa, Morocco and the Atlas, to the Indian Ocean, La Reunion and Mauritius, as narrated in *Across the Territories* (2004). The project is about rediscovering the world, and giving sensation to it. Because of his openness to the cultures of the world, White received the Edouard Glissant Prize attributed by the University of Paris VIII for World Culture, in March to April 2004.

White practises geopoetics. He has travelled worldwide, but space has not allowed to further examine his 'waysbooks', besides his 'staybooks' — as he calls them. He walks, and walks, and walks. The way he has architected his house, and the choice of its location, is also a way of expressing fondness with nature as the source of 'primordial life' and the way to reach the essential self.

How do I relate to geopoetics? In so many ways that only sensation can describe. I grew up in a village, surrounded by mountains, trees, rivers, birds and domestic animals. I grew up amidst very modest people. I saw how they live on a daily basis, and how they support each other in need, though all of them appear in need. I loved farming, swimming in natural rivers, and drinking water from a spring without fear. I could walk miles alone to the far school, with no fear of nature. I then moved to a town, then a city, then to capitals in Europe. These are worlds apart in terms of how people relate to the world, nature, and each other. The life I experienced in my early eight years in nature has impacted me ever since, and I feel it is a dream life, something far. This concerns human relations as well, and human relations with nature and its elements, animals and plants and mountains. The sensation of being part of the world is different from the way one perceives it in a village, surrounded by nature, from its counterpart, surrounded by cement, cars, undergrounds lines, various means of technological communication. Despite the greatness of human achievements, there is something on the way that is being lost: that contact with nature and the humility it teaches in relation to other elements of nature and other human beings. There is always a middle way, a *wasatiyyah* spirit, that one has to seek. Geopoetics can be very inspiring in that regard for people of various traditions in a gradually multicultural world. The 'open world' of geopoetics can be so enriching for common human creative serenity.

VICEGERENCY AND NATURE

Munjed M. Murad

And when thy Lord said to the angels, 'I am placing a vicegerent upon the earth,' they said, 'Wilt Thou place therein one who will work corruption therein, and shed blood, while we hymn Thy praise and call Thee Holy?' He said, 'Truly I know what you know not.' And He taught Adam the names, all of them. Then He laid them before the angels and said, 'Tell me the names of these, if you are truthful.' They said, 'Glory be to Thee! We have no knowledge save what Thou hast taught us. Truly Thou art the Knower, the Wise.' He said, 'Adam, tell them their names.' And when he had told them their names He said, 'Did I not say to you that I know the unseen of the heavens and the earth, and that I know what you disclose and what you used to conceal?'

The Qur'an, 2:30-33

He it is Who appointed you vicegerents upon the earth and raised some of you by degrees above others, that He may try you in that which He has given you. Truly thy Lord is Swift in retribution, and truly He is Forgiving, Merciful.

The Qur'an, 6:165

Humanity is the vicegerent of God on earth and thus the steward of nature. This paraphrases one of the main rallying cries of today's environmental movement in the Islamic world, paralleled to a significant degree in other religious traditions. That humanity is both vicegerent and steward implies a specific trifold relationship between God, humanity, and nature. In other words, it implies a metaphysics, which is what I seek to expound here.

The leading voice in today's Islamic intellectual response to the ecological crisis, Seyyed Hossein Nasr, has provided the following definitive summary of the status of the human being in relation to God and the world from an Islamic perspective:

> Pontifical man is the reflection of the Centre on the periphery and the echo of
> the Origin in later cycles of time and generations of history. He is the
> vicegerent of God (*khalīfatallāh*) on earth, to use the Islamic term, responsible
> to God for his actions, and the custodian and protector of the earth of which
> he is given dominion on the condition that he remain faithful to himself as the
> central terrestrial figure created in the form of God, a theomorphic being
> living in this world but created for eternity.

In order to fully appreciate the significance of this statement and of the
aforementioned slogan of the Islamic environmental movement, we must
examine their origins. We can say with confidence that Qur'anic verses,
such as those quoted above, and Prophetic teachings are at the heart of all
of this. We are in need, however, of recourse to Islamic intellectual literature
for a deep understanding of what these statements mean and of their
implications for the contemporary Islamic perception of the ecological
crisis. Thus, in this paper, I turn to ibn 'Arabī (d. 1240), the Great Master
(*al-Shaykh al-Akbar*) of Islamic metaphysics, for a detailed exposition.

Muḥyī al-Dīn Muḥammad ibn 'Arabī was an Islamic metaphysician born
in what today is Spain and in his time was the Islamic land of Andalusia. For
centuries he has maintained a profound influence on Islamic intellectual
traditions. A great many of the explanations of the cosmological and
metaphysical dimensions of reality that the Islamic tradition offers today are
formulated through his teachings.

For the Shaykh, the whole of the Islamic creation story is summarised by
the *ḥadīth qudsī* of the Hidden Treasure:

> I was a Treasure but was not known. So I loved to be known, and created the
> creatures and made Myself known to them. Then they came to know Me.

In ibn 'Arabī's metaphysics, mankind and the rest of creation were created
for the fulfilment of the wish of God expressed in this one statement. The
single purpose of a human being is to know God in a total way. The
epistemic faculty that allows mankind this knowledge is unique to humanity.
It is made possible by the potential to reflect God's totality within the
human soul. A full and clear reflection constitutes the realisation of a total
knowledge of God, as well as the spiritual realisation of the human soul. In
attaining this, one fulfils the primary responsibility of vicegerency. This
double-realisation is reflected in another famed *ḥadīth qudsī*, 'Whosoever

knows himself knows his Lord.' The implication of the trifold relationship between God, the world, and the human being viewed in light of the possibility of such realisation is what I investigate here. Simply put, I wish to explain the metaphysical foundation of vicegerency, as it has been expounded by ibn 'Arabī.

As for terminology, regarding the object of human vicegerency, ibn 'Arabī does not use the Arabic equivalent of 'nature' in the writings of his that concern us here, but rather that of 'the world' or 'creation'. However, it is a logical next step to transpose findings on the implications of mankind's vicegerency for creation to those for the natural world. Indeed, it hardly seems like a transposition at all, especially given the nearly synonymous relationship that the two concepts have in Islamic cosmological literature, particularly the writings of ibn 'Arabī that we examine here. Of course, there are dimensions to the word *al-'ālam,* that do not immediately refer to the natural world. For the purposes of this essay, however, the dimension that refers to 'nature' is all that concerns us. This is evident in the analyses that I provide, but not the translations. For the latter, *al-'ālam* is rendered by 'the world' or 'creation'. I do this for the sake of staying true to the Shaykh's terminology when citing him, although preferring a more relevant term in my own writings. Ibn 'Arabī's reference to God (*Allāh*) as the Real (*al-Ḥaqq*) is also worth noting when reading the translations.

While many works of the Shaykh address the topic at hand, the questions that this essay seeks to answer are treated in detail in the first chapter of *The Ringstones of Wisdom* (*Fuṣūṣ al-ḥikam*), namely 'The Ringstone of Divine Wisdom in the Word of Adam' (*Faṣṣ ḥikmah ilāhiyyah fī kalimah ādamiyyah*), and it is this chapter that will be the focus of my attention, though I cite excerpts of it in an order that elucidates the sub-topics that we encounter in the following pages. I furthermore supplement the few gaps left unfilled by this chapter's treatment of the topic with other resources on the Shaykh's worldview or related matters.

It is only appropriate that we have started with the *ḥadīth qudsī* of the Hidden Treasure. It not only provides us with a rich paradigm in which to answer our questions, but also frames and structures this very chapter of the Shaykh's writings.

Understanding Mankind in Relation to What Is Above It

According to the ontological narrative that we examine here: The Real wished to see Himself through another. Thus, He created a comprehensive being that encompasses all truths and is able to reflect Him. Such a being is like a clear mirror unto God. The Shaykh so famously starts his first chapter to *The Ringstones of Wisdom*:

> The Real willed, glorified be He, in virtue of His Beautiful Names, which are innumerable, to see their identities — if you so wish you can say: to see His Identity — in a comprehensive being that comprises the whole affair insofar as it is characterised by existence and His Mystery is manifest to Himself through it. For the vision a thing has of itself in itself is not like the vision a thing has of itself in another thing, which will be like a mirror for it...

This is clearly a commentary upon the aforementioned creation story. Humanity is the instrument through which God facilitates the vision of Himself in other than Himself. This is made possible by mankind's formation in the image of God. The human soul is made to reflect the synthesis of the Divine Names:

> And so all of the Names, which are divine forms, are manifested in this makeup of man, and the function of encompassment and synthesis is achieved through his existence.

Being made in the total image of God, mankind enjoys the rank of vicegerency. The human purpose is to reflect God in a total way in the world and, by virtue of this function, to be His vicegerent on earth. The human being is thus defined by its encompassment of all truths and its consequential capacity for vicegerency of the Real. It is such that the Shaykh writes:

> And so the aforementioned was called Man and Vicegerent. As for his being Man, it refers to the totality of his makeup and his encompassment of all realities.

If the above makes reference to the makeup — and hence to the potentiality — of the human being, it must be noted that it is only the fully realised human being that facilitates the aforementioned full reflection of God in one single point within the cosmos. In the Shaykh's terminology, such a being is referred to as the Perfect Human Being (*al-insān al-kāmil*). Throughout this essay, his references to 'mankind', 'man', humanity', or 'the human being' in the generic seem to concern the Perfect Human Being alone, at least when read for the practical realisation of whatever he is writing about. Only such a being reflects God totally and so only such a being fulfils the responsibilities of vicegerency. In ibn 'Arabī's own words:

> Were he not manifest in the form of He who entrusted him with Vicegerency, within that over which he was made Vicegerent, he would not have been Vicegerent. If he did not contain all that was needed of him by the charge over which he was set as Vicegerent – and by reason of their dependence upon him he would have to possess everything that they needed – he would not be Vicegerent over them. *Vicegerency is only for the Perfect Human Being...*

Mankind is like a mirror before God. We can also say that mankind serves as the function of the pupil to God's eye. It is the means by which God sees Himself in another, thus giving fulfilment to the creation story with which we started.

> In relation to the Real man is like the pupil in relation to the eye, through which vision occurs. This is called the faculty of sight. For this reason he was called Man, and through him the Real looks upon His creation and shows mercy upon them.

Thus, regarding mankind's relationship with God, the human being is at once the reflection of the synthesised totality of God's Names, His vicegerent, and the facilitation of His sight in the world. This is such notwithstanding the ephemeral and mortal nature of a human being's life. There is something at once mortal and immortal, ephemeral and eternal, and created and uncreated in mankind. It is the latter aspect of each of these pairs that enables the human being's synthesised reflection of divinity and the former constitutes what is necessary for the existentiation of such a reflection outside of God as Uncreated.

Existence must be understood here as an attribute of creation and not of the Uncreated. The etymology of 'existence' is of use to us here. The Latin *existere* has the sense of 'to step out' or 'to come forth'. Creation, so to speak, steps out of God and comes into being. God, as Uncreated, is beyond such a phenomenon. With this in mind, we can make the following observation: Regarding its createdness, a human being can only be 'a comprehensive being that comprises the whole affair *insofar as it is characterised by existence...*' Regarding that which is divine about a human being, it is 'a comprehensive being that comprises the whole affair *insofar as... His Mystery is manifest to Himself through it.*'

Understanding Mankind in Relation to What Is Below It

Total knowledge of God is unique to the realised human state. Not even the angels – the seemingly loftiest beings – share in this prerogative. The Shaykh has made this clear: 'The angels did not possess the synthesis possessed by Adam...' Nor is the attainment of this knowledge within the capacity of the rest of creation:

> [The world's] perception of itself does not comprehend the Real. It shall ever be within a veil that shall remain unlifted, even with its knowledge that it is distinguished from its Existentiator by reason of its needfulness. Indeed, it has no share in that necessity of the Essence which belongs to the existence of the Real. It will never perceive God, and because of this reality, God remains unknown both to the knowledge through taste and that of witnessing, because what comes to be has no place in this.

> With Adam there were Divine Names the angels did not possess, so neither their glorification nor their proclamation of His holiness were like those of Adam.

It is thus that we can speak of the world as being below a human being. In reality, the world can only be such when the human being in question is fully realised as the Perfect Human Being. Several Qur'anic verses refer to unrealised human beings as being lower than others in creation:

> Or do you suppose that most of them hear or understand? Truly they are but as cattle. Nay, they are further astray from the way. (25:44)

> .. truly We created man in the most beautiful stature, then We cast him to the lowest of the low, save those who believe and perform righteous deeds for theirs shall be a reward unceasing. (95:4-6).

At the point of a total reflection of God, the Shaykh affirms that the realised human being surpasses in rank all else in creation:

... [God] is in every existent thing of the world in the measure of what the reality of that existent thing requires of Him, though not one of them possesses the totality of the Vicegerent. He surpasses not but through this totality.

If creation shares not mankind's prerogative of potentially knowing the Real, it neither shares its responsibility of serving as the Real's vicegerent. Mankind is the seal to what the world is.

He is to the world what the ringstone is to the ring, which is the place of the signet and the mark with which the king sets a seal upon his treasures. For this reason was he named Vicegerent, for through him the Real protects His creation, as the seal protects those treasures.

A human being is not the only reflection of God. The cosmos is such too. However, while the world reflects God in multiplicity, only the human being can reflect God in a synthesised unity. The Perfect Human Being and the *totality* of the cosmos both reflect God, but only the human being reflects God in one single form within a sea of multiplicity. In other words, while the world constitutes the very many loci of manifestation of the very many Names of God, the Perfect Human Being constitutes the locus of manifestation of the Name *Allāh,* which is the all-comprehensive Name of God that contains in a synthesised way all the other Divine Names. In light of this totality, ibn 'Arabī's school of metaphysics considers the Perfect Human Being to be like 'the Face of God in His creatures.' In an analysis of an explanation provided by Jāmī, the fifteenth century authoritative expositor of ibn 'Arabī's teachings, Chittick writes:

This 'two-pronged' self-disclosure of the name Allah is the basis for Jāmī's exposition of man's relation to the cosmos. Man the microcosm (*al-'ālam al-ṣaghīr*) is the mirror of the macrocosm (*al-'ālam al-kabīr*). But in man the name Allah is manifested in such a way that each one of the individual names that are comprehended by it is equivalent to all the others. In other words, the divine unity is manifested directly in man in the midst of the multiplicity of the world, but the world itself, though also a reflection of the name Allah, is so in a particularised mode and manifests the relative multiplicity inherent in that name.

Mankind is the spirit to the world as form. The world, without mankind, is an unpolished mirror. The spirit to the form – mankind to the world – is the cleansing to the mirror that is otherwise unpolished. The existence of the world is thus intimately dependent upon that of humanity.

The Real had existentiated the entire world as a body made ready, in which there was no spirit, and so it was like an unpolished mirror... The situation required that the mirror of the world be clear, and Adam was the very clearness of this mirror and the spirit of this form.

Some Qur'anic commentators have understood the term *khalīfah* as rooted in the word *khalafa*, which means 'to come after', implying that 'human beings come after all creatures and all grades of being are summarised in the human state,' complementing ibn 'Arabi's description of mankind as a 'seal' to the world. This parallels the role of the Prophet Muhammad as a seal to the prophets, ending the cycle of prophecy and encompassing within him the realities of all other prophets.

One may be tempted to ask, 'What of the world before the arrival of humanity?' A response has already been provided by Chittick:

> Before the actualisation of the human form the world existed and the planets revolved. So how can you call man the Pole (*quṭb*) of the cosmos and the means whereby it is maintained? Jāmī replies that although man did not exist in the sensory world, he did exist in the spiritual world, and the effect of his existence was manifest in the lower world.

The time in which the world existed without human presence in the sensory world, but only in the spiritual world, is likely the time at which the world was like 'an unpolished mirror.'

Humanity Defined

The Perfect Human Being is the unique reflection of the synthesis and totality of the Names of God, the encompassment of all realities, the pupil to God's eye in the world, and His vicegerent on earth. This realised human being is also the spirit to the world's form, the clarity to the mirror that the world is, and, as we see further on, the protector of the world that otherwise would not be.

The makeup of a human being is what allows the Perfect Human Being to be a bridge between God and the world.

Were [Adam] not manifest in the form of He who entrusted him with Vicegerency, within that over which he was made Vicegerent, he would not have been Vicegerent... The makeup of his outward form is made up of the realities of the world and its forms, and his inward form is modelled on the Form of God Most High.

Mankind is addressed as, on one hand, the reflection of the synthesis of God's Names, and, on the other hand, the reflection of the synthesis of all of creation. The human being is the microcosm and the world is the macrocosm. One implication of this correspondence is that mankind can contemplate the signs of God that it holds within itself outside of itself. This act, which is done in the wont of God, as illustrated by the aforementioned creation story, is a sign that mankind is a bridge between God and the world.

Something must be said here about the two poles that define the human state. Given that which is above mankind and that which is below it, we can note that the Perfect Human Being constitutes the harmonious meeting between lordship and servanthood. The former is a quality of a human being in relation to other creatures, and the latter in relation to God. The two qualities are not necessarily opposed to each other, but rather support each other. Service of God informs lordship over creation. Righteous lordship over creation is a means of serving God.

Chittick explains humanity, in light of its relation to God and the world, as follows:

Thus, only through man does God gaze upon unity in multiplicity. In Himself He sees nothing but unity, and in the world nothing but multiplicity. But in man unity and multiplicity are combined in such a way that all of God's attributes – in other words the name Allah – are manifested within one unitary locus of manifestation in the midst of the plurality of the world. Without man, a certain mode of divine knowledge would not exist and the infinity of God would be limited. This is the same as saying that man must exist.

In Itself the Hidden Treasure knows its own Essence in a unitary mode such that every attribute is equivalent to every other. In the world, the Hidden Treasure observes each of Its attributes manifested in various combinations as semi-independent realities. Only in man does the Hidden Treasure know Itself as a unity objectified and externalised within the heart of multiplicity.

The Implications of Mankind's Purpose

Given the relationships that we have just understood – that of mankind with what is above it and that of mankind with what is below it – we can now address their implications. The former implies that, through the realisation of a Perfect Human Being, God is reflected in a total manner and He sees Himself in a thing other than Himself. This constitutes the fulfilment of the purpose of creation.

An implication of what mankind and the world are in light of each other, as well as each in light of God, is that mankind safeguards nature, if only through the presence of the Perfect Human Being. Such a being is the realised vicegerent of God on earth. The fulfilment of this purpose towards God – of reflecting Him in a total manner – implies, as the Shaykh explains, the protection of the rest of creation.

> He is Man, who comes to be and is beginningless, who is perpetual and endless in his makeup, who is the separative and unitive Word, and who is the subsisting of the world through his existence. He is to the world what the ringstone is to the ring, which is the place of the signet and the mark with which the king sets a seal upon his treasures. For this reason was he named Vicegerent, for through him the Real protects His creation, as the seal protects those treasures. No one would dare open them so long as the king's seal was still upon them, unless by his leave. It is thus that he is entrusted with protecting the world. *And so the world shall always be protected so long as this Perfect Human Being is found in it.*

Indeed, without the presence of a fully realised Perfect Human Being the world itself cannot exist:

> Do you not see that, when [the Perfect Human Being] withdraws and is separated from the storehouse of the lower-world, there shall remain none of what God had stored therein, and that what had been there shall depart away…?

Being uniquely made in the image of God, the human being alone can become vicegerent. This prerogative is planted as a seed into the human being's makeup, sprouting into life upon realisation as the Perfect Human Being whose purpose is to know and reflect God in a total manner. Such a being is the spirit to the world as form. Consequential to mankind's knowledge of God is mankind's protection of the world, and so of the natural world. Thus, the world cannot be without a realised human being, whose fulfilment of purpose towards That which is above protects that which is below. The very existence of the Perfect Human Being is that which safeguards the world.

Now you know the wisdom of the makeup of Adam, by which I mean his manifest form, and you also know the makeup of Adam's spirit, by which I mean his inner form. He is the Real/creation. You also know the makeup of his station, which is the totality by virtue of which he merits Vicegerency.

PALESTINE AND (HUMAN) NATURE

Naomi Foyle

1.

14 Feb 2016

I'm in an aeroplane, about as far from 'nature' as it's possible for an ordinary person to get: 30,000 feet above the earth, breathing recycled air in a giant plastic and metal sheath. I'm not even flying to Palestine, but Lebanon – but where are Palestine's borders? In addressing the decades-long struggle to resolve that violently contested question, I can only start from who and where I am. That first question is hard for anyone to answer, but it's fair to say I'm a middle-aged, middle-class, white British-Canadian of no fixed religion, still winging it through life, aware of her privilege and trying to put it in the service of humanity; paying her carbon credits and packing two passports to visit neighbouring countries on a permanent war footing. I'm on this plane because I'm en route to experience Palestine in the many dimensions of its threatened but undeniable existence – as land and occupied territory; place and memory; catastrophe and vision.

First I'm flying as a Canadian to Beirut with the UK charity Interpal, a member of its Bear Witness women's convoy to the Palestinian and Syrian refugee camps in Lebanon. Then I'll stop over in Cyprus, revert to my British passport, and journey via Tel Aviv to the West Bank, where I'll visit the Palestine Museum of Natural History in Bethlehem, and volunteer at Marda Permaculture Farm near Ramallah. Over the fortnight I'll be seeking to better understand how people in exile and under occupation experience and protect their natural environment – the more-than-human world of plants, birds, animals and the landscape itself. It feels an urgent question.

During the six years I've supported the Palestinian-led Boycott, Divestment and Sanctions (BDS) campaign against the state of Israel, I've observed – like anyone with a functioning sense of reality – each year get hotter and hotter, and global weather patterns more and more disturbed; and seen scientists confirm that human activity is causing not only global warming but the planet's sixth mass extinction, an event that threatens to wipe out half of all land and marine species by 2100. This won't be like going to the zoo and finding half the cages empty: such a devastating blow to biodiversity could shatter the food chain and destroy modern agriculture. In the meantime, climate change and environmental degradation are already causing widespread human suffering, largely to brown-skinned people: in 1991 in Washington DC, the First National People of Color Environmental Leadership Summit formalised the principles of environmental justice, a concept which recognises 'the disproportionate impact of environmental hazards on people of colour' and seeks, not to redistribute those hazards more evenly (so that poor whites suffer too), but to abolish them.

There could be no clearer example of such environmental injustice than the Israeli-Palestinian conflict, in which a nationalist settler movement led by wealthy Europeans and bankrolled by America has dispossessed the indigenous Arab population and laid waste to their remaining natural resources. The environmental impact of settlements includes the depletion of groundwater supplies; air, land and water contamination by raw sewage and factory outlets; and the deliberate destruction of olive trees: throughout the West Bank Israel burns and bulldozes the *zaytoon*, that ancient, silvery symbol of *sumud*, the philosophy of steadfastness that sustains Palestinians in place of hope. In Gaza, under siege, the situation does look hopeless. Israel Defence Forces (IDF) bombardments have left the strip suffering from infertile soil, loss of biodiversity, an increase in nuisance animals and plants, air polluted by toxic demolition waste, and a barely drinkable water supply that is now damaging unborn children. Yet against this apocalypse, Palestinian ecologists, almost unnoticed, are leading their own environmental revolution. I want to meet and write about these people because, working as they do under military occupation and an apartheid regime, they surely have much to teach the world about resilience, resistance and regeneration.

Maybe, though, I am well-intentioned but naïve. In a geopolitical economy geared to profit from colonial oppression and environmental destruction, is the dream of an egalitarian green future for Israel-Palestine simply that: a dream? Given the rate of settlement expansion, perhaps it is now too late for peace in the region; and beyond that, perhaps, as green guru James Lovelock claims, it also is too late to entertain romantic notions of 'saving the planet'. Maybe we're all up to our nostrils in a planetary oil spill, and there is no longer a safe shore to swim to. Personally, I consider myself an idealist, but I still like to base my arguments and actions on scientific evidence. And on the question of how long we have to halt global warming, there is no consensus. Against Lovelock's pessimism, climatologist Jean Jouzel, a leading member of the International Panel on Climate Change, insists that by abandoning fossil fuels and achieving carbon neutrality by the end of the century, we can still keep from exceeding a 2°C rise in global temperatures. Dismantling the international oil industry may seem as impossible as dissolving Zionism, but cynicism is a self-defeating prophecy, and one we cannot afford to fall prey to. While there's still hope for humanity to halt, slow or reverse climate change, we must keep up the pressure on governments and corporations, at least for other species' sake. But also for our own.

We are an adaptable and populous species: global warming will not wipe us out in one thunderous crash. It will, as it is already doing, cause massive social upheaval. The current refugee crisis was arguably triggered by conflict over oil, and droughts, flooding and coastal erosion will inevitably add to the current epidemic of displacement. But here is where an idealist sees opportunity: while images of Europe's borders slamming shut against floods of desperate people fleeing genocidal warfare can look like the ultimate failure of compassion, they might equally represent the red dawn of humanity's long day of reckoning. For with this migration of vulnerable populations, sustained by family bonds, faiths and cultures, comes a colossal opportunity for the rich West to morally evolve – and the world to politically devolve into an equitable internationalism. Angela Merkel's generosity in opening Germany's borders to one million refugees demonstrated that Europe need not be ruled by fear. Individually and politically, this crisis asks us to conquer our habit of dehumanising the other, and instead treat all people as members of the same human family. From that immersive vantage point, we may even radically relax our relationship with borders. Arguing this now, as Europe begins illegally deporting refugees back to Turkey, and Britain contemplates Brexit, may seem utterly deluded. But the nation state is a recent phenomenon, and there is no reason to believe that over time – and under pressure – it cannot mutate into other, more organic arrangements. The chaos of war has already aided this process: in Syria the revolution has by necessity produced over four hundred, hugely under-reported neighbourhood councils. And under the Turkish thumb, the Kurds have developed a vision of democratic confederalism, based on the anarchist model of bioregionalism.

For now, though, violent conflict still defines our realpolitik. What is needed (and utterly lacking in most political leaders' approach to the challenges we face) is unity: a powerful but humble sense we are all one, interdependent, and dependent on all of creation. In Southern Africa this philosophy is known by the Nguni Bantu word *Ubuntu*: 'the belief in a universal bond of sharing that connects all humanity.' For atheists, this translates as solidarity, and history demonstrates its potency: Marxism, the civil rights movements, feminism and disability activism have all proven that collective protest can force societies to become more inclusive. But the concept also has a spiritual dimension. A belief in universal sharing flies in the face of the materialist conception of human nature as fundamentally driven by the biological imperative to reproduce our 'selfish genes', and re-ennobles the concept of altruism, which evolutionary psychologists interpret as self-sacrifice to benefit younger generations. People inspired by universal consciousness act on behalf of others they are only in the most general of senses 'related' to. And while I'm no expert on world religions, research for my science fiction has convinced me that the philosophy of *Ubuntu* beats at the heart of the three Abrahamic faiths. Though Christ is usually credited with advising 'do unto others as one would have them do unto you', it was the first century BCE Jewish sage Hillel who claimed: 'what is hateful to you, do not do unto your neighbour: that is the whole of the Torah'. You might call that a philosophy of enlightened self-interest, but its light is cast by a profound understanding that we all are equal in worth. Later, Islam, of course, brought its own signal message of unity. The doctrine of *Tawhid* is usually interpreted as a rebuke to the Trinity or earlier polytheisms, but also, for the growing eco-jihad movement, 'gives expression to the fact that everything in the world is part of creation and is related to everything else, which makes the entire world significant, valuable, and worthy of protection.' And just as *Khilafa* and *Amana* emphasise humanity's stewardship of and responsibility for the Earth, so too does contemporary Judeo-Christian environmentalist thought. If the natural world is the ground of all sharing, then nothing embodies *Ubuntu* more than the co-operation of interfaith and non-religious groups in support of environmental justice. And nowhere do such activists work with greater tenacity and vision than in Palestine. From the people seeding a green future in the open air prisons of refugee camps and walled in towns, cities and hills, I know I will learn far more than facts.

Now it's Valentine's Night and I'm in a boutique Beirut hotel, touched to find a plate of heart-shaped chocolates on my pillow, but still digesting my first ever evening in Lebanon. Our convoy arrived to a burst of fireworks honouring the late prime minister of Lebanon, Rafic Hariri, assassinated eleven years ago today in a mass murder widely considered the work of Bashar al-Assad. Over dinner our guides from the Interpal Field Office explained the current crisis in the country. Hezbollah has been boycotting presidential elections since 2014, and the vacuum in government has resulted in civic chaos: after no garbage pick-up for months, Beirut's rivers of refuse are now causing outbreaks of disease. When a country can't protect the health of its land and citizens, you have to fear for refugees within its borders, and sure enough, the news here is bleak too.

Lebanon hosts half a million Palestinians, and the Syrian influx of nearly a million people means that refugees now comprise a quarter of the country's population. Compared to the derisory British offer to take 20,000 Syrians over five years, Lebanon thus sounds incredibly generous; in reality, though, its hospitality is far less impressive. Unlike Jordan (and previously Syria), Lebanon forbids Palestinians from working in most professional jobs, and from owning property or businesses. Dependent on aid and meagre wages scratched from day labouring and cottage industries, generations of people have been condemned to poverty, and their situation is getting worse. UNRWA, the UN body set up in 1948 to administer to the Palestinian refugees, now also supporting approximately 44,000 Syrian Palestinians, has recently announced cuts to its medical services. Hundreds of jobs have been lost in the camps and at least four people have died on hospital doorsteps, after being turned away without treatment. One man, our translator said, set himself on fire in protest. He survived, and his medical bills are now being met one hundred per cent. That's a good news story here. I'm glad my trip has started with the gift of a few extra hearts, as mine is already working overtime.

15 Feb

Barelias and al-Farah are two of the over eighty Syrian refugee camps in Bekaa Valley, a fertile plain between Mount Lebanon and the Anti-Lebanon mountains – across which lies the carnage of Syria. Looking at those low grey peaks from the tour bus today, and knowing that Hezbollah fighters traverse them to support a regime many Lebanese blame for their prime minister's murder, it struck me that Lebanon is fortunate to have thus far avoided another re-eruption of its own internal conflicts. Those wrinkled flanks seemed like sleeping bull elephants, only one prod away from rampaging.

But for now they are bulwarks against insanity, if not much else. The Syrians in the valley live in containers and tents, and barren socio-economic conditions, lucky to pick up seasonal or day labouring work. Barelias and al-Farah, two of the better-organised camps, sharing a school and a medical clinic, offer only scant shelter against the elements. People here might have smartphones and televisions, electricity, food and water, but little else except each other, their small dwellings meagrely furnished with gas-burning stoves, shelving units and stacks of foam mats that double as sofas and beds. It was an unexpectedly hot winter's day, and the containers we visited were surprisingly cool inside. But later on my laptop I saw footage of the tents flooding in a storm, the bed mats afloat in muddy water: here, amidst breath-taking scenery, nature is still a force that can undo you.

There was harsh irony too, in the camps' locations, surrounded by arable pastures, but pitched on stony ground, with not a leaf or blade of grass in sight. In Barelias I asked our Lebanese translator if there was any possibility for people to grow plants here. 'No, there is nothing for that,' she replied shortly, as if the question was frankly idiotic. Of course, water must be expensive, and I didn't press the point. Later though, I spied a row of healthy shrubs in plastic containers behind two men playing chess. Not wanting to interrupt the game, I hovered, taking photos. The tableau, framed by the tent's cleverly modified arched frontage, could have been transplanted from a Damascus café, and sparked the old argument about painting murals on the Apartheid Wall: is it wrong to try and beautify monstrosities? But while permanent structures in supposedly temporary camps are an ominous development, here in this necessary if inadequate refuge, I was heartened to see people wresting creative control over their monotonous, sterile environment.

Otherwise, people sat on plastic stools outside their dwellings, peeling potatoes, hanging out washing, and watching the children play. Everywhere, the gleeful children racing about, clamouring at the school gates, injected the listless streets with a noisy sense of purpose. The adults occasionally burst out with crueller truths. 'We're dying here' one woman told us, while Fatima, a seventy-eight-year-old doubly-displaced Palestinian from Tabariyya via Yarmouk, recently bereaved of her husband, complained bitterly that there was nothing to do and no-one to visit with in the camp. And of course, many people are traumatised. Five women spoke of barrel bombings, sniper fields, shrapnel wounds, sons taken into Assad's jails never to return. But despite all they'd been through, none wanted to join the exodus to our hostile political climate. We met Da'ad, who had lost a child and a brother to tank fire, and whose husband was killed in their home by soldiers, high on a gunfight, who barged in and accused him of setting off the device that had just destroyed part of the house. Da'ad told us that even though there is no war in the camp, she would rather be in Syria, because 'at least in your homeland you can smell the place where your son died'.

16 Feb

Lebanon's two most northerly Palestinian camps, al Beddawi and Nahr el Bared, are large, long-established but in many ways precarious shanty towns. Forced to grow vertically to accommodate new generations, the buildings are haphazard and unsafe, while during Lebanon's twenty-five -year long civil war, refugee camps were often the most vulnerable places to be. Now, riddled with illegal Syrian militants, they are still afflicted with violence. In 2007, in an effort to rout what I was told was a Syrian branch of Al-Qaida, the Lebanese army shelled Nahr el Bared, forcing the evacuation of its 45,000 inhabitants to al Beddawi. Nine years later, al Beddawi's resources are seriously strained and Nahr el Bared is only half-reconstructed and repopulated.

Morale though, was high. In home visits we met families who had accepted their existential limbo with what seemed miraculous grace. And at the Nahr el Barad Women's Programme Association, the calm, glowing centre director Manal Hamled Abdel Aal, embodied the camp's reputation for enterprise. Before the shelling, Nahr el Barad ran a thriving market and Manal's capable leadership has revived this spirit of entrepreneurship: her WPA runs occupational training courses in sewing, sells its traditional cooking in Beirut, and has a women-only gym. Here, seeing steps lined with potted plants, I asked Manal if she had any plans to encourage home food production. Warmly clasping my hand, she said yes, she had a roof-top garden herself, and had tried to get funding for a pilot project, but the NGO involved had pulled out. Hearing this, I offered to put her in touch with the Palestine Museum of Natural History in Bethlehem. Her dream was a seed that deserved water.

Indeed, growing plants in a refugee camp didn't seem quite such a frivolous Western notion here. Later we visited the Green Land Project, a large walled vegetable garden decorated by murals of women in traditional dress. Soaking up the verdant peace of this place, I thought again how vital it was that the Palestinians, deprived for decades of their land, should not suffer also the loss of the ability to work the soil. But for me, the most moving moment in the camp came on the tour bus. Passing a razed stretch of rubble and sand, we gazed on a small mound of jumbled tombstones and shrubs: the camp's oldest cemetery, the green graves of Nahr el Barad's grandmothers and grandfathers, who had died without ever seeing their beloved homeland again, and are now buried in a bombsite.

17 Feb

Today, at the Women's Programme Association in El Buss camp in Tyr, we heard distressing stories about the increase in child marriage since the Syrian influx. Impoverished Syrian parents offer their fourteen-year-old daughters as second wives to Palestinian men, many of whom snap up these bargains then return the pregnant girls to their families a year later. Though these marriages are illegal, social workers are reluctant to involve the Lebanese police because jailing the parents will only make matters worse. While understanding the predicament, we nevertheless pressed for answers. Centre director Hanan Jadaa responded with the story of a Syrian girl who ran to the WPA to avoid being married off to a fifty-year-old man. In this case she was sent to the police, who kept her safe for a week while camp residents put pressure on her family, their landlord threatening to evict them if the marriage went ahead. The parents relented, the daughter returned home, received occupational training and is now working as a hairdresser. This success story reminded me of the cliché that war brings out 'the best and the worst in humanity'. Like most clichés it's largely true; what is vital is to identify and develop whatever that 'best' behaviour is: here, an inspiring example of a refugee camp's leadership in the field of restorative community justice. Hanan's response also encouraged me to ask again my now familiar Englishwoman's question about gardening. She replied that space is at such a premium in the camp that even when the WPA had tried to get permission to create children's playgrounds in the crowded camp, the neighbourhood councils had been unable to agree on a proposal. This example of El Buss's participatory democracy demonstrated just how far removed camp conditions are from Western conceptions of 'normal' life. Later a question about sporting opportunities for disabled children dried on my lips as I realised that here, football fields and swimming pools were facilities just seen on a screen. But the case of the Syrian girl had not been unique. Again and again in this materially impoverished place, we encountered world-class social care: a tiny baby getting expert physiotherapy for a frozen shoulder; bright, happy students with hearing impairments being taught by a deaf former student of the school, which is also proud of a graduate currently working in an advertising agency, earning four times more than the average Palestinian wage.

I'm also becoming increasingly impressed by Interpal, which clearly supports the strong ethos of self-organisation at work in the camps. A Muslim charity, it has built trust through a sense of shared faith – shared also with me, who prayed in a mosque today, for the first time invited by women I know – but also by honouring principles of popular sovereignty, employing Palestinians and Syrians as medical and social workers. The latter are exclusively young women: a man could not speak alone to a Muslim woman, and Muslim men in the camps tend to believe that family difficulties are a wife's responsibility, even (or perhaps especially) if these involve the husband's emotional problems. But while more needs to be done to involve men, it's clear that the profession's language of care, inclusion and child protection makes a vital contribution to a culture of respect and opportunity for women in the camps, empowering them to work toward a future return to Palestine or Syria. Altogether, today nurtured hope.

18 Feb

Near Saida, south of Beirut, stands the largest Palestinian camp in Lebanon, its one hundred thousand inhabitants pulsing against the walls of a volatile, over-crowded, concrete maze. Between buildings collapsing in storms, and the illegal Syrian Islamists who frequently clash with its internal Fatah security force, Ein el Hilweh is a dangerous place and we were assigned an armed guard: three strapping khaki-clad youths and their grizzled commander, charged with keeping us safe. Kidnappings of foreigners by Palestinian militants are virtually unknown but, aware of the 2011 capture and killing of Italian activist Vittorio Arrigoni in Gaza – a murder condemned by all major Palestinian factions – I was glad of protection from any publicity-seeking Salafis. Our guards escorted us first to a medical clinic that has to apply for permits to leave the camp to refill its oxygen canisters, then to private homes, where we heard stories of complete despair. A young man with a damaged leg, earning five dollars a day, can't afford surgery. A mother of five, abandoned by her husband and suffering from depression, lives in a dank room with a tiny high window, breastfeeding by candle light in the middle of the day. Her eldest son, a twelve year-old, runs wild in the camp and sleeps in the graveyard. Nearby, lives a family of school drop-outs, where a sixteen-year-old girl is not permitted to study hairdressing because her parents fear she won't be safe walking to the centre, and her older brother – who could escort her, but won't – doesn't think his sister should learn a trade.

Interpal can't necessarily help these people, as the sums needed and the sociopsychological challenges are so great, and sitting on these sofas with my notepad and pen I felt increasingly helpless, as if I were playing a part in an absurd charade. Decompressing later in a play park, the first we had seen in the camps, I had to sternly remind myself that all these people were receiving professional attention, and my role was simply to bear witness — as much as I could bear. There was no grass in the park, and its cages of lethargic monkeys disturbed us all, but wandering in the sunshine between a carousel and colourful murals I began to regain my equilibrium. Then, in a meeting with young Palestinian human rights workers and a journalist, my spirits lifted. Articulate, confident, connected with the diaspora, West Bank and Gaza, these young women are fully committed to the struggle of being Palestinian. They told us of recent political initiatives to end the restrictions on employment and give the Palestinians Lebanese citizenship. Though the Syrian catastrophe has interrupted these campaigns, and caused so many other difficulties, all three were deeply involved in helping Syrians. Their jobs are tough, but when the stress mounts, the journalist takes out her skipping rope.

Buoyed up myself, I confess I flirted with one of our guards as we re-boarded the bus. Tall and bashful, he had a fluttery way with his eyelashes that provoked me to say goodbye with a playful 'Shukran, habibi!' Naturally, in one of the most densely populated places on the planet, I was overheard. 'Habibi?' one of his brothers-in-arms echoed incredulously as my new sweetheart smiled coyly into his beard. 'Why him habibi, no me?!'

All right, I flirted with two of the guards … 'Stay human', Vittorio Arrigoni urged in his signature to all of his messages.

19 Feb

Our last day in Lebanon took us to UNRWA, where the communications officer insisted that the recent cuts to the health care budget were not in fact cuts, but a reallocation of funds. Knowing of daily protests, deaths, the man who had immolated himself in despair, and hospitals holding children hostage until parents could beg or borrow the money to pay their bills, we were shocked by this disavowal of responsibility. Next the Chief of Education, a soft-spoken Palestinian, himself from a camp, spoke of the importance of encouraging creativity, and empowering women as students and mothers. I warmed to him, but found myself getting confused. When the rest of the staff rushed off to attend an emergency meeting, I wondered aloud why the words 'international donors' kept being repeated, as though the UN were a kind of glorified charity, and asked the two Palestinians remaining how, in their view, UNRWA could best advocate for the most fundamental of the refugees' rights – the right to return to their homes. The Chief of Education's diplomatic response was that UNRWA schools teach the right of return as part of a human rights based education. Although I had seen the positive effects of such a curriculum in the camps' social centres, it was not a highly satisfactory answer. In the hallway afterwards, I spoke to him privately, and he clarified that UNRWA does not receive core funding, but is dependent on voluntary contributions from individual governments, the most generous of which is America. Suddenly, I got it. The country that bankrolls Israel also exerts the most influence over UN support to the Palestinian refugees. A shift in the balance of sponsorship might push the agency into active advocacy – while Saudi Arabia and Kuwait rank high, looking right now at the 2015 list of donors, the contribution from the League of Arab States is pitiful, and Qatar, which independently funds reconstruction projects in Gaza, fails to put money where it would have significant political clout. Currently, I am afraid I agree with those who argue that UNRWA is part of the Palestinians' problem. Under its guardianship a 'temporary problem' has become permanent crisis management.

Finally, we ended our tour of Lebanon in the camp that, more than any other, is synonymous with the brutal persecution of the Palestinians: Shatila, in the neighbourhood of Sabra. Here, between 16 and 18 September 1982, a right-wing Christian Lebanese militia, assisted by the IDF – who sent up flares to turn the night skies as bright as a football stadium – raped, tortured and butchered as many as 3,500 people. The Phalangists left the camp and surrounding streets strewn with grossly mutilated bodies – and survivors waiting indefinitely for justice. The UN officially blamed Israel, the occupying force in the country at the time, for the massacre, while even an internal Israeli investigation held Defence Minister Ariel Sharon personally responsible for not doing enough to prevent the killings. But no prosecution for war crimes resulted. Sharon was simply forced to resign.

Now Shatila's mosque has become a martyrs' cemetery, and the declassified camp also houses Lebanese people and Syrian refugees. Its reputation as a lawless jungle means taxi drivers often refuse to drive to it, while most Beirutians are so scared of the place they don't even know where it is. But for us it was the simplest of the camps to enter: no longer constrained by a Lebanese army checkpoint, people walk freely in and out. Due at the airport, and lacking time to pay our respects at the graveyard, we visited Basmeh & Zeitooneh Relief and Development Agency, an ambitious start-up NGO supporting Syrian refugees. In a few rooms at the top of a narrow building, we found a school, theatre, art therapy room, library, and media and communications training room, and met a class of young students studying Peace Education. Syrian children have been so traumatised by their experiences that teachers now build psychosocial support into the curriculum, including training in non-violent communication and conflict resolution. It's yet another way in which catastrophe has made moral leaders of the dispossessed.

From the rooftop patio we looked out over the hectic streets to a massive cliff of buildings, its rough-hewn, shambolic composition of balconies, cables, drab curtains, black plastic water barrels, satellite dishes and cindercrete extensions somehow serene in the sun. Yet again, I could see no trees, but Basmed & Zeitooneh had found a way to bring nature into the austere chaos of the camp, hiring local craftsmen to etch brutalist reliefs of tree trunks and traditional doors into the stairwell walls. I snapped away, but found the final, iconic image of my visit while leaving Shatila, looking up from the road at a giant rust-red key mounted to a water tower. It was, of course, the key to resolving the misery and violence of these camps, easing the pressure on Syrian refugee services in Lebanon, and replanting half a million parched souls in their native soil – the return of the Palestinian refugees to their homeland.

2.

20 Feb

I switched passports in Cyprus, and – after the ludicrous but unsettling experience of being interrogated by Israeli security about my copy of Khalil Gibran's *The Prophet* – have made it in to Tel Aviv. It's sad and sobering to be arriving just after another three people, two Palestinian youths and one Israeli settler, have been killed in the wave of violence that has consumed the region since October. To the on-going series of stabbings and car-rammings committed mainly by young Palestinians on settlers, soldiers, and police officers, 28 of whom have been killed, Israel has responded with force: reflecting the endemic disproportionality of the conflict, over 180 Palestinians, including 49 children, have been killed during this period, many in incidents that Israeli human rights organisation B'Tselem terms 'public, summary street executions, without law or trial'. Some have dubbed this period the 'knife intifada', but the Palestinian attacks are random, committed by unrelated individuals; not an organised protest, but expressions of hopeless fury at the ever-mounting injustice of the occupation. The tragic deaths on both sides, as well as the hundreds of injuries incurred, should be a powerful motivation to find, at last, a political solution to the conflict. Instead, Netanyahu ramps up the 'terrorist' rhetoric and implicitly endorses a shoot-to-kill policy; Palestinian anger grows; and more despairing adolescents are drawn toward the shallow promise of martyrdom. Ultimately, the cycle of violence works in Israel's favour, distracting world attention from its seizure of what is left of Palestinian land.

The volatile situation is not, though, a reason not to visit: Israel shouldn't be allowed to completely cut Palestinians off from the rest of the world. I'm here to see friends, some of whom are unable to travel to see me, simply because they are Palestinian. Coming here is a humbling privilege I am all too conscious of after visiting the refugees in Lebanon. I also feel tense and paranoid. Here in a hotel with paper-thin walls, I'm too nervous to watch videos sent by a new Facebook friend, Ahmad in Gaza. What if someone hears the Arabic, and reports me?

21 Feb

In Bethlehem, my birthday (officially tomorrow), has started with a flourish of Arab hospitality. Having insisted over email that I phone him should I encounter any problem at all in Palestine, Mazin Qumsiyeh of the Palestine Museum of Natural History came with his wife Jessie and their American volunteer Deb to my Franciscan guest house, and treated me to dinner in the colourful foyer restaurant. It was almost far too kind. Mazin, a Christian Arab from Bethlehem, is a world-renowned scientist and indefatigable human rights activist whose work promotes a refreshing, pluralist approach to the Israel-Palestine conflict, most fully explored in his book *Sharing the Land of Canaan*. Jessie, a former accountant whom he met in America, is the co-founder of the museum and its parent organisation The Palestine Institute of Biodiversity Research. Deb is a permaculturist, artist and political activist. Scanning the menu, discussing the fact that all its dishes are made with Israeli produce, and looking around at well-heeled Italian and Japanese tourists, I had the sinking feeling that I was dragging the leadership of the Palestinian Green revolution into horrendous complicity with Zionist industrial agriculture and international apathy to the occupation. Mazin though, sensed my discomfort and waved it aside, commenting, 'Nearly everything we do damages the world in some way – so order what you like.'

I did, and soon we were talking permaculture, GM crops, Lebanon, mutual friends – Jewish ex-Israelis who'd insisted I meet Mazin – and finally Arabic. From Anthony Shadid's *House of Stone*, the late journalist's account of rebuilding his ancestral home in Lebanon, I had learned that *beit* – as in Beit Lehem and its neighbourhoods Beit Jala and Beit Sahour – means 'house', and by extension 'family' and 'village'. The word also refers to a line of poetry in the Arabic and Urdu form the *ghazal* and, I reflected, like the Italian *stanza*, which means 'room', gives a reassuring sense of a poem as a dwelling place. Mazin reached for a paper table mat and drew the letter *bā*, with its curved wall and single dot: 'The centuries have turned it upside down, but it looks like a house, see?'

It did. And I felt as though I was being made welcome inside it.

22 Feb

Funded by Mazin and Jessie's initial sizable investment, The Palestine Museum of Natural History rents land and buildings from Bethlehem University, where Mazin is a professor. The main sandstone building contains an office/library, a conference/research room, and a hall that will eventually host the Museum's full collections. Here, Environmental Biology MA student Elias Handal proudly showed me trays of butterflies, dragonflies, grasshoppers, and his personal speciality – raptor pellets, from which he has recently reconstructed the hedgehogs eaten by a pair of Eagle

Owls nesting near Wadi Mahour, Beit Jala. Keen to deploy my limited Arabic, I asked about the *hudhud*, or hoopoe, a quaint, colourful bird prominent in the Islamic and Judeo-Christian myths I'd researched for my last novel. Elias was more taken with the iridescent Palestine sunbird, the country's national symbol. Then, next to a large map of the ethnically cleansed villages of 1948, he pulled out a drawer in which, limp as if sleeping, lay a giant kingfisher, a porcupine, a fruit bat Elias had personally killed and skinned, and a barn owl corpse he – no doubt noting my growing look of alarm – assured me had been found on the road. Moving on to the reptile, amphibian and biogenetics section he casually pointed out a jam jar containing a human foetus: there is more than a whiff of the Victorian cabinet of curiosities about the Museum. You won't smell formaldehyde though in its preserved frog jars – a heavily proscribed substance due to its potentially explosive qualities, formaldehyde is rarely approved for import into the West Bank and what Israel does allow through is saved for human tissue samples: the Museum uses alcohol for its specimens. As Elias agreed, you ask a simple question in Palestine and the answer is likely as not to expose the impact of the occupation.

A showroom too for the Palestine Institute of Biodiversity Research, the collections hall also houses a research display, including Mazin's landmark work *Mammals of the Holy Land*, and papers on geotoxicity and declining biodiversity. The research dimensions of the Institute are manifold: visiting scholars learn how the occupation not only damages the land, but curtails Palestinian scholarship. In this context Mazin, also the author of *Popular Resistance in Palestine: A History of Hope and Empowerment*, talks to guests about the boycott, divestment and sanctions movement. It was immediately clear that the nascent Museum is no pet project or dusty archive; rather the living embryo of a highly effective international environmental justice organisation.

The Museum grounds, then, are its green, revitalised womb. Owned by the church, the land was preserved from development by being used as the university's dump site. The adjacent fields are still home to farmers and wild dogs, but a school, shops and houses now overlook the plots, while across the valley, a stark reminder of what the Museum is up against, a white stone settlement marches down the crest of the next hill. Israel, Mazin informed me, has annexed 87% of the land around Bethlehem. This, of course, makes taking full ecological responsibility for the land that is left to the Palestinians nearly impossible, but even more important. Mazin and Jessie's first priority was water management; having constructed a rain water collecting pool, they then built greenhouses and removed asbestos from the roof of a shed intended for a bird rehabilitation and aquaponics centre, where fish will produce nitrogen for fertiliser. They also planted chickpeas and plum trees, installed a clay oven, and established a compost heap and a vermiculture farm: an old enamel bathtub filled with compost-creating worms. Jessie also showed me the *Hugelkultur* bed – a German innovation in which buried wood enriches the soil – and spoke of plans to encourage long-stay volunteers by opening a cafeteria, covering the old cistern with a grape trellis and converting three containers into bedrooms: Deb has been painting images of lynx and kingfishers on the doors. The site also hosts wildflowers, bee hives, fruit and nut trees, two species of endangered orchid and the now rare Star of Bethlehem, nearly driven to extinction in the area by the local practise of pressing the blossom in glass to sell to tourists. The Museum's olive trees, ignored for decades, are now increasing their yield annually. It's a peaceful oasis – except for the conflict. Tear gas regularly rolls down the hill, and while studies have yet to be done on the environmental effects of the chemical, one bee hive swarmed after a dose of it and, down in the town, a Christmas tree hung with gas canisters as a piece of public art died within a week. Mazin winced as he told me this story: he had tried to insist that the artist wash the canisters thoroughly, but somehow the message did not get through. It is early days though, for the Institute's environmental activism. Financially, things should improve: the honey, fruit, vegetables and herbs produced on the site can be sold, while the Museum is now applying for grants to support its educational programme. I was only too pleased to spend my birthday helping Jessie and Deb draft a proposal for a project that would teach children from local Middle Schools, including two in the Bethlehem refugee camps, about recycling and composting. After collecting plastic water bottles to use as planters, the students will build 'green walls' in which to grow food. It's hard to imagine a better symbolic riposte to the Apartheid Wall, that illegal brutality that makes a mockery of the 'green line' of Palestine's 1967 borders. In the meantime, the Museum has taken possession of the dead Christmas tree tear gas canisters: washed, filled with soil and mounted on an olive tree, they are now sprouting za'atar and geraniums.

26 Feb

After a warm farewell to the Museum, and an evening in Ramallah, I arrived at Marda permaculture farm, where my feverish diary keeping has given way to a run of early nights. Owned by Murad Alkufash, the farm is a smallholding in the village of Marda, which sits downhill from the sprawl of Ariel, the fourth largest settlement in the West Bank. Notorious for founding a university on stolen land, Ariel, built on arable hilltops once used for winter crops, is surrounded by a barbed wire fence that has also separated farmers from long swathes of their olive groves and cut villagers off from the nearest town – what was once a five minute drive to the hospital now takes forty minutes. Crowning its abuse of the village, Ariel periodically flushes its raw sewage out down the hills, torrents of faeces diluted with rainwater that erode the soil, pollute the streams and pool in the streets. Seeing photos of Murad's house befouled by this disgusting assault, I could only think that, while the Palestinians may have lost their land, the Israeli settlers are losing their souls. Things have otherwise been quiet with Ariel, Murad says, but in Palestine violence is never very far away. I got a lift here from a friend of his, who pointed out the spot at a checkpoint where a young Palestinian woman was shot and killed during the on-going cycle of attacks.

Against this tense background, the farm flourishes, just as it was carefully designed to do. Permaculture, an ethical system of sustainable and 'permanent agriculture', was developed in Australia in the early nineteen seventies by David Holmgrund and maverick biologist Bill Mollison who, with the publication of *Permaculture: A Designers Manual* became the guru of a movement that aims for nothing less than to dismantle industrialised agriculture, and replace it with a global society characterised by self-reliance at the personal, local and regional levels. In a sense, though, the utopian aura of the term 'permaculture' is misleading: as Mollinson points out, permanence and sustainability are not synonymous. Feudal permanence, in which peasants work the land, provides stability until the inevitable revolts provoke state-engineered famines. Baronial permanence, in which large fields are devoted to single crop cultivation to profit their owners, can be sustained in low-tech societies, but once mechanised monoagriculture quickly depletes the soil resulting in desertification.

Permaculture, in contrast, was devised as a system of 'communal permanence' that could deliver both food security and social justice thanks to its study of the inherent patterns of nature and adherence to the central concept of beneficial design. Thus, planted strategically, trees provide windbreak for more fragile plants; star-shaped beds increase the length of edge; circular beds embrace the plant, ensuring no wastage of water. Space is maximised by vertical gardening and companion planting: Murad sows his herbs and cabbages in 'tyre tiers', using old tyres he gets for free from local mechanics; and lets beans, for example, grow up the stalks of corn. As well as cultivating long greenhouse beds, he plants outside in a mosaic of mainly circular plots arranged between beehives, citrus fruit and olive trees, a worm farm and a chicken and pigeon coop. But while in many ways the farm deploys traditional and low-impact knowledge and practices, permaculture also embraces modern technology: from the beginning Mollinson was enthusiastic about the use of computers to model designs. And as a revolutionary, future-oriented method of planning sustainable human settlements, the practice naturally supports urban life.

In Bethlehem, permaculture had yet to gain traction at the Museum. While the Institute officially promotes the philosophy, and does not till its soil, it has not yet committed to a full permaculture design plan, partly because not all the local Palestinians involved in the project are interested in this approach. Some may feel that permaculture, developed in Australia, is a 'Western import', but although not yet widespread, permaculture has a long history in Palestine. Murad attended his first course in 1991 when some Australians established a training centre in Marda, an organisation that lasted until the IDF shut it down in 2001, declaring the area a military zone. The land was never returned and the main building is now a restaurant for settlers and soldiers. Murad, who could have easily been driven mad by this, used his Chilean passport, a legacy of his father's time in exile, to go to America to gain further qualifications, returning to Marda in 2006 to get married, cultivate his land, and resume teaching. His experience is of strong local interest: the farm's next course, running in April, has so far attracted nine students, none of them international.

For Murad, this is only logical. Permaculture, for him, harmonises with the Muslim faith, and forms the basis of his political position as a Palestinian. Permaculture's devotion to patterns is shared by Islamic architecture, of course, but Murad also believes that 'Islam tells a man to support his own family'. This is not a patriarchal rejection of women's economic empowerment: his wife is currently returning to work part-time in Ramallah. Rather it is a philosophy of radical self-reliance. Murad not only provides food for the table and an income from his produce sales and courses, but a political education for his three young daughters and son. For no one living in the shadow of neighbours who literally shit all over you can be anything but politicised. And as Murad says to volunteers, and in his presentations at international peace and democracy conferences: in Palestine, permaculture is a form of resistance.

To start with, all kinds of farming are under grave threat in Palestine. Whenever, uprooted or destabilised, Palestinians leave their land, Israel claims it for settlements or national parks. Israel has also destroyed the millennia old practice of seed-sharing, its companies encouraging Palestinians to use patented seeds and bioengineered fertilisers. Currently, in a development even Orwell couldn't have made up, the Zionist assault on Palestinian farming allegedly extends to pig warfare. Growing up, Murad never saw a wild boar, which formerly existed only in the north of Palestine. Now there are thousands of them, a genuine plague of huge ferocious beasts that hold night orgies in farmers' fields and groves, devouring crops and trampling the fragile roots of the olive trees. Murad himself lost a thousand lettuces and cauliflowers, and nearly his life after he charged at a sounder of boars that had broken into his farm. Fortunately the boar leader was a wily one, and did not attack, just snorted at Murad long enough to allow his pig family to escape. It was a good story, but the problem is huge, and deeply political. Villagers report seeing IDF helicopters landing to release pairs of the animals, and Palestinian Authority President Mahmoud Abbas has accused settlers of 'training dogs to attack us and sending wild boars to spread corruption on the face of the earth.' B'Tselem more cautiously conjectures that the rise of the boars is a result of decreasing biodiversity, a decline attributed to ... you guessed it, the settlers' shit. But whatever caused the problem, Israel has blockaded a solution. Palestinians are not allowed guns to cull the beasts, and cannot poison them because strychnine is now banned from import. Tranquilliser guns were prohibited at the same time, when Israel passed a law forbidding the hunting of these dangerous predators – straight-facedly citing a threat to biodiversity.

Murad reinforced the fence around his farm with recycled tyres, so far a boar-proof barrier. He is not, though, just interested in protecting his own business. Against the Zionist stranglehold on his people's aspirations, he has a vision of national food sovereignty and economic independence. Palestinian land – what is left of it – he told me, is mostly countryside, and even in cities and towns there are large gardens and fields in which fruit, vegetables and grains could be grown. I nodded, thinking of the wild, enchanting olive groves I'd stumbled on in East Jerusalem and Ramallah, and the scores of open hilltops I'd passed through on my way from Bethlehem – and of the refugees who could live on them instead of yet more illegal settlers. In the meantime, for urban and rural Palestinians, the ability to grow food without expensive chemicals or patented seeds would save money, while even rooftop and balcony gardens would help relieve hunger, particularly important for the people in Gaza, suffering economic siege and Israel's grotesque policy of 'putting the Palestinians on a diet'.

Food sovereignty would also support the boycott of Israel, a campaign Murad actively endorses, checking labels in his local shop, and working as a translator for researchers into Israel's illegal activities in the West Bank. Yesterday afternoon I accompanied him and two Methodists investigating the predictably ill-effects of two Israeli factories on nearby Palestinian villages: cancer rates have rocketed, we were told by the Mayor of Deir Balut, possibly because every autumn the factories blow a thick white dust over the olive groves, which cannot be harvested until after heavy rains. The Methodists, currently reviewing their investments, will be making a report to the German parent company, Heidelberg Cement. But if money talks, permaculture also has a growing voice of its own. Murad's farm attracts not just aid but commercial opportunities: the UK soap company Lush, which buys olive oil from a consortium of the villagers, is interested in funding a permaculture project with him next.

All of this is possible because permaculture is very well-suited to a Middle Eastern climate. Marda farm yields harvest all year round. Right now, the oranges and lemons are ripe on the trees, the radishes big, bright and crisp, and the lettuces as long as my forearm. This time of year the main task is weeding. Leaving, as instructed, the peppery nasturtiums to attract aphids away from Murad's planned cucumber seedlings, I've cleared a raised bed and a path in the greenhouse, and a row of bushy za'atar outside in the shade of the olive trees. I like the job, which I also did at length when volunteering years ago on organic farms in Australia, most especially the satisfying feeling when the root clump comes up all in a soft earthy rush. Though how aggravating when, despite being whacked at with both ends of a pick mattock, the taproot refuses to budge, and I have to saw through its fibres and re-bury the tenacious sign of my failure, feeling like an un-re-educatable extra in a Maoist revolution. Nearing fifty now, I sense it's unlikely I'll ever be more than an apprentice gardener. Today I even walked down to the farm with my reading glasses stuck up on the top of my head, so it's a good thing Murad is the very opposite of the Chairman in philosophy and disposition. 'Take it easy,' he says. 'Take a break now.' And then we stop to eat, and laugh with his kids, or go for a walk round the village, stopping every ten minutes for Murad to conduct voluble exchanges of opinion and news with his various relatives. 'You're the *malak* of Marda' I teased him today – remembering another word from *House of Stone*, and thinking also of *King of Kensington*, the classic Canadian TV show about a generous convenience store owner and his multicultural neighbourhood in downtown Toronto. No, Murad demurred, genuinely shocked, the first time in three days I had seen this visionary eco-dynamo lost for words.

15 April

Thinking of that moment with Murad as I finish this essay, I realise anew that my involvement in the Palestinian-led resistance to Zionism challenges the very notion of leadership itself. Most activists I know are deeply disillusioned by the official Palestinian leadership: corrupt Fatah polices the West Bank on behalf of Israel, while Hamas is locked into a grim cycle of violence with the IDF it can never militarily win. It is oft complained that the Palestinians lack a Gandhi figure, but when people can be jailed indefinitely without charges, simply for organising a weekly demonstration, how can such a peaceful superhero emerge? The answer, as I have learned from Manal Hamied Abdel Aal, Hanan Jadaa, Mazin and Jessie Qumsiyeh, Murad Alkufash and his family, and the self-ironised 'leaders' of the BDS movement I've worked with for years, lies in civil society: Palestinian leadership has to be shared.

And is stronger for it. You can jail individuals, but not – despite Israel's best efforts in Gaza – a whole people, or a vision whose strength is attested by its growing reach. On my trip I also met with Jewish Israeli human rights activists and boycott campaigners, as well as a publishing professional in Tel Aviv who hates the apartheid in her country, intends to send her son to an integrated school, and reluctantly supports BDS. Undeniably, the skies are dark over Israel-Palestine. But powerful rays of light are breaking through: visionary projects like those I visited radiate hope, while every month the boycott movement announces significant victories, most recently the withdrawal of two huge multinational corporations, Veolia and G4S, from the Israeli market. Zionism is not invincible. All empires must fall in the end, and the long-term future of Israel-Palestine may yet lie in a shared state, or even bioregional governance. For now, let Mazin Qumsiyeh, himself a recent visitor to Beirut, explain how appreciating the multifarious blessings of (human) nature can help achieve a just peace in a land which, like all land, is holy:

> Lebanon, like Palestine, is such a beautiful rich country but its political leaders do not seem to get their act together. Being divided into sometimes intermixing and sometimes contending communities is not a bad thing if you think in terms of healthy diverse human communities just like a healthy diverse ecosystem (many species competing, conflicting, sometimes cooperating). It is fertile ground for innovation ... in Palestine, we just need to collect all those good people in networks to better help young talent to grow and promote collaboration and healthy but not destructive competition. Our museum motto is RESPECT (for ourselves, for others, for nature) ... Come visit us.

WILD IN THE FOREST

Zeshan Akhter

There are moments of insight in life that stay with you forever. Invisible to all except you, they are there, making minute adjustments to the meanings that you assign to what you see, think and learn. One such moment for me came many years ago during a marine science lecture.

At that time, I had been going through a period of asking myself where I belong. Pakistani by parental heritage, Yorkshire lass by birth and Glaswegian by upbringing, I wondered where was home for me. As much as Scotland is the only home I have known, and where I happily feel I *am* home, I don't have roots here in the way that native Scottish people do. I don't know how it would feel to have ancestors who were born here or to associate different towns and cities with my family or ancestral history. Yet, in Pakistan, I am regarded as an outsider – one of those odd people who choose to live permanently elsewhere as a minority. So where did I truly belong?

I pondered such thoughts during the class for my marine science course. The lecturer was explaining how the moon's gravitational pull causes the earth's tides. No matter where on Earth you go, tides ebb and flow, caused by the moon, 238,855 miles from Earth. It is a planet-wide phenomenon; the moon's gravity affects the whole globe, not just particular areas. Photographs of earth taken by astronauts from space tumbled into my mind. Earth appears as a blue marble floating in the dense blackness of space, its swirling white clouds veiling the life below. I realised that humanity is akin to a child utterly unaware of the wondrous context in which it has come into existence. From space, there are no barriers describing where different groupings of people live. From space, Earth is one world where humanity resides. Indeed, one of the images taken from space, 'Earthrise' by Apollo 8 astronaut William Anders, is often credited with having been central to galvanising the environmental movement.

It suddenly occurred to me that this planet is my home. No matter where I go on Earth, I am home – there is comfort in knowing that I belong everywhere. The Prophet Muhammad is reported to have said: 'the earth is beautiful and green and Allah has made you stewards over it. He sees how you acquit yourselves.' I remember feeling simultaneously astonished and delighted the first time I came across this hadith in my go-to university text book on nature conservation. I was familiar with many hadiths but this was the first one that deeply impressed upon me that my faith is steeped in nature. In fact, I learned, Islam has much to say about our human relationship with creation. The Qur'an refers both to its own verses and the verses of nature as *ayat* – which means 'signs' that point to Him. This symbolises creation also as revelation, which points to the existence of God in the same way as the verses of the Qur'an. We treat the Word of God with deep reverence. So why should we not treat the other revelation, His creation, which includes ourselves and the natural world, with equal reverence? If I had no other knowledge of Islam's teachings about my relationship with Creation, this one realisation would be enough.

One of the fundamental concepts of Islam is *fitra* – the divine spark with which we are born. It is the natural disposition to be aware of our origins as the purposeful creation of God. But we are in danger of neglecting this innate awareness, or losing that light in our own selves, if we do not strive against unrefined thought and action. It is our role to consciously use our free will to keep polishing that divinity that emanates from within. This is from where our relationship to Earth and all that lives on and in it stems.

One of my favourite verses in the Qur'an appears in Surah An-Nur: 'Do you not see that all those in the heavens and earth praise God, as do the birds with wings outstretched. Each knows its [own way] of prayer and glorification. God has full knowledge of what they do' (24:41). This verse brings the believers' attention to the way in which Creation is engaged in silent worship of Allah, each in its own way. Whereas humanity accepted free will and therefore chooses to worship Allah where, when and how it decides to, animals, plants and every aspect of the world worship Allah constantly although we are unable to perceive their method. The verse exhorts the believer to respect nature, but also points to something deeper. Ours is not an ecology because we are facing catastrophe: it is an ecology of principle and it does not come from risks or dangers. Surah An-Nur also reminds us of our origin: that we have been created out of dust and this is what Satan objected to: that he is made of light and we are dust. We are also reminded that we have been created out of water. So it is important to remember that our origins are of the Earth. No wonder, traditional Eastern and African spiritualities regard earth as the mother and the source of all life.

It was these realisations that motivated me to work for nature conservation. The organisation in which I am employed, Scottish Natural Heritage (SNH), believes that nature has an intrinsic right to exist without reference to its utility to human beings. It also stresses the benefits that flow from nature to people – benefits we have come to take for granted. The benefits that are meant to allow people to meet their essential needs for food, clothing, shelter, medicine and the very air we breathe. Without plants on land and microscopic phytoplankton in the oceans, and the oxygen they produce, we would not be able to breathe. Without bees to pollinate many kinds of crop plants, we would not have fruit, vegetables and spices such as tomatoes, coriander, cardamom, mangoes and pomegranates.

But our appreciation of plankton, bees and forests, and complex interconnection between man and nature, did not emerge overnight. It took a long and meandering journey for us to arrive at the realisation that we actively need to conserve nature.

The modern countryside landscape of Britain, far from being a natural, wild environment, has been profoundly changed after millennia of being utilised by human beings to meet their needs. Britain was once entirely covered in woodland. In Scotland, a special kind of forest enveloped a large part of the country. It was called the Caledonian forest, after the name by which the Romans knew Scotland – Caledonia – meaning 'wooded heights'. This forest was a kaleidoscope of colours and types of trees such as pine, birch, rowan, aspen and juniper. It was home to large mammals such as brown bears, moose and wolves as well as the European beaver. People initially felled the trees for firewood and timber and then as the British Isles developed, and people went from hunter gatherers to farmers, they cleared the forests to grow crops and to provide grazing land for livestock. Villages, towns and cities evolved and people moved out of the countryside and into urban settlements. Signs and remnants of the original lost forest can still be seen in Scotland. In old Gaelic, the town of Kingussie in Invernesshire is called *Ceann a' Ghiùthsaich*, meaning the end of the pine wood because at one time, the Caledonian forest extended down to that point. Britain's countryside, especially in Scotland (where this is still the case), was held in large estates that were owned mainly by individuals, often aristocracy. Whilst the wild landscapes were valued, there was no overall concept of what we would call nature conservation.

Following the Renaissance and Enlightenment periods, scientific discoveries and new advancements in the eighteenth century led quickly to the industrial revolution. Even more people moved from the countryside into centres of urban population in search of jobs and a better life. Cities became centres of activity that fed mechanised mass production. People gave up their old ways of living from the land; their connection to nature and their lives became centred on division of labour: mill workers, machinists, ship builders. Whilst mechanisation did make people's lives easier in many ways, increasing city sizes led to grime, pollution and poverty for many.

Industrialisation corresponded with the rise of Romanticism, an intellectual and artistic movement that arose in the mid-eighteenth century in response to the scientific rationalisation of nature. Poets, writers and painters, among others, observed how nature's bounty in the form of water, coal, cotton and precious metals, was being sucked out of the Earth and used to power mechanised production. They also reacted to the increasing alienation of people from nature. Poets such as William Wordsworth and Samuel Taylor Coleridge, with insight into the renewing capabilities nature possesses, wrote about nature as a healing and spiritual force. Their words captured people's hearts and imagination. Here, as an example, is Wordsworth:

> Sweet is the lore which Nature brings:
> Our meddling intellect
> Mis-shapes the beauteous forms of things
> We murder to dissect.
> Enough of science and of art:
> Close up these barren leaves:
> Come forth, and bring with you a heart
> That watches and receives.

People from cities who could afford to travel went to the places the poets described to discover for themselves the vistas that the artists spoke about. The concept of caring for the landscape in Britain is considered to be deeply indebted to the Romantics.

Increasing agriculture, growing towns and cities, then the industrial revolution and finally the two World Wars took a heavy toll on Britain's forests. Cumulative human activity resulted in Britain almost completely losing its woodlands. How Britain set about recovering its forests is closely linked with its colonial history in India.

In the nineteenth century, the demands of the industrial revolution were consuming increasing amounts of nature's riches. Timber, in particular, was greatly in demand. Britain's empire, stretching far and wide, allowed it to import wood from overseas more cheaply than to grow it at home. There were closer timber markets as well, particularly in Scandinavia and the Baltic regions. Thus Britain was not too concerned about its own forests or sourcing timber locally. However, by 1874, India was experiencing a grave loss of its forests, which had been felled to make way for massive colonial agriculture. Britain had also instigated the construction of a railway network that spanned, by 1910, over 51,650 kilometres. The railway construction called for huge amounts of timber because the tracks that were laid down, were of course, made of wood. Nine hundred sleepers were needed for just a two kilometre piece of track. Teak and sal as well as deodar cedar (Cedrus deodara) were three of the preferred tree species used for this purpose because of their strength and the belief that they were resistant to rotting. The Latin name *deodara* actually comes from the Sanskrit word *devdaru* meaning timber of the gods: the cedar was used for building temples in India. The curative properties of deodar cedar are well recorded in Indian Ayurvedic medicine. Interestingly, the deodar cedar is currently the national tree of Pakistan.

India's forests were reduced to such an extent that the authorities finally realised that intensive extraction of timber could not be sustained indefinitely. This seemingly very simple realisation is constantly being relearned over and over again in different parts of the world and in relation to different animals and plants. Nature cannot bear endless exploitation without her treasure trove eventually being emptied. Botanists and other scientists in the colonial service in India became convinced that deforestation was resulting in the land surface drying out. Soil was being degraded, rainfall was declining, flash floods had become common in rivers silting up.

In 1854, the colonial administrator of India, Lord Dalhousie (1812–1860), realised that a forestry policy for India at a country-level was urgently needed. Subsequently, in 1864, the Indian Forestry Service was established; and a German Botanist and Forester called Dietrich Brandis (1824–1907) was appointed Inspector-General of Forests in India. Brandis had already impressed the British with his scientific approach to forest management during his ten-year stint in colonial Burma – where the forests were declining just as rapidly. Britain had its estates and foresters but unlike France and Germany, it did not, at that time, practice scientific forestry methods. Scientific forestry requires knowledge of the size of forests and this demands surveys and mapping. It is also necessary to understand how rapidly trees grow yearly so that it can be calculated how many, and how often, trees can be felled without completely destroying the forest and ensure that it can continue to regenerate and grow. Germany and France had become concerned about their own dwindling timber supplies in the late eighteenth century and had developed quantitative methods to manage their forests. They had foresters with skills to address the timber problem in India.

The German quantitative approach to the management of forests had a serious flaw. Forests were managed for the sole purpose of growing timber in the shortest time and in the most efficient way. A few particular tree species were favoured over a more natural balance consisting of the full range that would naturally occur in certain areas. No consideration was given to the ecological functioning of forests and the relationship that local communities had with them. Many of the uprisings against colonial rule in India resulted from people objecting to being forbidden from accessing and using forests in customary ways. Dietrich Brandis did try to include ways of managing the forests in collaboration with local communities through what he termed 'forest villages' but the priority for the British was to secure the supply of timber, both for India and Britain, and his idea was rejected. Eventually, a Forestry School was established at Dehra Dun and gradually India became a centre of expertise in forestry science. The flow of knowledge and expertise reached Britain under Dietrich Brandis and his

German countryman William Schilch (1840-1925) who essentially became the founder of forest science in Britain. Forestry schools, university lectureships and forestry departments were established. Edinburgh University was the first place in Scotland to have a forestry lectureship.

Britain had inherited a way of practising forestry that was informed by German (and French) scientific methods. After the First World War, this efficient way of growing and managing forests became vital for its severely depleted forests to be replenished. Timber was particularly important during the war and was used in myriad ways, including as fuel in factories in which firearms and ammunition were assembled, but also in the trenches for infrastructure. After the war, only five per cent of Britain's land area was covered in forest. Much of the timber used in the war had come from privately owned British estates.

The British government considered how best to address this problem and decided to set up, in 1919, a government agency called the Forestry Commission with a remit in England, Scotland, Wales and Ireland. In those early days, the organisation's priority was to buy land and plant trees. Large swathes of the countryside and lower hillsides were planted with conifer trees such as Sitka spruce and Douglas fir.

These trees however, are not native to Britain. They are found on the west coast of North America. They are fast growing. Sitka spruce in particular is the fifth quickest growing tree in the world. Its wood is white with long fibres, making it ideal for the production of high quality paper. It was felt that these tall trees, which grew well in the British climate, were ideal to restore British forests and to quickly re-establish a domestic supply of timber. Once again, their impact on local ecology was ignored. By contrast, the planting in India led by Brandis and others did at least use native trees.

The Forestry Commission still exists today (although, Scotland has its own agency now called the Forestry Commission Scotland) and the production of timber to meet Britain's increasing consumption of wood-based products is still a core part of its work. However, in many other ways the organisation is very different. It actively and successfully promotes the forests as places of sanctuary for people and encourages recreational access for a range of activities. In Scotland for example, Galloway Forest Park has been designated the UK's Dark Skies Park. The

Park is one of the darkest places in Britain where people can go to escape light pollution from cities. Over 7,000 stars and planets are visible as well as the silver band of the Milky Way. Visitors can observe the stars clearly while experiencing the forest and its beauty at night. Nowadays, encouraging people to go outdoors and experience nature is a core part of the work of nature conservation organisations. To experience the natural world and reflect on the cosmos and His signs in them is a core message of the Qur'an. Yet this message is rarely heard amongst Islamic teachers instructing young people today.

After the two World Wars, Britain set up special protected areas of the countryside in order to provide sanctuary for the most precious wildlife and natural places, and also for people. Awareness had been growing for some time that Britain's countryside and wildlife was under increasing pressure from a variety of different ways that the land was being used. It was felt that the best of what remained should be protected as jewels in the crown of the British natural landscape. In Islam, the concept of protected areas, called *hima*, has existed since the Prophet declared Mecca and Medina inviolable sanctuaries where not even a fly or plant can be killed. Tragically, in modern times, these blessed cities are the last places where we might expect to find the environment treated with respect. In classical Islam, the concept of *hima*, and a second kind of inviolate zone, *haram*, were an integral part of the Shariah. *Hima* zones were reserved for forests in which cutting of trees was forbidden, grazing was restricted to certain seasons, and the whole zone was managed for the welfare of the community; and the community itself was responsible for its protection and conservation. Around *haram* zones, which were located near wells, rivers and other areas, development was forbidden. The purity of the water had to be conserved. Many historic Muslim cities, such as Fez in Morocco and Aleppo in Syria were built around *hima* and *haram* zones. But all this is history.

However, there are indications that the concepts of *hima* and *haram* may emerge in contemporary times. A good example is provided by the Birmingham-based Islamic Foundation for Ecology and Environmental Sciences (IFEES). During the last few years IFEES has worked with the NGO Care International to persuade fishermen in Zanzibar to employ sustainable fishing methods. The fishermen were under tremendous pressure from international trawling ships that scoop up the schools of abundant fish in areas the local people had traditionally depended upon. This had left the local fishermen no option but to fish in the areas that were too close to shore for the huge fishing ships to approach. There, the catches were poorer and the fishermen were using dynamite to maximise their returns. Verses from the Qur'an were related to the fishermen who were reminded that Allah requires believers to care about nature and other creatures. Once they learned about the Qur'anic verses and Prophetic examples of caring for nature, the fishermen agreed to designate their diminished fishing grounds a *hima*. They could still make a meagre living but in ways that are kinder to the important coral reefs that surround their island archipelago. The international trawlers, however, carry on emptying the seas of its fish at a rate that is simply not sustainable.

In Scotland, there are now over 2,000 protected areas, covering 18 per cent of the country. Twelve different types of designations identify the level of international or national legislation or policy under which the areas are protected. Laws and special arrangements apply in order to protect these places from certain kinds of human activities such as development that might harm them. One particular kind of protected site is named after the Iranian city, Ramsar, on the coast of the Caspian Sea where the international conservation community met in 1971. At that meeting, it was decided that it was important to protect wetlands of particular uniqueness and to use them sustainably. The fundamental ecological functions of wetlands and their economic, cultural, scientific, and recreational value were acknowledged in that agreement.

Up to now, the world had sought to preserve the most precious places of nature as 'islands' that were protected against human activities. Gradually, the thinking would change and move towards understanding that we cannot go on isolating areas and protecting only those whilst surrounding them by human activity that negatively impacts their ability to exist. In his book *The Song of the Dodo*, David Quammen makes the point that for some time ecosystems have been unravelling like a richly and intricately woven Persian carpet to which a hunting knife has been taken and cut into thirty-six pieces. Each resulting little piece of carpet does not become a perfect miniature piece of Persian carpet. What you are left with are pieces of worthless, ragged, rapidly unravelling carpet-like stuff, not a perfectly functional whole. This, he explains, is roughly what scientists discovered happens when habitats such as forests are cut into segments for agriculture, transport infrastructure and other forms of development. The bigger the piece of carpet – meaning, the bigger the piece of unspoiled habitat – the better. Or, as John Muir (1838–1914), Scottish-American naturalist and environmental philosopher who was instrumental in the creation of national parks, points out: 'when we try to pick out anything by itself, we find it hitched to everything else in the Universe'.

The nature conservation community in Britain has gone through a process of realising that the Persian carpet needs to be stitched back together. Colleagues at my agency, Scottish Natural Heritage, are poring over maps to study where parcels of land can be connected through planting trees or by creating other types of natural corridors. Attention is now on understanding how a whole landscape works with the aim of looking after it in a more holistic way. This involves viewing people as integral components of the ecosystem, and inviting them to take part in dialogue about how to manage land and water, taking into account their own and others' needs as well as the manner in which nature works and the benefits that flow from it. Thích Nhất Hạnh, the Vietnamese Buddhist monk and peace activist, explains how various components of nature come together in a holist way with a pertinent example. 'You can hold an orange in your hand', he says, 'but it does not really exist as an orange. That is, it does not exist apart from the tree, the sun, and rain, the soil and its organisms, the farmer, the truck driver, and so on. One could say the orange is actually made up of "non-orange elements" – a set of conditions that allow the orange to be here. If you really look at the orange, you can see the entire cosmos at play.' People are wired into the Earth for every aspect of their existence.

A key moment in the global environmental movement came in 1992 with the famous United Nations Conference on Environment and Development – otherwise known as the Rio Earth Summit. The agreement that nations pledged to honour was to stop the loss of biodiversity by 2010. Most countries have now signed, or are in the process of signing, that agreement which is formally called the Convention on Biological Diversity. The term biodiversity means the variety of life. There are different ways of measuring the diversity of life on Earth: one of them is simply the number of different species of plants and animals that exists – which is estimated to be perhaps up to 100 million species or more.

Britain's hard working nature conservation community swung into place and developed plans at the national and local levels to protect particular habitats and species. Whilst successes were achieved in different countries, globally, the target was not met. The scale of the problem is truly monumental. The Royal Zoological Society of Britain announced that the world is currently experiencing a sixth mass extinction event; a point well argued in Elizabeth Kolbert's recent book, *The Sixth Extinction*. Mass extinction events have occurred five times in Earth's history and were catastrophic events during which much of life was wiped out. One of the theories put forward to explain why dinosaurs disappeared is that a meteor hit the Earth, the resulting debris that was thrown up into the atmosphere blocked out the sun, causing the plants to die out which in turn decimated animal life. Right now, human activity is having the effect of wiping out species at a rate that is analogous to that meteor strike. We have entered, it has been argued, a new geological age – the Anthropocene epoch. Human activities now have unparalleled impact on Earth's geology and unimagined consequences for its ecology.

The Global Biodiversity Outlook reports, produced by the Secretariat of the Convention on Biological Diversity, regularly issue dire warnings about the ecological health of our planet. A recent report states that 'natural systems that support economies, lives and livelihoods across the planet are at risk of rapid degradation and collapse, unless there is swift, radical and creative action to conserve and sustainably use the variety of life on Earth'. The report concluded that 'we can no longer see the continued loss of biodiversity as an issue separate from the core concerns of society. Realising objectives such as tackling poverty and improving the health, wealth and security of present and future generations will be greatly strengthened if we finally give biodiversity the priority it deserves'. It is not just that we need to avoid 'economic meltdown' but we also need to 'avoid a much more serious and fundamental breakdown in the Earth's life support system'. If nature is to be saved, the report states, all of society needs to be involved, not just the scientists and nature conservationists. Society needs to find ways of living and having its needs met without damaging the natural world.

The good news is that public understanding about how keeping nature intact helps people is slowly increasing. For example, over the Christmas period of 2015, flooding was in the news as communities in many areas of Britain experienced the results of high and sustained rainfall. Factors that can contribute to flooding include hillsides that are bare of trees. Tree roots slow and hold water in the soil rather than letting it sweep down valleys unimpeded. Grassland that is wet and boggy can help hold water too. If homes have been built on flood plains, there is a likelihood that a river could spill over during periods of high rainfall and inundate homes and businesses that have been built too close to its banks. Being aware of these aspects of how nature works and planning settlements in a way that works with this knowledge, has helped some communities better defend themselves against the prospect of flooding. In the English town of Eddleston natural flood management has helped to protect the community. It involved planting native woodlands on floodplains, installing log-jams in the headwaters to slow down run-off, and creating new water retention ponds to capture flood water.

However, ethnic minorities are lagging behind. Public attitude surveys in Britain consistently find that people from Asian and Muslim backgrounds have the least understanding about nature and spend the least amount of time in it undertaking any kind of activity in the countryside, parks or other types of green spaces in towns and cities. They are considered 'hard to reach', meaning that they do not respond to mainstream efforts that aim to inform the public about the environment and to encourage them to spend time outdoors. There are multiple underlying reasons for this disconnection. The first generations to arrive in the UK for economic or political reasons endured a severe kind of social, cultural and environmental severance from their home countries. They were often from rural backgrounds and may have made their living wholly or partially from the land. They brought knowledge of the medicinal properties of plants with them. But it would have been, and continues to be, impossible for them to translocate the meaning that they attached to plants, animals and nature from their countries of origin to the countryside of the UK.

The generations born in the UK, unlike their parents, would have had absolutely no historic sense of connection with the environment or nature. Most people who love to spend time in natural places – camping, hiking, sailing, gardening – tell how their love of nature began during childhood. Indeed, research shows that by the time a child is twelve years old, his or her formative reaction to nature has already developed and will accompany the child into adulthood. The practical realities of making a living dominate the lives of this generation. Only what is necessary is given attention: when people are under pressure, anything that is not essential to survival is marginalised.

Perhaps now, two or three generations along, Muslims in Britain can rediscover Islamic teachings on nature. After all, can we regard ourselves as complete and holistic Muslims without giving due attention to God's other book of revelation – the verses of nature?

GO SLOW

Lali Zaibun-Nisa

When I was living and working in London there were many times when I would have the urge to get away from the city. I needed to escape the blinking lights, the constant noise, the ever present pollution. At that time, my brother was living in Brighton. It too is a city but there was one big difference between London and Brighton: the sea. That's why it was the focus of my attention.

I would take the short train journey to Brighton and sit on the pebble beach. With my back to the crowds of people streaming towards the pier, I would look out across the coast. There was the flat line of the horizon. There were the seagulls soaring in a cloudless blue expanse. There was the tremendous sound of the waves crashing against the shore. As I sat taking in the scene, the salty sea air would whip around me in unpredictable motions, dizzying and uplifting. An hour or two would stretch out and seem to stop so that I would eventually lose track of time. It was enough to just sit and be and let myself be taken in and enfolded by the seascape; the power of nature evident in the movement of the waves that beckoned both to lose myself in them and recover something lost living in the city. My senses were awake and my heart full. I felt whole and connected to nature.

Time spent communing with nature is a luxury for most of us who live in the modern developed world. Compared to even fifty years ago, the accelerated pace of technological change and development has transformed the way we live so that we spend the vast majority of our time in artificial environments in which there is little chance or time for connecting with nature. We spend our lives indoors in climate-controlled buildings and homes. We consume food that has been manufactured, processed and treated in industrialised farms and factories. The average person's leisure and work consists of staring at a screen. Our instinctual selves, evolved over thousands of years to survive and thrive in harmony with the cycles of nature, have had to adapt to an onslaught of modernisation that has greatly reduced the quality of our lives. And so along with the vast changes to our lifestyles, we've seen a dramatic change in our health as a species: despite the fact that we now on average live longer, our global mental and physical health has deteriorated.

To put things into perspective: in 2008, 63 per cent of all deaths globally were due to non-communicable diseases (NCDs), principally cardiovascular diseases, diabetes, cancer and chronic respiratory diseases. These NCDs are projected to increase by 15 per cent between 2010 and 2020. Once thought of as 'diseases of affluence', these conditions have spread from the developed world to the developing world reflecting the negative effects of globalisation, rapid unplanned urbanisation and increasingly sedentary lives. Likewise, the obesity epidemic sweeping the world attests to the destructive influence of these factors: in 2008 more than 1.4 billion adults were overweight and more than half a billion obese, these figures having doubled since 1980.

Hand in hand with this is the increasing deterioration of our collective mental health. Globally, mental health conditions account for 13 per cent of the total burden of disease, with depression likely to increase to become the highest contributor to burden of disease by 2030, even more so than heart disease, stroke, road accidents and HIV/AIDS. Worldwide, one in four people suffer or will suffer from a mental health condition. In low-income countries, depression represents almost as large a problem as malaria. There is also a correlation between physical and mental health problems: a 2012 study found that 30 per cent of people with a long-term physical health problem also had a mental health problem and 46 per cent of people with a mental health problem also had a long-term physical health problem.

The sharp dichotomy between an increase in material wealth and comfort on the one hand and the increase in disease on the other reveals a fundamental chasm between our expectations of what constitutes a good life and the stark reality on the ground. Organisations such as WHO which monitor and report on the health of our species outline strategies to tackle the 'disease burden' through material interventions such as improving our diets and tackling the 'lifestyle factors' which contribute to our suffering. While we need to understand the material causes for our decline in health, we also need to go deeper than this. We need to discover the cultural bedrock upon which our civilisation and our lifestyles have been built. The real medicine for our times, as the archetypal psychologist James Hillman once said, is to identify the ideas that shape our relations with the world; to enact a 'therapy of ideas'. Only by doing this cultural forensic work will we move closer to restoring health to its fuller meaning of wholeness, as suggested by the etymology of the word.

Let us start then with the idea of 'progress' – an Enlightenment ideal which has its origins in the understanding of our world, arising and concretised during the European Renaissance, as an inanimate place subject to mechanistic laws which are discernible to the rational mind. Scientists and philosophers, as American philosopher and historian of science Carolyn Merchant points out, regarded nature as a woman: 'as woman's womb had symbolically yielded to the forceps, so nature's womb harboured secrets that through technology could be wrested from her grasp for use in the improvement of the human condition'. So the idea of progress is tied up with the accumulation of knowledge for the improvement of the human condition through extraction – forcefully if necessary – of nature's secrets. Whilst no-one can argue with the multitude of material improvements that have arisen in the wake of this revolution – increased life spans, better medical care, curing previously incurable diseases, to name a few – running parallel to these developments has been an increasing sense of alienation from our bodies and disconnection from the natural world. This is because at the heart of the idea of progress is the dualistic worldview that the self is located in the mind and is radically separate from nature. Rene Descartes, acknowledged by many as the 'father' of this modern worldview, encapsulated this separation perfectly through his famous words 'I think, therefore I am'. The power given to the thinking, rational mind over and above the 'inert' world of matter secured nature's subservience to 'sovereign' man and the body became mere housing for the mind.

One needn't go very far to trace the overwhelming influence of these two ideas on our modern-day sensibilities: the natural world continues to be pillaged, polluted and turned into 'resources' to be efficiently used and disposed of, our bodies are something we control, abuse and shape as our 'sovereign' desires dictate, and the animals we eat and rely on are assembly-line, factory-farmed 'products' manufactured under grotesquely inhumane conditions. Only the mind which sees itself as separate could enact such violence against anything it saw as outside of it. Only the mind hell-bent on 'improving the human condition' at the expense of everything else could build an entire civilisation over a nexus of unacknowledged suffering. And thanks to colonialism, globalisation and neo-liberalism which spread this model of progress to the non-European world, there is nowhere on our planet which hasn't been free from this suffering.

The global deterioration of our health is, I believe, the revolt within our bodies to these ideas. Though our 'rational' minds might dismiss any such notion, I believe we need to acknowledge that the suffering we create outside ourselves is tied up with the suffering we ourselves endure. To recognise our kinship with the natural world is to undermine the idea that we are separate and that progress has to be predicated on having an exploitative and extractive relationship with the world around us. Most importantly, our deteriorating health is a signal that we need to find ways to reconnect what has been split apart; that what we are experiencing is a direct outcome of our disconnection from nature.

One step in the right direction is the hypothesis of 'Nature Deficit Disorder' (NDD) postulated by the author and journalist Richard Louv, which offers us a methodology by which we can improve the human condition, not through exploitative means but through recognising the huge part that regular nature interaction can play in our health. His theory stresses the importance of reconnecting people (children especially) with nature, either through direct contact in the form of wilderness immersion practises such as forest schooling, or indirect contact in the form of increased visual access to the natural world — such as being able to see trees and plants from school windows. In *The Nature Principle*, Louv cites research that supports the positive impacts of these strategies: for children, who are perhaps most vulnerable to the negative effects of modern civilisation, the beneficial impacts to the state of their psychological health include a reduction in the symptoms of Attention Deficit Hyperactivity Disorder (ADHD), a heavily diagnosed mental health condition; increased ability to pay attention; improvement in test scores and scholastic ability and motivation; gains in self-esteem; even improved conflict-resolution and cooperation skills. Similarly, for adults too the gains are immense, both psychologically and physically: a reduction in the symptoms of mental health conditions and recovery for otherwise intractable conditions; an enhanced ability to cope with stress; faster recovery from illness and injury; better pain management in conditions such as heart disease; enhanced immune resistance; and improved mood and self-esteem. Through recognising that there is a 'deficit of nature' in our lives, we can ameliorate symptoms which conventional medicines and therapies cannot assist with.

NDD theory also encourages us to reflect on the gradual dulling of our sensory capacities thanks to the artificial environments we live in. Louv makes the distinction that diminished sensory awareness impacts the quality of our life and suggests that NDD 'by its broadest interpretation… is an atrophied awareness'. He cites the work of American poet and naturalist Diane Ackerman, who writes: 'People think of the mind as being located in the head, but the latest findings in physiology suggest that the mind doesn't really dwell in the brain but travels the whole body on caravans of enzyme, busily making sense of the compound wonders we catalogue as touch, taste, smell, hearing, vision'.

It is crucial not to overlook the immense impact of this simple statement. According to the latest scientific research, there is no division of the mind from body. The self, located as it has been in the mind since Descartes, is now expanded to include the body and its processes, including its sensory capacities. This suggests that to be fully realised people – to be fully human – we need to be able to access and exercise these sensory capacities. Many people (including myself) report a greater satisfaction with life when they are able to commune with nature on a regular basis, and as the results of the studies cited in Louv's book show, 'nature' can be as simple as being able to go for a walk in the local park or gardening in our backyard. But why would this be so? What makes the natural world so potent a panacea that even just looking at it from a distance, as some of Louv's cited studies show, can bestow healthy benefits? Though a park might be highly landscaped and manicured, there are immense variations between the plants themselves. No tree is exactly the same as another. Neither can we stop a bird from landing two feet away from us, or a fox passing us by. Simple as these things might be, they are in stark contrast to the highly regulated and artificial environments we surround ourselves with. Modernity prescribes that we live in a world of boxes and straight lines, that our schedules be highly repetitive and structured, that we interact daily with machines, and that we consume mass produced goods. This linearity and dulling sameness stems from our mechanistic ideas about the world and is the outcome of a desire to enact sovereign control over it. The language and methodology of materialist science – controlling variables, standardisation, efficiency – dictates and shapes our culture to an extreme degree, suppressing our sensory capacities and limiting our ability to fully engage with the world. So increasing our sensory fitness through participation with nature is one of the keys ways by which we can reclaim our wholeness and, therefore, our health.

However, as with the medical establishment's strategies to address our collective 'disease burden', talk of 'interacting with nature' and 'communing with nature' falls into the same dualistic trap of dividing human from nature. Nature is still outside ourselves, objectified and made into an Other, much in the same way we separated mind from the body. As helpful as the theory of NDD is in addressing the problems of a disconnected modern society, we need to go further still by recognising the delusion that human and nature are separate. Rather than merely interacting with nature as if it were an entity outside of us – an object that exists for our pleasure and health – we would go one step further and say that we are nature itself. This holistic perspective does away with the subject-object divide and encourages us to see our deteriorating health as reflected in and symptomatic of a wider crisis in which the world itself is sick. The implications of this radical reunification of human and nature is that we can no longer see health as a solely individual concern; for we see that at every turn we are surrounded by life-destroying processes. When we destroy the natural world through pollution, we are destroying ourselves. When we are abusing animals in the name of meat production and science, we are abusing ourselves. When we poison rivers and oceans, we are poisoning ourselves. We recognise that we are part of a movement and a process in history which tricks us into believing that there is a divide between us and the non-human. We understand that the longer this dividing wall stays up, the more we will increase our own suffering. This is what a 'therapy of ideas' looks like – to see the sickness originating in dualistic ideas and to find ways to challenge them.

A more comprehensive approach then to tackling both our own health and the health of the planet is to 'think in systems'. This is where we recognise that humans are a niche, a part, within the wider system of the earth community. Systems theory, deep ecology and the permaculture movement, which is a marriage of the two, are concerned with the principles which allow a system to function at its highest integrity. The fundamental tenet of permaculture is learning from nature, which means observation of natural systems and applying this learning to the man-made systems we create. Part of learning from nature involves increasing our awareness of feedback mechanisms, which are the regulatory responses from a system to any changes made within it. This means any action we take incurs a negative or positive response from the system in order to maintain balance. If more of us thought like systems, we would soon come to understand that the main strategy for our own health would be to make changes to those systems we create which are generating negative feedback responses. Can we see then that a consumption-based society that depletes its 'resource base' is a system that needs re-organising based on the feedback from our bodies and the ecologies of which we are a part? Might recovering our health as a species amount to recovering a way of life that is more 'natural' or at least doesn't harm the systems we depend on for our survival?

'Pre-modern' cultures and the few surviving indigenous societies that remain today are characterised by the way in which they are deeply embedded in nature, that it is difficult not to think of them as nature itself. Many of them lived for thousands of years in harmony with the systems around them, recognising and preserving the complex and symbiotic interrelationships which characterise a well functioning system. Whilst I am not advocating that we go and live in forests in order to become more 'natural', I would stress the importance of learning from indigenous cultures and maybe thinking more like them as a way to regain our full humanity. In his autobiography, *Memories, Dreams, Reflections,* Carl Jung recounts the story of meeting a chief of the Pueblo Indians in the US. The chief believed that the Europeans were crazy since they thought with their heads. Surprised, Jung asked how he thought and the chief replied with his heart. This simple interchange illustrates the central dilemma of the modern human: in thinking solely with our heads, we have lost touch with our heart, that locus of feeling and empathic awareness which, I believe, connects us to the world around us. By neglecting the 'thought of the heart' we lose access to the guiding compass by which we can acknowledge, feel and know the suffering of all – human and non-human – and block ourselves from participating in wholeness, in health. On the other hand, when we open up to and feel the truth that our suffering is intimately tied up with the communities of which we are a part, we can move closer to 'thinking in systems' which is what I believe our cultural predecessors did. Can we see then that strategies like reforestation, reducing consumption and pollution, and conserving and regenerating natural habitats might make more sense as concrete strategies for reducing suffering?

Through accepting the indivisibility of the earth community, which is the outcome of thinking, feeling and sensing with our full human capacities, we neither negate nor demonise our rationality but rather see it as one mode of interacting with the world, which must be balanced with what our hearts, our bodies and what the world around us tell us. This new stance requires that we accept the underlying uncertainty that confronts us when we embrace the creative chaos of living in a universe that speaks to us through feedback mechanisms. Complex adaptive systems, which is what we are, are most resilient when they are poised between chaos and order – on the edges and margins where they relate in a recursive feedback loop to the world they are enfolded in. It is the 'edges' of a system where creativity, potential for change and response-ability arises, and where also the most danger lies. This is what ecology and systems thinking teaches us but many of our spiritual traditions speak to the same idea. In the Islamic tradition, for example, the heart (*qalb*) is seen to be the locus of awareness and consciousness and the meaning of *qalb* is closely tied to a sense of movement and fluctuation. In other words, the heart is permeable to both negative and positive influences from without, meaning it is in relationship and responsive to feedback mechanisms. So when we live solely with our *aql*, our reasoning, we are not in our full awareness; reason and rationality can only take us so far. It is through the awareness of the heart that we are tested, we are engaged and we become responsive to our environment. We learn to live on the edges between chaos and order when we include the thought of the heart. Naturally, this means that our pace must be slow, for the faster our actions the less opportunity for reflection on what is and isn't working. The traditional Nigerian proverb 'the times are urgent, we must go slowly' reflects the counter-intuitive attitude we should be taking in these testing times and is wisdom that is echoed by many cultures, spiritual traditions and sciences like systems thinking and ecology.

Along with increasing our response-ability, slowness also enhances our appreciation of the world. Seeking solace in nature is to seek solace in slowness whereby slowness is the attempt to appreciate the world we inhabit. Slowness allows us to return to the 'eachness' of things where the particular events or things we encounter are given the chance to reflect on the beauty inherent in them, something we gloss over when we are rushing to and fro. Slowness is a legitimate response to the big problems that face us. If we learn to slow down, we appreciate where we are at and so 'lose our appetite' for events and things. We consume less because we are sated with what is already ours. The need to possess and have and do more, to be more than what we already are – a reflection of the gigantism and titanism that is perfectly tied up with the enlightenment ideal of progress – would be virtually extinguished because all around us there would be treasure to be noticed and appreciated. How would this simple shift in attitude impact air travel, consumption levels, GDP? How about stress levels, CO_2 emissions, our relationships to our neighbours and our loved ones? There is a kind of magic in the act of slowing down, where through our noticing of the particulars around us, we are weaved into the greater fabric of the earth's life. In this way, we grow down and into the earth, rooted in a particular place, a particular time and we recover our wholeness.

So without objectifying the natural world, without seeing it as something that exists for us and outside of us, we must learn to relate to it again with the full awareness of our hearts, our minds and our bodies. We must slow down and notice what is around us to awaken our aesthetic response, which yearns for the opportunity to witness beauty in the world. We must witness suffering from the seat of our hearts and awaken our response-ability to this suffering, awaken our ability to perceive how the delusion of the separate mind creates suffering and ill-health. We must gaze at the ocean or at a tree or a bird and know that it is our own complexity reflected back to us, that we too are nature, despite modern culture and our abstractions suggesting otherwise. In small moments by the shore, or in a park, or a forest we listen and we hear the way our ideas shape and influence our shared reality, for good or bad, and how we ourselves are shaped and influenced in turn; we recognise that sanity and health require seeing through our most cherished and entrenched ideas if these ideas endanger our shared reality, our shared planet. We must recognise that enlightenment is not human progress at the expense of the non-human or the feats of a mind fixated on improvement but that it is to be intimate with all things. To be connected to and intimate with all things is to be truly whole – to be healthy.

OUR MULTIPLE SELVES

Shanon Shah

In English, the word 'sex' can refer to biology – the kinds of reproductive organs a living organism has. It can also refer to a particular human act or family of acts that can be reproductive or recreational or both. What counts as a sex act can be contested, however, as in the infamous defence by former US President Bill Clinton against allegations of sexual misconduct with Monica Lewinsky: 'I did not have sexual relations with that woman.' To the rest of the world, it seemed like an outrageous lie. Clearly, some sort of sexual activity did take place.

Not all languages use the same word to refer to anatomical sex and sexual acts. In Malay, for example, the translation for 'sex' in reference to anatomy is '*jantina*', which is a portmanteau word from the component words '*jantan*' (male) and '*betina*' (female). To determine the *jantina* of humans, animals and plants, we need to ascertain the nature of their *alat kelamin* (sexual/reproductive organs). Sexual intercourse is therefore more accurately translated as '*hubungan kelamin*', not '*hubungan jantina*'.

This kind of pedantry is pointless at most times but becomes significant when we need to make sense of sexual acts and identities that are controversial or stigmatised in different societies – not just on a Clintonesque level. Take the term *liwat*, which was developed by pre-modern Islamic jurists. The word does not exist in the Qur'an, but was coined to refer to what jurists understood as the sin of the people of the Prophet Lut. Many interpreted this as penetrative anal sex between males. Jurists from different schools or *madhahib* would disagree on what exactly constituted *liwat* and would often try to narrow its scope. If an adult male fell madly in love with a handsome adolescent, did that constitute *liwat*? If they kissed passionately, would that constitute *liwat*? Was non-penetrative, non-anal erotic activity between two men equivalent to *liwat*? According to the historian Khaled El-Rouayheb, these minutiae were discussed in great detail in the Ottoman Era. By the way, the answer to all three questions was no.

For the most part, *liwat* can effectively be translated as 'sodomy'. Just as the word '*liwat*' does not occur in the Qur'an, neither does the word 'sodomy' occur in the Bible. Just as the term '*liwat*' was coined by Islamic jurists to refer to the sins of the people of Lut, 'sodomy' in Christendom came to refer to the sins of the inhabitants of the Biblical Lot's city of Sodom. In both traditions, the narrowing of '*liwat*' and 'sodomy' to focus primarily on sexual relations was a gradual process and which was subject to considerable debate. However, the two terms emerged in distinctive cultural contexts and eventually entailed slightly different political and legal consequences. While classical Islamic jurists took great pains to limit exactly what counted as '*liwat*', medieval Christian theologians often stretched the concept of 'sodomy' to include a broad range of sexual immorality. These differences in scope probably explain why so many Victorian travellers to the Orient were scandalised by the visible, socially accepted and even romantic relationships between men. On the other hand, Muslim travellers to the West in the early nineteenth century found it surprising that European men did *not* court the romantic affections or sing the praises of male youths. What was acceptable to natives of the Orient because it did not constitute *liwat* was tantamount to sodomy for blushing Occidentals.

Islamic jurists agreed, however, that whatever was ultimately defined as *liwat* was a corporal crime. Yet before the Ottoman Era, jurists disagreed on the premises for criminalising *liwat* which then influenced the extent of the prescribed punishments. The majority view in the Maliki, Hanbali and Shafi'i schools in Sunni Islam was that *liwat* was analogous to *zina* (fornication) and therefore punishable by stoning to death for those who were married and lashing for the unmarried. The Ja'fari school in Shi'a Islam mirrored this logic and prescribed similar punishments. However, the Sunni Hanafi school held that this was flawed *qiyas* (reasoning by analogy) – *liwat* does not result in procreation and so could not possibly be likened to *zina*. The punishment, according to the Hanafis, was thus a maximum of 40 lashes at the discretion of the ruler. According to the extant Zahiri school – which flourished in Al-Andalus before the Catholic

Reconquista in the fifteenth century CE – the punishment for *liwat* was only a maximum of ten lashes if it caused a public nuisance.

Furthermore, the Ottoman legal system contained a complex interplay between what was officially termed *shari'a* (divine legislation elaborated by Muslim jurists) and *kanun* (state laws promulgated by the Sultan). Under the Ottoman system *kadis* (judges) were trained in *madrasas* (state-funded religious schools) to adjudicate according to both systems of law. The *shari'a* in the Ottoman Empire was also never fully codified, which was significant when it came to judgements about sexual offences. The prevailing stereotype of *fiqh* (Islamic jurisprudence) now is that it is inflexibly intolerant of sexual offences, whether heterosexual or homosexual. For example, under the Ottoman *shari'a* legislation, married adult men and women who engaged in *zina* faced the death sentence. Under *kanun* provisions, however, the same offence was punishable only by a fine for both men and women. In principle, *kadis* held that *shari'a* punishments should apply in all circumstances but noted that, in practice, it was usually impossible to meet the *shari'a*'s stringent demands for evidence. Thus, in the vast majority of cases, *kanun* regulations would kick in. This logic also applied to sexual offences between people of the same sex. And actually, only *liwat* was punishable under both *shari'a* and *kanun* regulations – sexual offences between women were punished solely under *shari'a*, and much more lightly at that.

Apart from outright *liwat*, rigorously defined by jurists, there is evidence of socially accepted same-sex relationships in the Ottoman Empire and other parts of the pre-modern Muslim world. According to the gender historian Afsaneh Najmabadi, before the nineteenth century in Iran adult males developed romantic and sexual relationships with *amrad*, or adolescent males, without being stigmatised or punished. However, through increased cultural contact and exchange, Iranian elites became aware that these sorts of relationships were viewed as vices in the European society of the late Victorian era. This is what led Iranian cultural elites to conceal, deny and eventually condemn homoerotic relationships. The desire of adult males for *amrad* went from being regarded as legitimate to ridiculed and reviled, as twentieth century Iranian society competed with European society for moral and civilisational legitimacy.

The Victorians and then the Edwardians were shocked not only by what they perceived as perverse sexual behaviours among non-European humans but those they found in the animal kingdom, too. George Murray Levick, a scientist with the 1910–13 Scott Antarctic expedition, was particularly unnerved early in his research by the sight of a male Adélie penguin trying to have sex with a dead female. And that was only the beginning. Throughout Levick's time there in the summer of 1911–12, he witnessed penguin males having sex with other males and dead females, including those that had died the previous year. He also saw them sexually coerce adult females and chicks and occasionally kill them. Imagine his horror at witnessing 'carnal intercourse against the order of nature' (the wording of the anti-sodomy provisions that the British introduced throughout their Empire) occurring so profligately in, well, nature. So traumatised was Levick that he wrote these observations in Greek so that they would be intelligible only to a fellow educated gentleman. When he eventually published his scientific paper (in English) on the Adélie penguins, he omitted all references to their sexual proclivities. He did go on to write a short paper on penguin sexual habits but circulated this privately among only a handful of experts. It took another fifty years for the remarkable sexual antics of the Adélie penguins to be recorded and disseminated widely among the scientific community.

So has this empirical evidence from nature challenged predominant assumptions that homosexuality is unnatural? Not really, judging by opinions that hold sway in some religious circles. On his television talk show in 2006, broadcast by the Qatar-based *Al Jazeera* network, the influential Sunni Egyptian scholar Yusuf Al Qaradawi dismissed all scientific research on homosexuality as evidence of Western corruption and cultural imperialism, saying:

> It is totally reprehensible of so many of our scientific scholars and medical doctors that they submit to the Western culture that is dominating the whole world. Westerners want to justify what is happening among them. It is a shame that so many scientific opinions are suspect.... What is publicly known about these [the positions of the World Health Organisation] is that it is their desire to market and sell by trickery a new culture that wants to make this matter seem natural, to attribute it to nature.

Denouncing the West is one thing, but what would Qaradawi say about non-Western societies which historically tolerated or even integrated 'third gender' cultures, that is men who adopted women's roles and formed relationships with other masculine men? Anthropologists have long documented such realities, including among Native Americans/First Nations, the Tanala of Madagascar, the Mesakin of Nuba, and the Chukchee of Siberia. And what about 'third gender' cultures that were historically tolerated in Muslim societies, from the *yan daudu* in Nigeria, the *khawaja sira* of South Asia and the *khanith* of Oman? Qaradawi would probably denounce all of these as 'unnatural'. In fact, unlike medieval Islamic jurists, he does not bother distinguishing between biological sex, *liwat* as a sexual act, and the individual's inner disposition. During the same *Al-Jazeera* talk show, he defined 'nature' as follows:

> The word 'nature' (*fitra*) is derived from the term for creation (*al-fatr*), as in the verse: All praise belongs to God, the creator (*fatir*) of the heavens and earth (Qur'an 35:1). It refers to the original nature with which each person is born that is not acquired or learned or attained; each and every person has it without entering school or being taught by parents or being effected by environment. Such things are natural things.... The human being is created with innate disposition to feel attraction to the other sex, with man attracted to woman and woman attracted to man.... I mean, this is a matter of biology (*amr tabi'i*) .... That is the meaning of 'nature.' The religion of Islam came to preserve the original human nature, not to oppose this nature by rebelling against nature.

So, according to Qaradawi, homosexuals are choosing to defy divinely ordained human nature and should be punished with:

> The same punishment as any sexual pervert.... The schools of thought disagree about the punishment. Some say they should be punished like fornicators, and then we distinguish between married and unmarried men, and between married and unmarried women. Some say both should be punished the same way. Some say we should throw them from a high place like God did with the people of Sodom. Some say we should burn them and so on. There is disagreement.

This kind of logic is not peculiar to so-called custodians of Islam like Qaradawi. The sodomy laws that spread throughout the British Empire in the second half of the nineteenth century also outlawed anal and oral sex for going against 'the order of nature'. And before sodomy was partially decriminalised in the UK in 1967, thousands of homosexual men were arrested for 'gross indecency' in the first half of the twentieth century. Many were imprisoned or forced to undergo electro-shock therapy to rehabilitate their supposed sexual deviance.

Perhaps this is why gay and lesbian activists in the West became more and more adamant that sexual orientation is innate – people are born straight, gay or lesbian and that is that. The gay and lesbian movement of the 1970s grew into the lesbian, gay, bisexual and transgender (LGBT) movement, and the acronym keeps growing in the spirit of inclusivity. Some organisations are now LGBTQI (with 'Q' standing for 'queer or questioning' and 'I' for 'intersex') and there are also newer references to LGBTQIPA (i.e. including 'pansexual' and 'asexual'). Many of these movements stress the importance of distinguishing between the concept of 'gender identity' (the 'sense' of being a man, woman, or transgender, etc.) and 'sexual orientation' (the type of romantic or erotic feelings an individual has). But then in 2012, Cynthia Nixon – one of the stars of TV's *Sex and the City* – triggered the fury of many LGBT activists by asserting that she was 'gay by choice'. She told the *New York Times*:

> I gave a speech recently, an empowerment speech to a gay audience, and it included the line 'I've been straight and I've been gay, and gay is better.' And they tried to get me to change it, because they said it implies that homosexuality can be a choice. And for me, it is a choice.

The LGBT establishment immediately hit back saying that sexual orientation is inborn and never a choice. Nixon clarified that what she meant was she is bisexual, which is not a choice for her, but that she had chosen to be in a gay relationship. She explained, however, why she was less comfortable identifying publicly as 'bisexual': 'I don't pull out the "bisexual" word because nobody likes the bisexuals. Everybody likes to dump on the bisexuals. We get no respect.' And she's right. Bisexuals are certainly affected by anti-homosexual sentiments, but they also upset the idea that people are born either exclusively heterosexual or homosexual. Appalling statements like 'bisexuals are just greedy', 'bisexuals should just make their minds up' and 'bisexuals can't ever be faithful in a relationship' are still commonplace examples of anti-bisexual prejudice, even in gay and lesbian circles. So Nixon was put in a very awkward position — from initially celebrating her gay identity as a matter of choice, she ended up reluctantly highlighting her bisexual identity as self-defence.

The fallout of Nixon's 'gay-by-choice' controversy tells us that sex and gender labels are never settled — being 'gay' sometimes does not mean the same thing to different individuals in different contexts. During my research in Malaysia, I met Amin (not his real name), a Muslim who identifies as 'straight', had girlfriends in the past, but is now in love with another Muslim man, Ebry (not his real name). I suggested to Amin that perhaps he was technically bisexual but he said the concept felt alien personally. To him, a true bisexual is someone who could be attracted to masculine men and feminine women whereas he was only interested in feminine men and women. Perhaps many might regard this explanation as dishonest or that Amin is an anomaly. But even Ebry's understanding of himself did not fall into neat boxes. When he told me he identifies as gay but feels like a woman in a man's body, I asked if he would prefer being thought of as transgender. He said no, because he was not interested in undergoing sex reassignment. Yet I know of other individuals who identify as transgender and are not necessarily interested in transitioning through medical or surgical intervention.

So when I have to discuss sex, gender and sexuality, I sometimes feel a bit like Levick might have felt when he was unnerved by the necrophilia, homosexuality and rape among his Adélie penguins. Not that I am likening Ebry and Amin to penguins nor did I become squeamish like Levick but my point is that they too confound plenty of conventional wisdom on sex and nature. And while I think it is important to include them as an example here, I do not want to exoticise them, however inadvertently, or make them seem like freaks.

Once upon a time it was so easy. I thought I had the answer to clinch any arguments about the relationship between sex and nature. 'Sex' refers to our reproductive physiology, whether male, female or intersex. So physiological phenomena such as menstruation and pregnancy in females and the deepening of boys' voices after puberty relate to sex. 'Gender' refers to the social and cultural expectations that get loaded onto us because of our biological sex. An example would be the idea that women give birth to children and are therefore more suited to caring professions or even to staying at home. Or when we use phrases like 'boys will be boys' to explain away certain rambunctious behaviours. Then there are the neat boxes that many people put either masculine or feminine characteristics in – there are several expectations that men and women should dress, talk, walk, speak or even laugh differently. In many cultures, a male person is expected to identify as a man and behave in masculine ways and a female person is similarly expected to identify as a woman and exhibit feminine behaviour. Many of us are brought up to take these associations between sex and gender for granted and to see men as naturally strong and aggressive and women as demure and passive. Finally, there is the dominant idea that men, by this very nature, must be sexually attracted only to women and vice versa.

There are so many ways that these links in the chain can be broken, however. What happens when a biological female identifies as a woman but behaves in a stereotypically masculine manner – playing aggressive sports, dominating group discussions and belching loudly after meals? Or when a masculine man is intensely sexually attracted to another masculine man? Are individuals like these anomalies, wilfully defying the laws of nature? These questions remain salient in the majority of the world where gendered hierarchies largely still privilege heterosexual men over women and non-heterosexuals.

Take the example of the biological functions of menstruation and childbirth that are used to justify the inferior status of women. Historically, menstruation was often seen as polluting – literally and symbolically – and was the basis for justifying why women should be segregated or regarded as unreliable for certain professions. But the definition of pollution and how it affects human interactions can vary drastically from culture to culture. The Kaulong of New Britain in Papua New Guinea consider women polluting from before puberty to after menopause. Women are particularly 'dangerous' during menstruation and childbirth, when they must stay away from gardens, dwellings and water sources. Adult men might become ill by eating anything that a polluted woman has touched or simply by placing themselves underneath the woman or a contaminated object. Women are thus isolated during childbirth and menstruation, away from homes and gardens.

The strength of Kaulong beliefs that menstruation and childbirth are polluting, however, means that many adult men are terrified of having sex with women. Sexual intercourse must take place in the forest, far away from dwellings and gardens. And because Kaulong culture equates sexual intercourse with marriage, many men are therefore afraid to get married and it is the women who take the dominant role in courtship. Girls may make offerings of food or tobacco to the man of their choice or they may physically attack him. The man can flee or stand his ground, without fighting back, until both parties reach an agreement. Girls are raised to behave aggressively towards boys and if a man were to initiate an approach towards a woman it would be considered akin to rape. Women are free to choose their husbands although they often consult with their close kin. Brides have been known to deceive or lure reluctant grooms into their 'fate' but women are very rarely forced into undesired marriages. Additionally, Kaulong women appear to have considerable economic independence. So this example upends the usual notion that beliefs in menstruation as pollution necessarily lead to the subordination of women.

The Kaulong example shows how gendered relations and stereotypes are culturally constructed based on biological functions relating to sex. In fact, all the examples so far – Clinton, the Ottomans, the Qajars, Levick and his Adélie penguins, Qaradawi, Nixon, Ebry and Amin – have focused on the ways that our ideas of sex and what is considered natural are socially constructed. I've been unpacking assumptions that link sex with nature but have not yet explored if the two *are* linked and in what ways. The challenge here is that so many efforts to discuss sex in ways that are 'purely' biological or scientific have actually been shaped by ideologically-driven gendered assumptions.

For thousands of years, the dominant medical paradigm in Europe held that women had the same genitals as men, albeit inverted such that these stayed *inside* their bodies. According to the historian Thomas Laqueur, the vagina in this world was imagined as 'an interior penis, the labia as foreskin, the uterus as scrotum, and the ovaries as testicles'. This logic owed much to the second and third century Greek physician Galen, who argued that women were essentially men lacking a vital 'heat', resulting in reversed anatomical structures that were outwardly visible in men. It followed, for example, in much ensuing theorising, that procreation was only possible when both the male and female partner achieved orgasm. A woman who did not achieve sexual climax could not by definition become pregnant.

By the nineteenth century, however, this one-sex model in the West was replaced by a two-sex model positing that men and women were different in every conceivable aspect of body and soul, physically and morally. These sexual differences, it was increasingly argued, were solidly grounded in nature. And guess what? The idea that female orgasm was a prerequisite to pregnancy quickly disappeared. In fact, it became increasingly common for intellectuals of this era to cast women as far less libidinous than men – a precursor to present-day stereotypes of men as obsessed with sex while women yearn for romance. Laqueur argues that actual scientific discovery can only partly account for this paradigm shift – women have faced different varieties of subjugation under both two-sex and one-sex regimes. The difference is between whether women were regarded as being altogether separate from albeit inferior to men in the two-sex model or if they were simply inferior versions of men according to the one-sex model.

A variation of the one-sex model was even more entrenched in the medical discourses of the Ottoman Empire, which were also heavily influenced by Galenic medicine. Man occupied the apex of terrestrial creation whereas woman was regarded as a less-developed version of man. Women's genitals were seen as flawed versions of men's genitals. The historian Dror Ze'evi suggests referring to this as the 'imperfect-man' rather than 'one-sex' model. Furthermore, in the Ottoman context, the lack of a two-sex model meant that same-sex relations were rarely discussed in medical circles in terms of what was 'natural'. For example, the ninth century physician Al-Razi regarded a man who enjoyed taking on the passive sexual role with another man as biologically but not morally inferior. Later physicians such as Ibn Sina (980–1037) and Ibn Hubal (1122–1213) disagreed and characterised such behaviour as a sinful cultural disease. All, however, only focused their judgements on the man taking the passive sexual role – the penetrating partner was not considered a problem in any way. And actually in the grander scheme, Ze'evi argues, Ottoman attitudes were mostly indifferent to what we would now categorise as active and passive male 'homosexuality' despite legal rulings on *liwat*.

Ze'evi further argues that the two-sex model that emerged in Western Europe only took partial hold over late Ottoman and post-Ottoman societies. This is partly because in Europe, the two-sex model evolved gradually and was driven by crucial factors outside the realm of medicine. This included burgeoning activism by women to participate more fully in politics and public life and struggles to define citizenship and the public sphere more generally. The idea of women as a totally different sex, rather than a flawed version of the male sex, was on balance an effective way of campaigning for their rights based on gender complementarity. This was the background against which new medical discourses on sex emerged in Western Europe and gradually took hold. There was not a similar trajectory of social change in the Middle East and so the new two-sex model could not be anchored by wider transformations in politics and public attitudes.

Whether in the Ottoman Empire or Western Europe, then, perceptions of biological sex were always informed by notions that heterosexual men (as we would now classify them) embodied the human ideal – women and non-heterosexuals were inferior. In particular, women were inferior under the one-sex model and, despite the proto-feminism of the Enlightenment, they remained inferior under the emerging two-sex model. How else do we explain the disappearance of the female orgasm in two-sex discourses and the ensuing logic under this model that women were naturally servile, delicate and less rational than men? Regardless of the scientific discoveries about males and females throughout the ages, the one-sex and two-sex models have largely served as political ranking systems ensuring that heterosexual men stay at the top of social hierarchies.

This is not to say that we should dispense entirely with thinking about the sexed nature of our bodies. And it would be ludicrous to argue that there are absolutely no differences between people who are male, female, intersex, transgender, homosexual, heterosexual or bisexual. The feminist biologist and historian of science Anne Fausto-Sterling even suggests a five-sex model now, encompassing: males; females; 'the so-called true hermaphrodites, who possess one testis and one ovary (the sperm- and egg- producing vessels, or gonads); male pseudo-hermaphrodites, who have testes and some aspects of female genitalia but no ovaries; and female pseudo-hermaphrodites, who have ovaries and some aspects of the male genitalia but lack testes'. We could agree or disagree with this classification. But the point is that we need better ways of analysing, reporting and representing sex and gender differences to challenge, or at the very least not perpetuate, hierarchies that punish those who do not conform.

It is therefore noteworthy that scientists in the academy are increasingly abandoning the nature/nurture dichotomy when it comes to sex – many argue that men and women are actually overwhelmingly alike. In proper scientific parlance, the human species is not particularly sexually dimorphic. In our traits, personality, cognitive abilities, temperament and motor skills, men and women are more similar than different, even in the face of cultures and institutions that maintain the gender divide. The two traits that show strong sexual dimorphism are sexual identity (most men identify as male and most women as female) and sexual attraction (most men are interested in women and vice versa).

Science demonstrates that society does also exert influence over biology, however – nurture can produce nature. One good example would be mental rotation skills, or the ability to imagine an object turning in our minds. The evidence for sex difference here is persuasive – in numerous experiments, the average man does better than 72–75 per cent of women. However, the gap between men's and women's mental rotation abilities can be significantly reduced through simple interventions. One study found that asking women to play a semester's worth of Tetris (that addictive, oh-so-90s video game involving rotating and fitting geometric shapes into one another) almost closed the gap between men's and women's scores. Another study found that just ten hours of video game play reduced the gap between men and women significantly. So perhaps we need to rethink our notions of what is natural for both sexes. Yes, the research so far shows that men are 'naturally' better at mental rotation than women, but perhaps women, more significantly, are 'naturally' able to catch up with men in this area.

Sex is thus only one piece in a more complicated puzzle of what is truly natural and what we perceive as natural. For example, gendered social rules in combination with hormonal and genetic factors serve to depress girls' bone-building activities and result in men having 20–30 per cent greater bone mass and strength than women. But this sex difference is reversed among Ultra-Orthodox Jewish adolescents – boys are expected to sacrifice play and exercise and study religious texts intensely while girls get to enjoy more sunshine and physical activity because of their lighter study loads. Many adolescent Ultra-Orthodox Jewish girls therefore have stronger bones than the boys in these communities.

So the idea that there are definite features of our biology that are immutable or impossible to change is no longer tenable, no matter what people like Qaradawi or Nixon's critics say. This realisation can be a double-edged sword, though. If what seems like someone's innate nature can be changed, what's to stop some overzealous anti-homosexual groups from trying to change people like Ebry and Amin to make them 'properly' masculine, heterosexual men? That's a deeply unpleasant possibility, but perhaps we can look at this in another way – the division of humans into 'male' and 'female' simply fails to capture the sheer diversity of human existence and our capacity to celebrate this diversity. Perhaps it would be better to ask in what ways we should protect diversity so that individuals may naturally flourish and harness their unique gifts for the good of the world. That means that you do not need to feel threatened or change anything if you are a masculine man who is a football fanatic or a feminine woman who loves makeup and romantic comedies. Just realise and accept that you will probably be joined by men, women, and non-binary individuals who break all the stereotypes and just want to be included in spaces that are theirs to enjoy, too.

For me, this sentiment is captured beautifully by this much quoted verse of the Qur'an:

> O mankind! We have created you from a male and a female, and have made you nations and tribes that you may know one another. The noblest of you, in the sight of Allah, is the best in conduct. Allah is Knower, Aware. (49:13)

ISLAMIC GARDENS

Emma Clark

Since the publication of his seminal book *Man and Nature: The Spiritual Crisis of Modern Man* in 1967, Seyyed Hossein Nasr has made the same vital point over and over again. There is no possibility of a solution to our ecological crisis unless a new approach is taken: an approach that sees nature, not as an 'it', 'not only as merely a source of raw materials to be exploited by man, not as a material reality devoid of innate spiritual significance, but as a sacred reality to be treated as such'. Remembering that nature is a sacred reality is fundamental to our reconnection with her. And this link between nature and the sacred is not particular to any specific religion or faith tradition but concerns us all, since by virtue of being human we are profoundly connected to nature, to the Divine unity that she both veils and reveals in the multiplicity of her beauty and glory.

Thus, when discussing the Islamic gardens of Paradise as an opportunity for this reconnection, it is important to make clear that these gardens are open to everyone, irrespective of background or creed: they are, as it were, a divinely-guided human interpretation of nature and as such may act as a universal symbol of the heavenly archetype. In a world facing drastic climate change, and where many people seem to have lost their way, it seems that nature provides the most wholesome (from 'holy') and uplifting solace, the potential to offer a path, not only of reconnection with the profound mystery of existence but also of recovering our sense of unity. Indeed, being in nature now even has a special name: eco-therapy! As the great Persian poet Saadi Shirazi (d. 1291) wrote, 'every leaf of the tree becomes a page of the Book once the heart is opened and it has learned to read.' He is referring to nature as a book of divine revelation that may be read and understood providing we have some knowledge of the language of symbols. Indeed, the word 'symbol' comes from the Greek meaning to 'throw together' – nature is in fact 'throwing' earth and Heaven together through her language of symbols – and if our eyes and hearts are open to this then we see every 'leaf of the tree' as a page of the divine book: the beauty of the outward appearance directs us both upwards and inwards, towards the essence.

The language of symbols has all but been lost to us today; and it is largely due to this loss that we have become so fixated on the one dimension, the material world we can perceive, forgetting our deep connection to both nature and the invisible world which she veils. As the late Martin Lings notes in his marvellous book, *Symbol and Archetype*, 'symbolism is the most important thing in existence; and it is at the same time, the sole explanation of existence.'

There is constant reference to the 'signs', 'symbols' or 'portents' in the natural world in the Qur'an, all of which are clear evidence of the Almighty: 'Another of His signs is the creation of the heavens and the earth and the diversity of your languages and colours. There truly are signs in this for those who know' (30:22). Similar also is the Native American Indian view which, in the words of Charles Eastman, 'holds nature to be the measure of consummate beauty and its destruction as sacrilege'; and this is why 'the Indian did not paint nature, not because he did not feel it, but because it was sacred to him. He so loved the reality that he could not venture upon the imitation'.

Islamic gardens of Paradise are the perfect vehicles both to reconnect with nature, and – most importantly – through this reconnection, help us to discover not only nature's sacred reality but also, since we are intimately linked to her, our own sacred reality: what it means to be human. Every true Islamic garden created on earth is, to a greater or lesser extent, inspired by the Heavenly archetype as described in the Qur'an and is thus both a reflection of the Eternal Paradise Gardens as well as a foretaste of them. By this very fact, they may awaken the heart of the visitor that is open and therefore serve as a powerful vehicle of remembrance and reconnection.

In its description of the Gardens of Paradise, the *Jannat al-firdaws*, the Qur'an frequently uses the phrase 'gardens underneath which rivers flow' (around thirty times). So immediately we understand the importance of water in these gardens. The religion of Islam was born in the baking hot desert region of the Arabian peninsular. So after spending even a short time here – or any similar climate – one longs for the sight, sound, smell, touch and taste of water: the blessed liquid, the source of all life. This is hard to understand when living in a temperate climate like the United Kingdom where too much rain and flooding have been the norm in recent years. However, with a little imagination, and some travel experience, it is easy to comprehend why Constance Villiers Stuart, writing in India in the early twentieth century, observed that 'the spirit of the garden paradises of Europe hides in the flowers, the grass, the trees, but the soul of the Eastern garden lies in none of these; it is centred on the running water which alone makes its other beauties possible'.

What then is an Islamic garden? And how is it different from other gardens? An Islamic garden is born out of what might be termed a divine meeting place between four principal underlying factors: the first three earthly, horizontal, factors are brought together and given new life by the fourth, vertical, transcendent one. Several key elements are added to these factors; when fully integrated, they make up a clearly recognisable Islamic garden, whether it is created in Mughal India, Andalusia under the Nasrid dynasty or Safavid Persia.

The first of these underlying factors is the concept of Paradise as a garden. It is a very ancient concept, pre-dating all three Abrahamic religions by centuries, going back as far as the Sumerian period (4000 B.C.) where the Paradise garden of the gods in the *Epic of Gilgamesh* mentions a fountain and shade. The second is the oasis, the quintessential desert garden of fresh water and shade-giving date-palms – the origin, it could be said of the Paradise garden, since if you have been trekking across sand and rock for days on end, as Vita Sackville-West vividly observes in her book *Passenger to Teheran*, first published in 1926, with nothing in sight but shades of brown reflecting the glare of the sun, then the green of the palm trees and the sight and sound of water will indeed be your Paradise. The third factor is the garden's geometric design based on the number four, deriving largely from the ancient Persian prototype, itself arising from the optimum method of irrigation. Finally, there is the defining cause of the Islamic garden, the Qur'an, with its sublime and enticing descriptions of the *jannat al-firdaws*, the 'Gardens of Paradise', infusing all of the other factors with a whole new spiritual and intellectual world vision.

Then there are the key elements, vital to a true Islamic garden, all of which, together with the all-important context, need to be taken into consideration when not only looking at an historic Islamic garden but also, and especially, if embarking upon designing one today.

There is no doubt that water is the supreme element in the Islamic Paradise gardens, both on a practical and symbolic level, closely followed by shade – indeed of course this second element is not possible without the first. These two go hand in hand and, for the pre-Islamic Arabs, they were indispensable for survival in the desert and were already revered as sacred. So when the Qur'an was revealed with its promise to the faithful of Gardens of Paradise with flowing waters and shade-giving trees, it resonated with the Arabs. The idea of water flowing 'underneath' possibly arose from the demands of a desert existence where the only source of water for most of the year was from the oases or underground irrigation systems such as the *qanats* in the Gulf and Persia.

Water is used to cleanse ourselves both physically as well as symbolically to 'wash away sins' and purify the soul: careful ritual ablutions are performed before prayer, *salat*, in Islam. Indeed, when visiting a garden, regardless of what tradition it may be, we always gravitate towards water and it is here that we decide to sit. Why is this? We all know that water is essential for our existence and to all life on earth but beyond this, more profoundly, water is a symbol of the soul. We feel a certain calm and contentedness when beside water – whether it is a still clear pool or a gentle fountain (the water should 'murmur' not be loud and ostentatious like many a municipal fountain today) – there is a strong connection and, for some, an opening towards contemplation. It is said that the fluidity and constantly purifying quality of water is symbolic of the soul's ability to renew itself.

How does the soul do this? Through, as they say in Sufism, the perpetual remembrance of God, or *dhikr*. Importantly, water is viewed in Islam as a clear blessing from Heaven: in the heat of the desert, water – and rain in particular – is seen as a direct symbol of God's mercy and is described throughout the Qur'an as a mercy and as life-giving. 'In the Qur'an', notes Martin Lings, 'the ideas of Mercy and water – in particular rain – are in a sense inseparable.' Shakespeare echoes this in *The Merchant of Venice:* 'the quality of Mercy is not strained, it droppeth like the gentle rain from

Heaven upon the place beneath'. The great Egyptian architect, Hassan Fathy, suggested that the fountain in a hot country was equivalent in importance to the open fire (in a fireplace) in a cold country – in terms of both practical use and symbolic significance. There is much to be said for this analogy as it brings home both the practical necessity and the intense symbolic significance of the fountain and of the fire alike: how both help equally to reconnect with nature and the environment through different ways, both practically and symbolically. Just as the fountain is a living grace as it were at the heart of the courtyard house, the garden or mosque, so the fire – to those who live in a cold climate – brings not only much needed warmth but also essential cheer and homeliness, the 'life and soul' of the house in fact. It is no accident that heart and hearth are etymologically connected.

In the Islamic garden, the water of the fountain should always be brim full to overflowing as it represents the eternally flowing waters in paradise. By extension shade is also a mercy from Heaven since it guards us from the burning glare of the sun's rays. The colour green, as an Arabic saying tells us, is 'cooling for the eyes' and thus is also a kind of mercy giving rest to the eyes and head. When green is fresh and bright it is the quintessential colour of spring and thus of rebirth, renewal, fertility and growth, indicating delight and hope.

After water and shade comes the third element of the Islamic garden: the four-fold design, which has come to be seen as the quintessential traditional Islamic garden, the *chahar-bagh*, meaning 'four gardens' in Persian. It has countless different representations all over the Islamic world all of which refer back directly or indirectly to the Four Gardens of Paradise described mainly in Chapter 55 of the Qur'an, *Surat al-Rahman*, in which four rivers are mentioned, as well as in an authentic tradition of the Prophet Muhammad: one of water, one of milk, one of honey and one of wine. There are also four fountains, one in each of the four gardens, and four trees: the date-palm, pomegranate, fig and olive tree. The four-fold plan is centred on a square, the geometric form of the number four, the quality (or principle one could say – as opposed to quantity) of which represents all things earthly: it encompasses the four cardinal directions, the four elements and the four seasons; and the cube, the three-dimensional shape of the number four, represents solidity, the Earth. The word Kaaba actually means 'cube' and it is said that the city of Mecca was traditionally divided into four parts by having lines drawn from the four corners of the Kaaba. The circle is the great symbol of the celestial realm, and when pilgrims make the *tawaaf* (circumambulation) we see a living symbol of the meeting place between Heaven and earth: a powerful and awe-inspiring reminder of our place in the universe, of our connection with the macrocosm. We also see this integration of the circle and square in Buddhist mandalas and in the art of other sacred traditions – the circle and square being universal symbols of Heaven and Earth, not particular to Islam. In an Islamic four-fold garden or *chahar-bagh*, the central fountain is often circular, representing one of the fountains in the heavenly gardens.

So the *chahar-bagh*, the quintessential Islamic garden, is a clear reflection on earth of the archetypal Heavenly gardens. By this I do not mean that there is a blueprint of the garden's design in the Qur'an; what I mean is that the descriptions of the Gardens of Paradise provide not only the inspiration but also the underlying meaning and motivation for the Islamic garden on earth. And one could say that it is principally for this reason that the Islamic garden is different from other gardens and why today it may offer more in the way of solace from the world since it is consciously founded upon a Heavenly garden and is therefore a reminder of our link with the Divine: a true form of Sacred Art in fact.

Thus the Qur'an provides the inner dimension – the *haqiqa* or the spiritual truth – which penetrates all traditional Islamic art, and indeed, the whole of the Islamic civilisation. This in brief is what is meant by Divine Unity (*at-tawhid*), the central message of the Qur'an. In such a civilisation, there is no separation between the sacred and profane and daily life is a constant interaction between the human and the Divine. Art, including the art of the garden, created in such a society is never simply aesthetically pleasing or a purely subjective experiment but is always a marriage between the practical and the spiritual. It is essentially a kind of prayer, a visual finite form offering a window onto the mysterious, invisible Infinite. This is precisely what is meant by the language of symbols – capturing the Infinite in the finite.

In Islamic gardens, due to the necessity of water preservation, pathways often replace rills; and it is these which create the four-fold design. A good example is the beautiful Al-Batha garden in Fes, Morocco – one of my favourite Islamic gardens – where the geometric pathways are balanced by the lush and abundant flowering trees, shrubs and plants. There is a wonderful combination of formality (the four-fold ground plan) with informality (the exuberant planting) something I always aim for in designing an Islamic garden today. Another beautiful example of this is in the gardens of the Seville Kasbah in Spain where narrow geometric rills run down the centre of the paths with planting overflowing from the beds. And in Mughal India at Humayun's tomb in Delhi, the geometric rills representing the four rivers of Paradise sometimes have a 'meeting place' in the form of an octagon pool. Indeed, the octagon, the number eight, symbolises the transition between earth and Heaven, signifying rebirth and renewal (a Christian font is often eight-sided): and the throne of the Almighty is said to be eight-sided according to a tradition of the Prophet.

A point worth emphasising is that the four-fold form, far from being exclusively 'Islamic', is universal. It may be adapted to constructing gardens in a wide variety of geographical areas, climates and environments, including Europe and the United States. The form provides the order and ground plan (the so-called 'hard landscaping') while the trees and abundant planting provide the 'soft landscaping', resulting in an harmonious balance between geometry (the crystalline element of nature) and flowing organic form – the basis of two of the three main elements of Islamic art, that is, geometry and arabesque or *islimi* (the third element being calligraphy). To draw a parallel closer to home in the United Kingdom, this is similar to one of the most famous gardens in England, Sissinghurst. The four-fold design may also be see in the great European medieval walled gardens, in the ground plan of the Monastic cloister gardens. The designs of both focus on the inward dimension, the heart, and the upward, the celestial. Monks would practise walking meditation around the cloisters looking within to the green enclosed square which rested their eyes made tired from writing manuscripts. A similar plan is also the basis of Oxford and Cambridge colleges, as well as the Victorian walled kitchen-garden, and has been adapted by Prince Charles in his garden at Clarence House and the so-called Carpet Garden at Highgrove – a thinly-disguised Islamic garden of Paradise in fact!

The fourth element of the traditional Islamic garden is enclosure. The word 'paradise' means, as many readers may know, 'enclosed by walls' (from the Persian *pairidaeza*) so we have the idea of an area isolated from its surroundings to create and protect a place of fertility and ease within. It is in the nature of paradise to be hidden and secret since it corresponds to the interior world – *al-jannah* meaning 'concealment' as well as garden. Thus, one of the characteristics of the Islamic garden is its seclusion: it is a kind of sanctuary for contemplation and is often represented in miniature paintings as being surrounded by high walls, the walled garden being a typical feature of traditional houses in many parts of the Islamic world.

Nowadays, maintaining water in the rills, pools and fountains of the gardens is often too expensive. There is also the concern for sustainability. Thus they are often left dry. Where there is no longer water in the channels, the heart, soul and spirit of the garden seem to die. Even if the rest of the garden is beautifully tended – the planting with scented flowers and herbs as well as shade-giving trees, all of the utmost importance, together with walls of magnificent patterned tiles – there is no question that life on both a superficial level and on a more profound mysterious level has disappeared along with the running water.

There is also a growing movement towards meadow planting in gardens and 're-wilding' of large areas of ground (for example, Knepp Castle in West Sussex, England) and the Islamic *chahar-bagh* with its emphasis on an underlying formal plan is becoming less fashionable. However, for the city, where the majority of people live, there is no doubt that such a garden offers not only a sanctuary away from the madness of contemporary urban life but also an opportunity for contemplation within a quiet and beautiful space. Increasingly, holidays are advertised as being remote from the city, as growing numbers search for meaning to their existence through contemplating nature and perhaps working on the land. Indeed, there has been a plethora of books in recent years with 'Wild' in the title: 'Wild Landscape,' 'Wild Swimming', 'Into the Wild' and so on. Most of us may not have the opportunity to access the wild but the garden may offer a taste of natural beauty. If we heed the advice of the Qur'an and open our 'eyes to see', and expose our hearts and souls to an awareness than the beauty of such an earthly garden may give us a taste of that Eternal Garden that, God willing, may be our ultimate end. It may also help us to a realisation that everything in nature truly is a sign or symbol of the

Archetypal Heavenly realm and thus guide us towards a deep reconnection with the sacred reality that is Mother Nature.

The fifth element of the Islamic Garden is the harmonious interweaving of architecture with the garden. Whether it be a small house, a palace, a pavilion or indeed a mausoleum (in which the Mughals excelled) this close link between the two is a distinctive and elegant feature. There is no question in my mind that the Taj Mahal would not be the celestial monument it is if it were not placed at the head of a magnificent *chaharbagh*, as well as on the edge of the River Jumna.

The sixth element is the great importance of an overall order, balance and correct proportion between all of the above ingredients, vital in determining the resulting harmony and beauty of the garden, water being the supreme unifying element. However, to reiterate an important principle in traditional Islamic art – as with the garden – the individual elements are not gathered together randomly as it were, simply because they look aesthetically pleasing, but rather they are the result of a pre-existing order and harmony: Divine Unity. 'Islamic art', the late Titus Burkhardt suggests, 'is essentially the projection into the visual order of certain aspects of Divine Unity.' This is indeed the key principle, and it is ultimately this which gives an Islamic garden its particular serene beauty and its potential to reconnect the visitor with the natural world.

Finally, there is one last, essential point to remember. It is 'Peace'; *Salaam* is the only word spoken in the Islamic Paradise gardens: 'there will be no idle or sinful talk there, only clean and wholesome speech' (56:25). This peace is promised to 'those who believe and do deeds of righteousness'. So what does this really mean? Is it peace from the world or is it, as is said in Sufism, peace from our own souls? Just as the external (*zahir*) garden needs constant attention to prevent weeds taking root and disease thriving so does the internal (*batin*) garden, the contemplative heart and soul. The great thirteenth century Sufi Jalaluddin Rumi suggested that 'the real gardens and flowers are within, they are in man's heart, not outside.' This inner garden is nurtured through prayer and the remembrance of God, and it is only thus that we may one day, by Heaven's grace, realise that longed-for peace. And there is no doubt that being surrounded by a lovingly tended and beautiful garden, which mirrors the garden of Heaven, not only aids us in contemplation and meditation but also gives us a taste of that everlasting peace 'which passes all understanding'.

The courtyards and gardens of the Alhambra and Generalife in Spain are some of the finest examples of Islamic gardens in the world, incorporating all the principles and elements in one harmonious and exquisite whole. The sense of being a sanctuary from the outside world, and bringing to life the phrase 'gardens underneath which rivers flow' is nowhere more visible than in the famous series of palaces and gardens that rise above the city of Granada in Andalusia. The intimate human-scale courtyards together with the many interlocking spaces or 'rooms' that make up a large part of these magical palaces and gardens have a quiet and profound beauty, most of which have water in the centre in some form or other. It is no accident that this is the most visited site in Europe – over 6,000 people per day. In such gardens, as with any garden created with a true sense of the wholeness and holiness of life, there is always a consciousness of the sanctity of the natural world, a consciousness that all levels of nature are interconnected: it is a living whole penetrated by the Spirit, and a true Islamic garden is always a mirror of the eternal Paradise garden.

Such gardens have the potential to become symbols of unity and hope, re-establishing our link to nature and the Infinite in an increasingly fragmented and one-dimensional world.

ARTS AND LETTERS

ONLY CONNECT

Daniel Dyer

Growing up near the Lake District, I was surrounded by the beauty of nature. Mountains, lakes, forests... all were on my doorstep, and the Divine hand was evident all around. When my wife and I decided to set up our own children's publishing company, we felt the need to be in nature and I found myself returning to the beauty of my childhood home. I was inspired to write a book about the 99 Names of Allah because I thought it would be a perfect way for children to learn about Islam, and a wonderful journey for myself.

The 99 Names of Allah is designed to help children discover the Names within themselves and in the world around them. Although 'the world around them' also encompasses the man-made world, for us it primarily means nature. We aim to help children build a spiritual link to the natural world, making them aware that God communicates to us through nature in the most beautiful, awesome, playful, sublime, and subtle manner. Children can begin to understand that they can learn spiritual and ethical lessons from nature, that they may draw sustenance, peace, and inner-calm simply by being witnesses within it, and that outside of the human soul, it is nature that is the ultimate playground for the manifestation of Allah's Names.

Hand-in-hand with this aim goes an attempt to build ecological awareness. Mainstream secular education is at pains to educate our children on our responsibilities in the face of environmental crisis. Much good work is being done in schools, yet the nature that is generally presented to children is one divested of meaning: it is a nature held at arm's length, a superficial thing separate from us and without spiritual significance. How much more invested we become when we understand the profound meaning within it, and our intimate spiritual connection to it. Ecological awareness becomes a matter of love.

At Chickpea Press, we believe all religions can help foster a spiritualised ecology, but perhaps none more so than Islam. The Qur'an is replete with exhortations for us to take care of the earth and witness its grandeur, beauty, and symbolism. Yet we might ask: how much does the religious education that Muslim children currently receive aid this process in an intelligent and informed manner? God willing, we hope that *The 99 Names of Allah* may go some small way towards aiding this process.

Each of the 99 Names is treated differently in terms of where we suggest children might witness signs. In many instances, attention is directed towards the natural world, though just as often it might be directed inward to some human quality children might discover within themselves. It is a holistic approach and the intention is to create balance.

The four Names presented here give only a snapshot of the information we present for each Name. In our full colour, illustrated guide, each Name is given a brief, easily understandable definition and is accompanied by a relevant quotation from the Qur'an and a quotation from a great Muslim teacher. In addition, each Name has four suggested activities and reflections and a deeper, more complex section for slightly older readers.

We use a broad range of Muslim teachers from Islam's classical period in order to explore the Names. In looking at the works of Rabiah or Rumi, for example, we readily find a sense of awe, wonder, and appreciation of the natural world:

O God,
Whenever I listen to the voice
of anything You have made —
The rustling of the trees
The trickling of water
The cries of birds
The flickering of shadow
The roar of the wind
The song of the thunder, I hear it saying:
"God is One!
Nothing can be compared with God!"

[Rabiah, *Doorkeeper of the Heart,* translated by Charles Upton]

In this world thousands of animals live happily,
without the throes of anxiety.
The dove on the tree coos gratefulness,
even though her food for the night has not yet arrived.

The nightingale's glorification is this:
"I depend for my daily bread,
on You who love to respond."
The falcon delights in the King's hand,
and no longer looks at carrion.

Look at every animal from the gnat to the elephant:
they all are God's family
and dependent on Him for their food.
What a nourisher is God!

[Mathnawi I: 2291-2295, *The Rumi Daybook*, translated by Kabir & Camille Helminski]

Giving an equal balance to male and female voices has been of great importance to us, especially given the history of cultural gender imbalance in Muslim societies and society at large. Indeed, we sense a very real connection between the exploitation of the natural world and the exploitation of women, and believe that it is not without reason that we speak of 'Mother Nature'.

Though this is a children's book, we do not shy away from passages that may be a little difficult or complex. Nature teaches that a seed can be planted that will bear fruit later: children do not necessarily need to immediately understand all the levels of meaning in the wisdom they encounter. Like adults, they can enjoy mystery and bewilderment, and their relationship with such sayings can flower over time.

This book is conceived as a resource children can continually engage with throughout their growing years, and perhaps once again when they themselves become parents. There are sections of each Name which children as young as seven or eight can read with guidance, whilst other sections give substantial and challenging material for young adults (and even parents and teachers themselves). The approach is holistic, and our hope is that the book will be seen as a family resource, a kind of tree from which people of all ages might pick fruit.

Al-Karim

The Most Generous

THE EARTH THAT WE WALK UPON is an excellent sign of the **Most Generous**. It produces the flowers and trees that bring joy to our eyes; the grains, vegetables and fruits that we eat; the stone, wood, and metals with which we build; and the fuels which give us energy. What could be a better reminder of the **generosity** of Allah?

Generosity is not just about giving though. It is also about taking in a responsible way. Treating the people or things from which we take in a thoughtful way is also a form of **generosity** and kindness. The Qur'an tells us to only take what we need, to never be wasteful and to treat the earth and all living things with dignity and respect.

Al-'Aliyy

The Highest

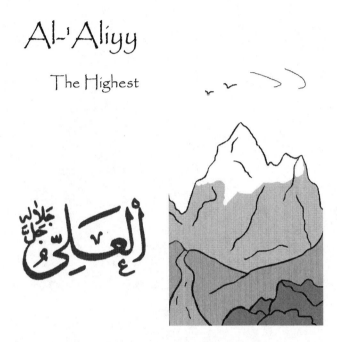

HAVE YOU EVER CLIMBED A MOUNTAIN? If you ever reach the top of one, looking out for miles **high** above the world, it may give you an idea of **al-'Aliyy**. When you reach the top you get a very special feeling. You have a sense of achievement, a thrill at being so **high**, and are filled with wonder at the splendour of nature. But there is something else: a sense of awesome silence.

There is only the sound of the wind. If you are there with friends, you often don't feel like saying anything. Words don't seem appropriate and you just want to look and take it all in. It is the same with the **Highest**: we feel an awe that makes us silent.

Al-Malik

The Sovereign

THE LION HAS BEEN CALLED "KING OF THE JUNGLE", and when we see him proudly staring out over the African plains we can understand why. The lion has a power and **majesty** that can remind us of **al-Malik**.

Human beings can also be a reminder. We have power over the animal world and it is our job to look after the entire planet on God's behalf. If the **leaders** we choose for ourselves are strong, wise, and kind like Muhammad, then they are the best reminder of the **Sovereign** that is Allah. They really care for the world and the people who live in it. They do not **rule** for themselves, but for **al-Malik** – the real **Leader** of us all.

Al-Muqit

The Nourisher

THE MILK THAT FLOWS FROM A MOTHER TO HER YOUNG is perhaps the clearest sign of the **Nourisher**. All mammals, including human beings, suckle their young. Watching a doe in the wild or a ewe on a farm as they suckle their young can have a powerful effect on us. We might think of the deep bond between a mother and her young, but we might also think of the deep bond between Allah and ourselves.

Though we might not see it, all **nourishment** (including mother's milk) is actually flowing to us from Allah. **Al-Muqit** never runs out of wholesome ways to **nourish** our bodies and souls, and all of creation is provided for in different ways.

ABDAL

Tam Hussein

Ba- Dal- Laam. Tinker with these Arabic triliteral roots and it will reveal many secrets. Those who believe language is a construct of the mind must look at Ba-Da-La; no human mind can conceive such mathematical order in such a complex language that organically sprang out of the bedouin as he recited poetry to urge his camel to move on. Ba-Da-La can both veil and unveil, deceive or reveal the truth. In terms of verbs it denotes exertion, substitution, exchanging and curiously, to prostitute. In terms of nouns it can be a suit, an allowance or it can refer to a person, a *badal* the plural being *Abdal*.

In Damascus these *Abdals* are simply known as the *Arba'een* or the forty. In fact a whole mountain has been named in their honour, *Jebel Arba'een*. Of course, there has always been a great debate as to who they were in the past and who they are now. As I explain to my students, these *Abdals* are mentioned in some narrations of the Prophet. In Sufi lore they are walking saints who hold up the very framework of the universe with their prayers and service to God. They are entrusted with some of the gifts of their predecessors, the Prophets, and they continue their work still. Sufi lore will of course go into greater depth and explain that sometimes the *Badal* will not even know whether he or she is one. Many of these *Abdals* are chosen from three hundred of the best or as they are known *Akhyar,* (which comes from the same root that denotes goodness). Once a *badal* dies he is replaced by another which makes sense since as we have said, *badal* also has connotations of 'replacing'.

Damascenes say that these Abdals are found in each continent of our planet but most of them are concentrated in Greater Syria. The head saint, the Qutb, resides in Mecca, in an unknown location and walks amongst the millions of pilgrims that visit the place. Be careful when you look down on that Sudanese fellow or the quiet *Takruni* woman who asks for nothing, for that one may just be the very embodiment of sainthood.

Even a taxi driver will point out the tombs of the ex-forties as he takes you through the city. He might, when driving past Bahsa Square point to a derelict shell of an incomplete mosque and a car park and tell you that the government tried to replace an ancient mosque where one of the forty used to worship with a car park. And although they succeeded in bulldozing the mosque and erecting the concrete structure, they discovered that deep below was an untapped spring which, if the car park was completed, would threaten to flood the whole city. Forget David Hume or ibn Rushd. Miracles happen in Damascus.

Most inhabitants will probably cite Sheikh Habbal as one of the elect. Certainly if one visits his work shop in *Midhat Pasha* where St Paul famously escaped his persecutors one can see why; an ancient man with a wispy beard sits working away; the very embodiment of piety, wisdom and industriousness. One of his numerous sons receives supplicants from the high and low, Presidents kill for that sort of adulation. Sheikh Habbal though spurns them, but they keep coming hoping that the blind man who sees with the eye of the soul will mention them in his prayer.

Whilst there is a degree of unanimity with regards to Sheikh Habbal the same cannot be said for Abu Muhammad. In the Old City at least where Time sits with you in the coffee shop, opinion is split. Some hold the blind beggar in high esteem. According to the party of Abu Muhammad as they are known, he is the ascetics' ascetic having worn the same clothes for thirty years. He has been spotted in two places at exactly the same time, in the Ummayyad Mosque whilst he was also seen snoozing at Ibn al-Arabi Mosque in Muhiyudin, his back turned oblivious to the tourists taking pictures of the address stitched to his back which read: 'Peace be on You, if you see me lost take me to Abu Salih's house in Qamariyeh, Damascus. May God bless you.' On other occasions he squats underneath the minaret of Jesus spitting out sunflower seeds whilst passing tourists grimace at his uncouthness. Their revulsion doesn't stop him from spitting out the seeds in their path. His eyes are in a dreamy opium like state, his face bearing an expression of joyous expectation as if the coming of the Messiah himself is imminent. His metal plate of food brought to him by his nephew's children, is untouched. The sight of cats sharing his plate, those rough leathery feet unhurt by the scorching cobbled stones, the patched blue thobe, all give him an aura of eccentricity and a touch of the uncouth Bedouin. When the party of Abu Muhammad say he is one of the Abdals, they have their reasons, after all this is a city of prophets, apostles, saints and miracles so why could Abu Muhammad not be of the Forty?

It is a proposition that his detractors do not deny. Abu Mazin, his foremost detractor, will tell you 'course he could be an Abdal but is it *plausible*', putting particular emphasis on the plausible, 'I mean is it plausible? A man with an address stitched on his back is a quack.' He would tap his finger on his head, 'plain loopy. How many saints do you know? We have to be rational about all this! He is the reason why we are so backward. Marx is right, religion is a *drug*.'

And the evidence, in fairness, is there for all to see. Abu Muhammad harangues them for their laziness at Nawfara café, he is restrained by the caretakers at the Ummayyad mosque for insulting rich Russians and their expensive wives whilst guiding total strangers and showing them nooks and crannies where no one else goes. Who is buried there, or what secret that part of Damascus holds only Abu Muhammad knows. 'Bonkers' Abu Mazin repeats, 'bonkers. It's his lot that gives Islam a bad name. It's the likes of him that get towns all restless and rebellious.' What else can Abu Mazin and his party do but laugh and inquire into everyone who pays too much attention to him? 'Why,' he says, 'if he is such a saint doesn't he pray to God to alleviate us from the Iraqis coming here? Why doesn't he pray for rain and sort out this drought in the countryside? Or reduce the prices?'

Whenever I return home, during summer recess, I am always pressed to approach his nephew, a childhood friend, especially, when Abu Muhammed becomes unbearable. I, being so far removed in Toronto and not so intertwined with the issue, am often asked to reason with his nephew, pressing him to keep his uncle in control using all the powers of rhetoric that an academic can muster. I always try to wriggle out of it but Abu Mazin always insists: 'you are your father's son! Speak to Abu Salih before his uncle turns this place upside down!' and so out of respect for my father's old friends I am pressed into action. But even with me Abu Salih is tightlipped. He always says he is too busy making furniture to give it much thought.

'No one wants good furniture any more,' Abu Salih says and keeps working without so much as a glance in my direction.

One day though when I pressed him too much, after Abu Muhammed had embarrassed Abu Mazin to tourists and Damascene alike calling into question his very manhood – that is his integrity and trustworthiness. It distressed him greatly. So I urged Abu Salih to place his uncle in a mental hospital where he could be cared for properly. That is when he stopped working and walked me out of his workshop.

'Abu Hamza,' he said, 'we have known each other since we were children, you have known my uncle ever since we used to play on the street gullies did you not?'

That was true. But my memory of him was often vague.

'Didn't you study Frankenstein?'

'Of course we did', I said, 'it is part of our degree to study Gothic literature.'

'Did you ever study why the monster became what he became?'

'You wouldn't,' I said, 'get a good mark if you didn't.' In fact one would fail if one did not at least broach the topic, you must try to understand even though one does not condone the actions of the Prometheus.

'So why don't you do that with my uncle? I have five mouths to feed, unlike you I don't have the time to keep my uncle in check. Unlike you I didn't get a scholarship and a cushy chair at a Western faculty where they have long holidays in between semesters. He is mad and God has lifted the pen of accountability on him. Leave him be.'

'Are you still sore about that scholarship after all these years?' I said surprised by my own temper.

'Me? Sore! No, not at all.'

'I scored the highest in French and English.'

'I didn't do too bad neither,' he said, 'I was top in Arabic and I was the school captain. God didn't write it for me.'

I don't know why but it wasn't the fact that Abu Salih had kicked me out of his workshop that made me angry. It was more the insinuations that I didn't deserve my scholarship. That night, during dinner with the boys I complained to my wife about Abu Salih's behaviour.

'He's just jealous darling' she said in that English accented Arabic that she hasn't managed to shed from the time I met her at McGill. 'Can you blame him? He is working away in the workshop and here you are, an academic at one of the most prestigious universities in the world!' Miriam turned round and pointed out the house that my father had made through sheer graft, despite the obstacles facing country bumpkins like him. Despite being a poor young man from Dera'a, he had worked and studied and now all I saw were framed certificates and pictures of past glory where father stands with notables from the highest strata of society, from the President to the politicians, from military men like Nasser to tea with Gaddaffi, conservative Saudi princes and to Beirut literatis. I don't know how he made it but he did. The square with the ornate octagonal fountain right in the middle of our house was proof of his greatness. My father had built this place. Planted the flowers and trees with his own hands and restored the colour of Umayyad brick work. The house that my father built was magnificent.

'Maybe,' suggested Miriam 'before pressing him again, maybe you should get acquainted with Abu Muhammad's story. Then he can't argue with you can he?' So this is what I set out to do in the semester of 2009.

***

Abu Muhammed or Zaid was not a bad painter in the 70s and the 80s. Even in those days Abu Mazin kept a close eye on him. In the morning Abu Mazin would serve him fresh bread. In the afternoon Abu Mazin noted that he sat on his fold up chair with a white canvas painting an arched portal with a winding alleyway concealing an ancient door perhaps from the time of the Ottomans. He loved painting streets with cedar wood beams jutting out of clay, plaster and mortar supporting creaking and groaning windows, balconies and floors. His streets were framed within in the Ummayad colours of black and pastel brown, sometimes there was a silhouette of a woman escaping into her home, perhaps after a secret tryst with her beloved. His paintings were beautiful. When inspiration seized him he'd paint the Ummayad Mosque itself. Abu Muhammad's paintings earned him patronage, fame and wealth. Before the civil war Lebanese businessmen purchased his paintings to hang them in their summer homes in Jubail, where they would be talked over and admired by European yachtsman stopping over. In the late 70s you could find him sitting in al-Rawdah café, smoking a pipe with the likes of Adonis, Marghout, and Tamer discussing the merits of some artistic movement or other. But after 1982, after Hama, things changed. His paintings had a certain darkness to them, the shades of dark became more prominent, the shadows in the alleyways became more profound. His women became veiled and his paintings took on a tinge of red.

Even in the Old City there were fluxes in the time and space continuum. Father Girges had an interview. Old Menhal to whom the caliphate had never ended woke up and realised that not only had it ended in 1924 but that his young nephew had vanished. Even Efraim the only Jew in Damascus was asked a question or two. But apart from that nothing much changed. Abu Muhammad, Abu Mazin noted, became more restless, more irregular in his work, it was as if a great thirst had opened up inside of him that could not be slaked. He was not seen frequenting Rawdah café any more. He would be seen skulking around at night or the early hours. In fact at one point, he was not seen for several weeks perhaps even months. No one in the Old City knew for how long but then many didn't ask. Some said he had gone to Beirut to ply his trade. Only Abu Mazin, kept count of the days he didn't buy bread from him. There were other rumours; Abu Muhammad was working on his master piece, the piece that would transcend all other pieces and everyone in the Old City awaited it expectantly. Abu Muhammad would always have his doors for the locals to come in and view his work. He was a painter of the people after all. But the piece never came, all that emerged one hot Friday, was a broken young man, blind, blabbering, lips caked with ink and an expression which veered from sheer terror to ecstasy. That day he earned himself the epithet of The Possessor of Muhammad on account of the unspeakable things he said about the Prophet which would offend even the most hard hearted of persons. Abu Mazin said the authorities carried him away to save him from the angry mob and cure him. After he was released he was handed back to his mother where he was nursed back by his mother and older brother, Hassan. He emerged one day putting his bare feet on the sun bleached marble on the Umayyad mosque and declared that 'Zaid al-Haddad is dead and has ceased painting.' It is difficult to shed light on the subject especially as his nephew, Abu Salih remains silent. No matter how much Abu Mazin plies him with tea and sweets, no matter how indirectly Hammad al-Kurdi, a close confidante of Abu Mazin questions him. The result of Abu Salih's silence has meant that two narrations have filled the vacuum which have in some ways been nourished by the smoke of cigarettes and strong coffee.

Hammad al-Kurdi is a strong proponent of this narration. He is my father's taxi driver he knows everything that goes on in Damascus. My father would employ him whenever he needed to attend some important function at the opera house. Whenever a young man wishes to hear a good yarn of the good old days they all go to al-Kurdi even in his retirement. Apart from a great story al-Kurdi also has a particular knack for geography. He'll tell you, whether relevant or not, that the capital of Kazakhstan is Almaty. This fixation with geography stems from him failing his secondary school geography exam. But is al-Kurdi reliable as an authority? According to Abu Mazin he is, because he has the privileged position of being with Abu Muhammad days before he stopped painting so it would be plausible that his school has a firm grounding. The only thing that may detract from his testimony is probably al-Kurdi's reputation for profligacy in his youth. As a young man he worked in Bulgaria and is considered somewhat international in that respect.

I found him where he was usually found for the past fifteen years, talking with Abu Mazin after Friday prayer at the Nawfara cafe. He wore a checked shirt and beige trousers smoking a big Zaaghloul which coloured his bristling mustachio with a darkish tint of pure tobacco pipe. Whenever he saw me he got up and gave me an affectionate kiss on both cheeks out of respect for his old patron. He inquired as was always the case about my late father and reminisced.

'I tell you', he said, 'the Ministry of Education has not been the same since his passing, God have mercy on him! Look how backward we are, all these kids sporting beards down to their legs! Monkeys! If your father was here this would never happen, God have mercy on him. Did I tell you he recommended me to Sharif Shami the Chief examination officer of Damascus?'

I knew that and I also knew how much Uncle Sharif used to complain about him to my father, but for some reason my father kept him on so did Uncle Sharif. Uncle Sharif was a generous soul. When I got my scholarship, he personally came to my father's house to announce the good news and presented me with the documents. No one had ever scored such a high mark in the exam. My father was pleased as if it was an inevitability. He never once doubted my academic ability, even when I did so myself and I

remember the personal attention he devoted to my education no matter
how busy he was.

***

Al-Kurdi told me that whatever happened to Abu Muhammad was
premised on a jinx.

'You see it all happened on the last day of October, I remember the first
cold winter's breeze hit me and thinking that winter is here and my neck's
going to give me grief. I was just about to start my shift and I was sitting in
Abu Ali's having a bowl of beans and a hot cup of tea when I sees Abu
Muhammad at the roundabout "Zaid," I says giving him a wave, "come over
here." He turns round and gives me a wave. I called him over, pointing to
me pack of cigarettes and me bowl – Abu Muhammad never used to smoke
cigarettes unless he snatched one off us. So he makes his way across the
roundabout and he's got one of his canvasses under his arm. I tells him to sit
down and order another hot bowl of beans. He reaches for me packet
straight away and lights one. I could tell that he wasn't too happy. His face
was all scrunched up and he looked upset. So I says, "What's going on man?
Things can't be that bad can it?"

"Not at all," he says with a shrug, "painting can get to you sometimes."

"Oh? Your artist friends did a runner on you did they?"

"No," he says dragging on his cigarette, "sometimes I get tired of painting
the same old stuff."

"He did have a point mind you, how many years can you draw arches, old
buildings and all that at some point you'd get tired – I know I would. Even
if like him, he'd do it in different ways. He must've been sick of it by now.
Know what I reckon?" I says.

"What?" he replies cynically, "that the capital of Bulgaria is Pristina?!"

"It's Sofia," I says, "listen I'm giving you some advice here. I reckon you
should change the stuff you paint."

"I've just come down from Mount Qasioun. Winter's arrived early, and I
probably won't finish my painting now because the wind will get into my
bones and you're talking about changing the subject?"

"That's not what I mean." I says, "why not draw animals and figures and wot not, like them artists in the West? You can be like that Leonardo. Do like a Mona Lisa or something."

"It's Leonardo da Vinci, I'm not doing that!"

"Why not?" I says.

"Because," he says raising up his hands as if he's talking to a fool, "I'm from the East, we have our own ways – besides in Islam its *haraam* to depict faces and living creatures."

"Since when did you suddenly get all religious and believe in all that?"

"Look," he says, "I might not pray but I don't think it's right."

"So you going to take on that commission you got about painting the President's son?"

"What?! How did you know about that?" He froze up, he looked at me suspiciously, "who told you?! There's ears everywhere these days."

"Come on," I am the driver to the Ministry of Education and Culture, I hear everything, "get with the times with all them loons in Hama rebelling what you expect? Everyone round here knows that Mr. Zayyat offered you the commission."

"Rebellion to you maybe."

"What you mean by that?"

"Nothing. Look, I swear I am never going to draw a living creature – and even if I were to, I'm not going to draw that arsehole – I'd rather accept a commission from Satan to draw his balls."

"Even if the President commands you?"

"President? You mean dictator?! Never. My paintings serve the people not tyrants."

"Alright, alright! Calm down! Never say never. Calm down! At least the Big Man is doing something about corruption."

Abu Muhammad was having none of it, "Since when did you become an ardent supporter of the President?"

"Always have" says I.

"Even now?" he came closer and whispered it, "Even when one of the most ancient cities have been flattened."

"They are enemies of Syria. Terrorists that want to destroy Syria."

"He bellows out a laugh and leaves me grabbing all me packet of cigarettes showering me with all sorts of affectionate insults. He shouts that maybe I could sort him out with some whore he could paint when I'm driving me taxi round Masakin Berzeh. "God knows," he says laughing "you supply it to the ministers." I was right though wasn't I? I always say never say never don't test the powers that be. He was painting a market scene down Souk Sarrujeh one day, and he came across this Yugoslavian girl working at the embassy and he must have been knocked out. I've seen her meself. Body like the Adriatic coast full of curves and waves, below the clear sea a hint of submerged white coast line. I'm telling you, whatever it was underneath her dress was pure magic. I think he saw her for months and just disappeared like one of them Shi'ite Imams. When I did see him he showed me a drawing of her in his sketch book. He looked like a drug addict, eaten up from inside but when I saw that rough pencil drawing, I nearly went blind, she was a houri or something. I remember ribbing him saying that it was all *haraam* in Islam and all that. He just shrugged it off saying that he's still not going to draw the President's son. I tells him that he could get loads of money and maybe marry her. Then he disappeared again for weeks and then comes out like he is now, bonkers. From the gibberish that he told me it was case of *Majnun* and *Laila*. He painted her, probably slept with her, because how could you resist? We're all human ain't we? And those lot in Yugoslavia are not like us here. We've got honour and morals. He must've thought that all the shagging was a prelude to marriage. But she was having none of it and told him that she was going to return to Yugoslavia and she couldn't marry him. She probably did it to make herself feel good. I mean every girl wants to be in a painting or a song? Women are fickle, they want to be little gods! All of them! He was gutted, probably painted her so well it seared into his brain and he went mad like rabid dog frothing at the mouth. That's probably when he threw a bit of turpentine into his eyes or scratched them out because he couldn't get her out of his mind. That's how he became Abu Muhammad. Your father would confirm it if he was alive, he knows the story better than me because he made inquiries for his mother when he disappeared.'

I was surprised because my father never mentioned it, even when I asked him about Abu Muhammed he never said a word, he used to walk past him as if he didn't exist even when Abu Muhammed threw him those long accusatory glances that was his custom to all those people he disapproved of.

***

The second account to Abu Muhammad's candidacy for being an Abdal is Mr. Rashid's. He is his cousin and childhood friend. I must admit though he is a local, I didn't know him even though my father did. There was a time when my father had appointed Mr. Rashid to teach at one of the local schools. For a brief period he had even tutored me. My father clearly appreciated his calibre, but for some reason those sessions stopped. Mr. Rashid didn't recognise me when I turned up on the steps and knocked on his metal door. He no longer looked like that slender young man but had aged much, when he saw me his face turned to a look of surprise that verged on terror as if he was standing in front of my father.

'Who are you?' he said searching my face as if he recognised me from his past.

'I'm Mr. Ammar's son,' I said, no response was forthcoming, 'I am one of your students.'

'My son, forgive me but my memory fails me' he said.

I was surprised that he was letting me stand outside of his porch when he was famous for his chivalry. Mr. Rashid was not just a man of probity and piety, he was chivalrous to the point of ridiculousness. Abu Mazin told me that once he found 2000 liras on the Jisr Ra'is, the bridge where all of the city's traffic congregated. Instead of pocketing the money or donating the money to charity like most sensible people, he placed an advert in all the newspapers announcing his find. Qamariyeh was swamped by hawkers, vendors and taxi drivers for days. Abu Mazin always says that he still lives in the era of Mutannabi. But Abu Muhammad spares him from his tongue lashings.

'*Ustaaz*,' I said 'don't you remember when you used to take me on a whirlwind tour of Arabic literature and history?' No response. 'Don't you remember the time when you explained my own house to me? You pointed to the wall and said: "We are not like the French who display everything beautiful to the outside world. They display their gardens, the charms of their woman all up front. We, on the other hand, are not ostentatious. When you walk past our home you will not come across showy gardens, rather a small door on a muddy wall, you have to bend to get into the home, to humble yourself, then are you let into a paradise, with the trickle of water, the shade of the tree, the light airiness of the stucco, the cedar beams. Hospitality is given and received. We are aware that all this worldly paradise is not for boast and ostentation. That is why our home may look miserly on the outside but they are certainly rich on the inside and that's our philosophy." It became almost an ode in homage of him. 'Sir, I think it was you who prompted me, much to my father's dismay, to switch to Arabic literature when I was at McGill.'

'Really?' his eyes came alive, 'so it's you?' He smiled at me like the sun and beamed. He hugged me warmly like I was that pupil many years back and brought me in through the narrow corridor. His warmth reminded me as to why I begged my father to continue our lessons but I was like a goat butting against a mountain. He just said that we Syrians needed to look forward and free ourselves from the slavery of our past. 'We need,' he said, 'to think anew my son, look to the future. The reason we are where we are is because we became prisoners to our past and we have Mongols knocking on our doors now both within and without.'

'But,' I said, ' the past is beautiful father, it's majestic. I love history, we can be like Baybars or Qutuz or Suleiman instead of being the monkeys that we are now.' 'Monkeys?' Father said and looked at me as if to say who taught you that? That was the last pronouncement he made on the subject and I was never taught by him again. In fact, he seemed to be wiped clean from my memory until I started digging.

We went through another door and entered through the courtyard into his study lined with magnificent tomes and books on all kinds of subjects. I had no doubt that some of his ancestors were mentioned in between those sheets of paper. Mr. Rashid belongs to the illustrious Haddad family – the same one which Abu Muhammad belongs to. The Haddads are considered to be of the *Shwam* that is, from the original inhabitants of the Old City. Their ancestry can be traced to the time of Abd el-Malik the Ummayad, and some of their ancestors have even graced the biographies of Damascus. And their brilliance meant that the Haddads could be found everywhere in society, from the artist's salon to the Ministry of Education, their brilliance meant that they could never be ignored. He poured me some tea with sage which had been quietly brewing on the oobia stove whilst I explained my objective. He was reluctant at first, saying that he didn't want to rock the boat. That he didn't want to be refused for a Hajj visa for the twentieth consecutive time. When I pressed him saying that this was for my ears alone he acquiesced saying that I said it the way my father did.

***

My son, I found Abu Muhammad on the tenth night of Ramadan at al-Nablusi's mosque in Salihiyeh. The Sheikh had finished the *Tarawih* prayers and had begun on the book he loved covering during Ramadan; the *Shama'il of Tirmidhi* — a collection of traditions related to the way the Prophet looked. It documented the minutest detail from the number of white hairs on the Prophet's beard to the way he behaved with children. The Sheikh always said that one could use the book to get such a detailed portrait of the Prophet's noble countenance that some Saints once they comprehended its contents were blinded by his magnificent countenance. He was the moon. One look at the countenance of the Prophet, Peace be upon him, would be like staring into the sun itself. You could go blind, the Prophet's Companions could see him because they were men of different constitution to ours. We are weaklings used to soft living. Our eyes cannot tolerate such a vision. 'He who wishes to stare into the sun- cannot' the Sheikh would say, 'therefore' holding aloft the *Shama'il* of Tirmidhi, 'let him stare in to the moon for it reflects the sun without its intensity.' The Sheikh had just finished reading the chapter on the way the Prophet, peace and blessings be upon him, wore his ring when I spotted Abu Muhammad sitting in the far corner of the mosque listening attentively, scribbling furiously in his notebook. It pleased me, it was proof of the healing of Ramadan, for during this blessed month even the Muslim who hardly ever prayed abstained from the world and turned to his Lord. After the Sheikh had closed his book I made my way towards him. Abu Muhammad was sitting on his knees deep in thought, he had a copy of the *Shamaa'il* on the rug. After exchanging pleasantries and inquiring into our respective families I asked him what brought him here to *Salihiyeh*. Abu Muhammad usually prayed at the Great Mosque in the Old City. He replied that he had wished to hear how the Prophet, peace and blessings upon him, looked like. I was pleased by that — for the only way to know God is to love His Prophet. I invited him to accompany me to *Maisat* where we could refresh ourselves with some fruit juice and he accepted my invitation. As we walked, he asked me how my teaching was going and I complained that I was having some trouble with officials from the Ministry of Education. 'They don't like the way I teach the syllabus,' I said, 'I thought they would like me teaching them the glories of the Arab peoples – but they are averse to it.'

'Isn't that the way these days?' he said.

I sensed that something disturbed him, because he was usually far more talkative than that. So I asked delicately: 'I trust that the engagement is going well?'

'It is as it should be.'

'Praise be to God. So when will you hold the engagement?'

'I won't,' he said bluntly, 'she has returned to Yugoslavia.'

'Only two weeks ago you were the happiest man alive.' I searched his face looking for traces of emotion but his face was a corpse in a morgue, 'Didn't she want to convert?'

'No, she converted and I'm glad she remains one – no dear friend, I broke it off.'

I touched his forehead to check his temperature and said: 'Do you remember when we used to talk about marrying a beautiful Circassian with green eyes, blond hair and pale skin?' He smiled as if he remembered those moments sitting in the inner courtyard of my house drinking iced mulberry juice, whilst the fig tree shaded us from the glaring sun. 'And now God out of His grace grants you one and you send her off packing?'

'I don't think you will understand the matter,' he said and changed the subject. He spoke no more of it the whole evening. I was not worried though he would explain in due course . He would find me when he needed to talk that had been his way ever since childhood. And he did. One evening when Mother and Father were visiting an uncle in *Midan*, I had just prepared some tea and was reading a novel in the courtyard, when the regular tap, the secret code of our childhood was heard. I went for the door without even marking the page I was on, I found him outside looking quite disheveled. His dark lank hair was greasy, his light blue shirt grimy on the collar and trousers creased as if he had slept in them.

'*Ahlan!*' I said looking round in case someone saw him, 'come in. Come in!'

He checked to see if anyone had followed him and came in.

'Has anyone been here asking about me?'

'No of course not. If anything I should be asking you.'

'You sure? You didn't see any one? A new street sweeper? Did Abu Mazin ask about me to you?'

'No,' I said concerned, 'but why are you in trouble?'

'Tea!' he demanded waving my question away.

I led him through the narrow hallway into the courtyard. I poured him a cup of tea. He sat down next to the fountain, placed his copy of the *Shama'il* and his sketch books carefully on the table. I noticed that he must have been working for his fingers were stained with ink and paints and he had the faint smell of turpentine about him. He drank his tea appearing very pensive, his handsome face was tired, his cheek bones sunken and his gait slightly hunched as if the days of fasting had taken its toll. I watched him silently waiting for it to come out.

'Cousin I am tired,' he said, 'tired of drawing market scenes, old minarets, and the ancient streets of the Old City. I need something different.' I concurred with this sentiment; all of us need a change of subject. 'Yes but, I mean I am tired of it – I need something more beautiful.'

'Why don't we visit my uncle in Homs,' I suggested, 'from there it is a short ride to Aphamiya or we can train it up to Lattakia. There's plenty of inspiration there.'

'I have already painted that, they hang on the walls of the wealthiest in Beirut.'

'So what do you want to do?'

'I wish to paint life, living things.'

'You know our traditions are not like that. You know that God will surely hold Michelangelo to account for demanding his statue to walk?! How dare he compete with the Most Magnificent?!'

'Yes, but we have also done so, we have drawn animals and human forms – just go and look at the Great Mosque. There are depiction of trees, birds and deer.'

'Yes it is true, we do have that tradition but they were representations of the real, our artists deliberately strove not to draw it realistically. They were illustrators who aimed to draw out the meaning of the represented, so that the represented does not become the focus itself. Our artists killed their egos.'

Abu Muhammad did not accept my reasoning and he dismissed it with a kiss of his teeth.

'Why can't I draw and paint like Leonardo Da Vinci? Even the Baroque artist Caravaggio?'

'I'm not questioning your ability, I have seen what you can do, truly there is something of the poet in your paintings, but I question your motives why?'

'Because I need it. I need something more than old buildings.'

'Is this why you broke off the engagement? Is she not enough? Is she not beautiful? Everyone says she is.'

He glanced at me impatiently.

'It's not that – you won't understand.'

'Try. Make me understand.'

'Don't you see?' He said excitedly, 'when Michelangelo painted the Sistine chapel it was as if his very soul was speaking to God with his very being? It is proof that we have an angelic nature.'

'Yes, truly in the remembrance of God do hearts find contentment but he depicted God as a man. He crossed threshold of the Law.'

'Can't you see that when Caravaggio painted Jesus it is as much a labour of love searching for meaning the same way our artists did with our Prophet?! Their journey is the same journey as that of the saints.'

'No!' I shouted him down. 'No that is a delusion! They do not know how Jesus looked like for they would be blinded by his beauty. It is true that some of our craftsmen depicted Muhammad, but they were done in the most unrealistic way, his face would have a veil, and painted for illiterate Turkish khans who wanted to know the story of our Prophet, peace and blessings be upon him, than to actually gaze at the real figure. They were illustrators. We do not do realism – those Renaissance painters will never understand the true meaning of Jesus!'

'There is no point in speaking to Philistines – there is simply no point.'

'Do not for a second think I don't appreciate the beauty of their paintings, for I often loved to go through your books of the artists, but I always realised that they deluded themselves. Do not think that you can achieve sainthood by seeking a short cut to God. Our Saints worked hard. They were chosen. You must ask Him if that is what you are *really* searching for.'

I wanted to say more but he did not let me. He had already got up was gulping the last of his tea and excused himself on a pretext of getting some fresh yogurt for the evening meal. I did not stop him for I, too, was flushed and vexed at the insolence of artists to break the rules set down by the Law. I was too distracted to notice that he had forgot his sketch pad and his book. When I did notice, he had already left and the courtyard was silent. I picked up the sketch book from the coffee table and casually flicked through it. In it were preparatory drawings of rings, turbans, swords, clothes, pictures from Topkapi palace in Istanbul of things having belonged to our Prophet, peace and blessings be upon him. My mind and heart began to race. I stared at the *Shama'il*, I opened its pages. To my horror I divined, through his copious notes his intention. I rushed out to catch him at home, I banged on the door and found his mother, Umm Hassan opening the door. 'He's out,' she said, and seemed reluctant to invite me in. I left a message for him to call me. But he did not return my calls. For several days I visited his house only to be given the same answer. Realising that he was at home all along I informed her of his design.

'Your son is in grave danger!'

'What are you talking about? He's been holed up here for days – there's no *Mukhabarat* snooping around. What are you talking about nephew?'

'I have seen his notes, he's trying to paint the Messenger of God!'

'I seek refuge in God,' she said exasperated and I heard the sound of her footsteps descend down the steps, the bolt unlock, Umm Hassan led me into the courtyard saying: 'That good for nothing's been in his room for days, I have hardly seen the fool.'

'Zaid!' I screamed looking up on the first floor towards his room. 'Come out.' There was no response from his room on the second floor. 'I know what you are trying to do – I have your notes.' Silence. 'Brother', I said, 'you cannot stare into the sun for it will blind you, stare into the moon instead and you will appreciate the rays of the sun. Don't do it for the love of God. Don't do it.'

'Go away,' said a muffled sound, it was a strange animal like sound, but nevertheless it was him. 'Go away,' he repeated.

'Zaid listen to me, Zaid! If a houri descended to earth the world would go blind. This enormity, to paint him is not only a sin, but his beauty will consume you.'

I heard a chuckle, a crazy laugh of a drunkard who had been warned about Scotch whiskey after he had already emptied it. 'Leave me.'

I left him having warned him. After two weeks Umm Hassan called me. She was hysterical. The three of us, me, and his brother Hassan managed to chase the half naked lunatic down, pin him down in Qamariyeh before the hard wooden police batons would find their mark on his body. I will never forget his expression, as I wrestled him, a blind wild beast with a tortured expression of ecstasy. He had gazed upon him! The police did swoop on us and after my release many months later, everything was in tatters. I lost my job and all I could do was to go to his room and with closed eyes and burn all the contents of that room. In the process perhaps I destroyed some of the best masterpieces that Damascus had ever seen. Perhaps even the world.

***

There were some questions that remained over Mr. Rashid's account. Stories that I had caught in passing. 'Isn't it true Mr. Rashid,' I said as gently as possible, 'that you were on a holiday for several weeks about the same time as Abu Muhammad's arrest?'

'Is that,' said Mr. Rashid as delicately as possible, 'what your father told you? Did he tell you that the Ministry accused me of burying some banned books in the cemetery? Did he tell you about the hard labour? The screams from the best teachers that Syria has ever produced?' He talked to me normally but his eyes were crying as if they had seen things that the soul could not comprehend.

I realised that this had become personal. It became clear that the man had lost his mind and I did not want to entertain such gibberish. I left him to his quiet idyllic indolence. I concluded there and then that there was no point in pursuing this line of inquiry. As the Prophet said: 'The best of you are those who leave those things that don't concern him.' I never bothered Abu Salih after that again. In fact, I consciously avoided him. As for Mr. Rashid that was the last I saw of the old man. Even my wife wondered why I didn't give him the courtesy to attend his funeral prayers when he died. My father had never mentioned the incident – ever. I am willing to wager all that I possess that my father had nothing to do with Mr. Rashid's arrests and the tortures he endured – or at least, he wasn't the one who sent out the order.

But I couldn't help it. Every summer whenever I saw Abu Muhammad sitting in that Grand Old Mosque, I fluctuated between those two accounts I had been told. Sometimes I inclined to the view of the youngsters who didn't have the same deference of the old. They politely inquired as to why Mr. Rashid had not been allowed to leave the country for pilgrimage since 1982. Perhaps Mr. Rashid is as mad as Abu Muhammad himself and the story of the forty Abdals and Abu Muhammad's candidacy was just a bit of nonsense keeping the people of Damascus sleeping. Other times, when I saw the old man with that turban wrapped just like it is found in *Tirmidhi's Shama'il*, his hands raised to heaven, his eyes closed, face wrinkly sunburnt with an expression of painful pleasure as if he had just made love to his newlywed for the very first time, could he be an Abdal? Perhaps there was something to that old lunatic. Sometimes I told myself that these Old Timers know what's what. Young scamps should mind their own business if they know what's good for them for after all did the Prophet not say: 'He who believes in God and the Last Day, let him speak good or remain silent.' And in this way I soothed my soul wishing at once to do away with Abu Muhammad who seemed so interwoven with my own past, and at other times, I wished to hug him and seek his forgiveness and ask him to pray for me and my father's soul. Over time Abu Muhammad seems to understand that longing inside me and is patient and waiting for me as if he knows that Ba-Da-Laam can both veil and unveil.

Tam Hussein wrote this story as Writer in Residence at the Muslim Institute Seventh Winter Gathering, 27–29 November 2015, Sarum College, Salisbury

M AND THE LAKE

Aamer Hussein

As a boy M had often walked by the lake. It mesmerised him in winter when it was glassy and in summer when it mirrored the sun's reddish rays. He'd play on its banks in warm weather with his friends. Some of the boys would take off their shirts, jump in, and splash around in the water, then come out shivering in their drenched trousers. But M, who couldn't swim, never joined them in the water, until one day one of his friends promised him to reward him if he did. The water was icy even though it was summer. He felt the lake would swallow him whole. His friends swam away and left him there, watching him from a distance as he spluttered and gasped until he struggled to the grassy bank, slipping and sliding on the glass-smooth pebbles on the lake's bed.

Later, he didn't remember whether his friend had kept his promise and rewarded him with a bank note or a book. But he always remembered the cold white water and his spluttering fear of drowning. Along with these fears he was afraid, too, of making new friends, who would leave him to flail in icy water as his playmates had done that summer day. At boarding school in his teens, he was congenial with his fellow-students and courteous to his teachers. He joined in discussions and debates. But he usually walked alone.

M liked walking alone and when he went home on his holidays from his first term at university he would set off on his own and stroll for miles, watching birds and squirrels on the greening branches of trees and rabbits and other little creatures scurrying in the bushes. One day, near the end of spring, he was walking on the path that led to a wooded hill, when he saw a deer sprinting ahead, a creature that seemed both remote and unafraid of him. It seemed to be leading him on, up the hill. Almost in a trance, M followed.

In a short while and M found himself at the peak of the hill at the edge of a lake he was sure he had seen before, though he knew it couldn't be the one he had played by as a child. He had lost sight of the running deer, as if it had vanished into the silver ripples of the lake. The walk had made him hot. He was perspiring and had long since drunk all the water in the bottle he had carried in his rucksack. He bent down, and sipped lake water from his cupped palms. Then he took off his shirt and vest and splashed cold water on his face and head. The sting of the water made him gasp but he went on splashing himself, bathing his shoulders and bare chest until he was shivering in the sunlight. He rolled up his trouser legs nearly to the knee, and washed his feet and his calves. For a moment he had the urge to dive deep into the lake's depths, but for now the bracing feel of its water on his skin was enough. When he had refreshed himself, he lay down on a reedy slope dotted with yellow-breasted white flowers, and closed his eyes for a while.

For a moment he wondered how it would be if someone were beside him to share the water and the sky and the silence. Then suddenly in his daydream he saw himself in his university classroom, seated beside a classmate who had always been friendly to him, in spite of M's reserved demeanour. Often the boy had offered advice, or to lend and share books. He had asked M, more than once, if he'd seen a certain film, or if M had ever used the swimming pool on campus, but before he could invite him to join, M had make awkward excuses to escape to his hostel room and the company of his books. Then one day the boy ran after him and told him he'd received a parcel from home with bread, biscuits, fruit, nuts and sweets which were hard to come by in the city and expensive too. Would M like to share a meal with him, right there on the campus, that day? M abruptly refused. After that he felt the boy had begun to withdraw.

But now, in the sunlight, he began making all sorts of plans for his return – he would make more of an effort with his classmates, and though he knew himself too well to think he'd ever make overtures to strangers, he would at least respond to the friendly gestures of others. But before he left and packed his bags, he was going for another dip in the lake. And when he went back to university, he would enrol for swimming lessons.

SIX POEMS

Paul Abdul Wadud Sutherland

White Deer In Bradgate Park

For Ayesha-Nur

Among groomed copses on trampled, bracken hills
that unfurl this way and that, with criss-crossing paths,
the white deer forage under a single tree. Their antlers
rise v-shaped towards a Spring day's prolonged blue
while their heads browse new greens in partial shade.
One, shy, absently, throws a dark-eyed glance at me.
'I'm safe, in this enclave, from your hounding world.
Here with my fellows, for hours we frisk, in innocence
hoof time, feign wounds, or lie prostrate as if a Muslim.
My whiteness has incited wonder and love; the humble
on quest, entranced in pursuit, dared torrents and cliffs.
Don't believe, I lack power to startle, if I look subdued.
My heart's weak, ready to break; I can't trot at your side
if you're kind you might see to whom — each night — I fly.

Swans on Kielder Water

The ochre borderland dips. Under greenest larch
on the water, white and trumpeting adults glide,
with heads raised, unseen, giant paddling webs
manoeuvre. Across an inlet swans crowd, idle
camouflaged but for their chatter, their beaks'
whooping horns among first light's reflection

Many, many more know the secret rendezvous
where to dive from the clouds, where to angle
towards earth, to gather. Alert to invading steps
half the company shrills alarm. They lift wings
to flap and flap as if against the solid water's pull
nothing could ascend. Yet snake necks straighten
to a flight of spears; wingtips slap with aching beat
till water gives and warning creatures rise to touch
– down in a more remote bay to speak their wisdom.

Three Birds of Prey

Three birds of prey
yesterday and today
high-pitched rotating

perhaps thunderbirds
with soul-signed wings
thermalling on my fears

or lusting after something
mantled by cumulus
that predicted a squall.

Frail rainbow through
a stone-split windscreen –
the second predator.

The first shirked-whined
patient not-stooping
on a little bird below

the day before over
a river-bank farmer's
ingathered ochre field.
The second above A1

spotted going south.
The third marauder north

my summer turned ice
the gyring talon searcher
billowed its feathers to flee

or give word to a lost other.
I looked long, drove slow
but never understood.

Miniatures from London

in Gatwick's flight path
lime green Parrots squeal in
and out of foliage –

*

only at twilight –
so many homes to serve –
this Blackbird's song

*

along the canal path
under sweet Acacia – a kid with a hoop

*

a white Rose has climbed
a Sycamore to see over
the railway wall

*

through bare seed-globes
a young Gull perches atop
Cleopatra's needle

*

glittering Thames
finds a stony shore
at Queen's Wharf

*

in Green Park, plane trees
bow under the strain
of holding up the sky

*

'In rooms of oceans'
a million fish suspended —
who can number them?

*

flourishing Milk Maids
at a glance a shy cosmos
in black holes of green

*

a discoloured stream
a tiny school shimmers through
summer shallowness

*

a green turban's brooch
one white blackberry flower
delighting in space

*

the meeting of trails
pretends without a signpost
every way is home.
Our path dies: it's sweet
to be condemned by a view
stretching to Allah.

Sawing

Creating falls of
dust — strenuous cutting
before snow begins

back and forth my limbs
sore and sawdust disperses
a golden-light rain.

The squall-weighted gale
staggers away — Orion
enlightens the sky

crescent — lifting off
its lunar back-side —
one star its witness

each male and female
serene in the duck pond —
a moon preening

indigo-crimsons
scintillating right above
a shimmering Birch.

Jet-streamers through blue
appear like some of mum's
long knitting needles.

Her knotted fingers
no longer kit a cardie
or write a letter.

She washed my brown hair
so calmly once — with me stretched
on the draining board.

Children rampage home
toward dismembered families
to dream of snowmen.

Along the B Road
rotary knives a-buzzing
leave mangled saplings

clouds give birth
instantly
Gulls in the wind.

Bare branches
of the rose — bloom
in winter moonlight

a child's bare bum
straining for relief
in an A1 lay-by

nearby – wiggling
on an Apricot
diamond buds

each so many miles
a car-driver's monument –
greyed wreaths, black skid marks.

An east wind chases
sawdust from the grooves
in the Cedar bark.

Atop
a Kilmarnock willow
crown of Sparrows

across
a hearse's rear windscreen
procession of Doves.

My hands mellowed
from sawing – the pruning steel
begins chanting

Walt Whitman reaching
his seventies began to sing
Allah Allah Allah.

From his log-burner
fragrances of Crab Apple
mingled with Date Palm.

Through frosted panes
like Bumblebees
yellowest Jasmine.

timber-dust swirling –
rain-pearls dripping
off Holly berries.

As if vaporous
a Roman Arch's studded stones
sometime move

the neighbour's baby
arrives
with midnight wails.

A timeless lady –
before fading from this plane –
murmurs she loves me.

What 'I' flits the womb
days from its own vanishing
at its first breath speaks?

She rescued loving
from chaos, contemplating
beyond here and now.

A treak
the blessed Hawthorn yields
to my exhausted blade.

On the repaired spire
an assortment of Pigeons
re-form to gargoyles

camouflaged snipers
traffic wardens sneak around
targeting soft cars

ex-soldier's cat
on a lean-to's roof — Venus
idles on the west wall.

Scraping off moss's
gold fur — the heart wood's the tint
of a Red Setter

snow closes in round
the Hunter — only nearby
Sirius glistening.

A Fig leaf
of a cloud distances
the winter sun.

I fan from a vase
Primulas with droplets
on their mauve petals.

My saw horse snorts and
squeals — wrestling it open
for another bout.

The empowered teeth's
flighty atoms — thick flurries
of a hand-saw's thrust.

the wood-forager's
muddy pathway stretches of
this morning in white

pink veins
of cabbage
snow-freckled

now the birth-giver
brings her son in a snowsuit
to the panting car

now the bed-bound dame
who gave me leave for one kiss
dreams from her ashes.

Atlantic salmon's
pink blush – inside
a Hawthorn's sawn limb

all that steals our breath
and we half understand is
nothing to what Is.

The Ascent

By a stratified ditch the bridleway narrows. You and I walk on Hajj this
afternoon fasting through sloe-berry mist with hawthorn and wild roses.
One prickly stem catches my prayer hat. I return to retrieve its Prophet
(saws) green. We climb the muddy path with a few birds flitting as if
between two Islamic traditions. Ochre, yellows, foxy brown, reds and
orange: leaves collect underfoot. No shuffle today. Who'll walk tomorrow
and hear their crispness? A robin convoluted branch to branch by the
waterless trench. The mist deepens. Yet the wind blows and leaves fall; the
way narrows and shrub limbs worry your coat with its house keys in a
zipped pocket. Neither of us properly booted. The hill's dampness oozes
inside; we step around horse-hooves' imprints. We trudge from the valley's
stillness to the top's ideographic gate with wooden planks; a windy peak. Yet
the mist stays unmoved as if waiting and you and I are unashamed to feel the
cold. An out of season pink flower can't give a perfume on our short Hajj.
All this is Allah's we remember. Then easily separate as if this climb was
isolated against the unseeing terrain that through Him sees everything.

   We've left the seventeenth century stone houses and the thatched roofs
of the village – the near empty, the noisy – and taken an upward track
wishing a vista from the hill's crest; but denied all but a hundred feet of

sightline into sheep or a few cows whose rumbling moos catch our wayward attention. We would long to arrive and are secretly disappointed to have to turn back towards the hamlet's predictability. Our limited vision, enclosed by expanded droplets, forces a quicker verdict of return and our need to pray, to do *sajda*, angled toward *qibla*.

What of nature? The passion in mist, in not knowing, catching only the smallest indicators of progress: red oblong rose hips or haws or a blackberry tangle – its fruit unpicked, or a sculpted tree – centuries carved to leave holes and eccentricity? Our ascent has no giant sky view planned, anticipated. If we'd walked on past twilight into darkness a moon would've broken through as a hazy traveller, hiding stars, would've tilted and rose and given light. But the haze disturbs us searchers. We want to see beyond; when beyond is denied – like the outcome of love. We only know to give ourselves to another, to take another cautious – sometime – step; our footfalls look impressive. We'll be able to clear our foot wear on return; we trust to return, to turn back and re-enter the patterned village, past Ivy House, under The Wispy, along side Manor Farm's cinder toffee blocks and Elizabethan windows, trust stepping back in time. We'd be surprised to walk out of our shoes into another age and place.

Similar an old man's broad brimmed hat and half a century of poetry in his black cloak pressing into the worn stones and mud and grassy middle with his walking stick. That pilgrim we could easily become. The one that didn't turn back due to the mist constricting his gaze – who studied the minor miracles in passing – a bird that zooms behind a trunk, of two trunks and remains songless as if the mist has stolen its voice, stolen the leaves' tremor, their swish and rustle. He sometimes walked on as if to endure the absence of vista was to accept death. I'm not sure why I should be frightened of death – he'd say – carrying his dream of one last poem, his best, his unwritten masterpiece. We are not him, neither of us impersonate that adventurer.

You say, 'you can go on if you want. I'm ok. Walking back on my own.' Your words lag in the trees like damp clothes suspended in the air. The grey with a hill's perhaps limit obscured with unseen promise. What's beyond that first up-lift's rim, more ascent or a careering descent, a plunge to a river's squashy sides? But I can't leave you to return alone; my Hajj has changed; slipped out of mist into interior worlds and vistas. I wonder how you would really feel stepping back down the narrowing way, unaccompanied by me, would you feel abandoned? Coming to the orange binding twine gate, where the rocky floor emerges from the mud – a firmer platform for return. I return with you, leaving the marked un-visualised prospect to another day. Yet bending back, hoping to avoid this time the pitfalls of the ascent, the hat snatching limb – to mention one or to be aware of what passed first time without much interruption of thought, the way back becomes miraculously the way ahead to a new set of probabilities. There is the expectation, already in *sajda* while gingerly keeping our feet; already the prayer mat's laid down in the small living room – waiting for us should we return or more properly arrive within the time accepted. The downward wandering becomes another kind of secret ascent – as hidden as what's beyond the mist that yesterday or tomorrow we might imagine to see. If I was asked why didn't I strive on alone that calm grey day, I would reply for love I returned and for love she allowed me to return, to walk hand pressed in hand as if we were our own leaves in a book. Calm grey implying that the passage to the next level though concealed, out of focus, was open, ready to welcome me. How many times the heart comes to the stile and turns back. It's colder up here than in the house-scattered village – compact in its manner. It chills our wrists though two black and white cows stroll without protection and the red and blue dyed sheep graze; chase and butt and ignore and spy us as what shapes – friend or enemy?

We turn round without re-tracing our steps. We know that illusion. Yet the opportunity hangs in space – a banner flapping mid-sky. Something else we've given up. I'm not sure if it can be recovered or has passed and must be found again on another day. I know there's peace at the threshold, a promise waiting inside as if our Hajj was completed, shortened for our sakes, made bearable and homely but still awe-fulfilling. We take off our coats and you your colourful wool wrist warmers and me my long green scarf – as if we have stumbled on arrival, without separation.

H2O

Tommy Evans

Study my game
I flow like blood in your veins
I'm puddles and rain
Thudding your pane
A deluge flooding the plains
I'm a lake underground
Grey cumulus clouds
Coming down
Accompanied by thunderous sounds
I'm jumping around fountains
Fires I'm dousing
When my high tide's rising
Guys are hiding on mountains
The vortex
Who's caught next inside of my down spin?
Down since prior to year nine hundred thousand
Peruse my movements
They're lunar influenced
I'm used for ablutions
My hue is translucent
Remove the pollutants
So my currents are clean
For mullet and bream
From the Gulf to my streams
My Gulf Stream engulfs steamboats
Hull to the beam
My colour schemes make waves
With multiple themes
I'm ultramarine

Green and sapphire bright blue
Moon light in my pools
A shining white jewel quite cool
Minus two degrees
An ice cube you see right through
Tsunamis and Typhoons strike soon
Life's cruel
Hand in hand with earthlings
We were working in tandem
Now they're worshipping mammon
Disturbing my balance
I'm hurt and abandoned
Lands deserted and barren
So scavenge and search
To quench your thirst with my gallons
Galleons gallop with a burst from their cannons
My surface is slalomed
By surfers and salmon
I'm Zam Zam
I grand slam sand banks
Cali to Cuba
Nuclear subs in my stomach
Spine carrying cruisers
Crude oil spoils barracuda
Halibut neutered
What's The Great Barrier's future?
Belize and Bermuda?
Pirates of the Caribbean:
Gangsters on waves
Like Francis Drake
Slave vessels anchored in bays
Ankles in chains
Captives anxious in pain
A vicious cycle entitled
The Triangular Trade
And we're still angry today

Demanding they pay reparations
But I doubt execs will pay them
You're The Big Boss?
I'm the Bosphorus
Coughing up octopus out of my oesophagus!

THREE POEMS

Michael Wolfe

Snap Shot: A Bend on the Yuba River

Water braiding down her wrists,
She spills lengths of the river at her lips
Just to keep up with it.

Others, downstream, kneel on boulders
Calling through the roar,
Grouped in twos and threes,
All of us drenched with it.

Still Life with Water Glass

Mercury, silver, lead of course, selenium and chlorine,
DDT, dioxins, PCBs,
The harmless (or not so harmless) fluorides,
Freon from a cast-off Frigidaire,

Sulfuric acid, sulfate, sulfites too in phantom traces,
Admixed to a spectral base
Of cellophane and fluorocarbons
From fifty million hair-spray cans a year

All dance together in a dark conjunction,
Spin tonight without even a ripple
Treading with me to your bedside table,
Who brought this glass while you were fast asleep.

All This

It's some great weight to have all this on loan, Sir —
Wheat fields breaking west from state to state
Bent down by thirst, stripped of lakes and ice caps
Backed up on bedded rivers drained and caved,
While mule deer patrol a hot Sierra
That half a life ago lay packed in snow.

All spring we set out starts in narrow rows,
Each weighing a half-ton on the palm —
Heavy futures riding on the outcome,
As promise rides the razorbacks of trout
And memory-laden salmon hurdle ladders
Bursting with orange eggs fatter than tears.

It is a lot to have upon one's platter —
This lack, these heavy absences gone missing
In the blindness of our want. Despite my part
In all this, which is certain, I still do hope
One day to see Your face, if just an instant,
Cloudy brightness freshening our canyon

The way after hard rains it used to do.

REVIEWS

POSTNORMAL FATHERS

C Scott Jordan

It seems rather fitting that I find myself trudging through snow, darkness, and the famous soul-biting wind of Omaha to see the latest work of Alejandro Gonzáles Iñárritu. The winters of the American Midwest, if nothing else, give one the sense that God, Mother Nature, or the Earth herself is quite mad at the human race. As the redness faded from my cheeks and my burning fingers reached for salty popcorn, I knew the discomfort I felt outside would be made no better upon the conclusion of the pre-show trailers. This film does not make its audience comfortable until several moments after one exits the theatre. One cannot afford to be comfortable at this time. Postnormal Times are not comfortable.

The Revenant at face value is a story of a man who survives a brutal bear attack to then seek revenge on those who killed his son and left him for dead. Could a story be more appealing to American audiences? Perhaps this is what drew me to see this movie! While Iñárritu's last film, *Birdman* (2014), was one of the best films I had seen in a long time, it is really curious why the Mexican filmmaker would chose such a subject as Hugh Glass. Glass is a nineteenth Century American frontiersman who famously survived and crawled to safety after being left for dead by his crew following a bear attack in modern day South Dakota. His miraculous journey was the subject of American West folklore and was immortalised in Michael Punke's 2002 novel of the same name; Iñárritu's film is roughly based on the novel. Punke's book was hailed as a classic revenge story, rugged, an ideal example of the American Western genre. Not exactly the calling of Iñárritu's worldly and complex style. Prior to *Birdman*, most Americans would probably confuse Iñárritu with Alfonso Cuarón or Guillermo Del Toro. Prior to *Birdman*, his works come from an international perspective tackling issues such as faith and Christianity or the struggles concerning justice with a Latino perspective. *Birdman* emerged completely out of left field. *The Revenant* came out of an entirely different stadium. Nevertheless, what remains throughout all of Iñárritu's films is a requisite of deep thought on the part of the viewer. I feel it is safe to assume he is not motivated to simply entertain predominantly white, American audiences. In this new phase of his career, we see a world in trouble. *Birdman* provides us with a society lost in complexity, riddled with chaos, reflecting on its own contradictions. Sardar's Postnormal Times on the big screen. In *The Revenant*, Iñárritu provides us with his attempt at a navigation of these worrisome times.

To set up our navigation, the film begins in a very weird place. Running water. Water, being a key element of life, is a fitting place to begin. From it rises trees, the Earth, and two humans. A father and a son. An almost unrecognisable Leonardo DiCaprio portrays the rugged Hugh Glass and Forrest Goodluck makes his debut as Hawk. Then there is something not of the Earth per say, their guns. A buck with countless delineation within its antlers, the tree of life made flesh. BANG! The unnatural sound begets our journey which will be rife with natural sounds of life's struggle. Nearby we see an encampment of men living in nature, yet slowly corrupting it, fires burning, the act of shaving, and the bundling of furs. The progression of morning is paused by the gunshot. John Fitzgerald (Tom Hardy) expresses concern over the unnatural noise to the authority figure of Captain Andrew Henry (Domhnall Gleeson). The ominous Other lurks all about.

The one unnatural sound launches countless arrows that lead the distant stomp of a herd of stallion's hooves. An endless and repetitive war cry plays first chair to the agonising cries and pleas made by the men under attack. The camera soars and swoops panning three hundred and sixty degrees. The audience is shown the entire world around, yet sees nothing. Suddenly the small eye the picture's view provides is not enough. Arrows come from ahead, behind, and beyond. All is insanity as the men seek to use the Earth to hide, seemingly, from the Earth itself which has launched this savage attack against them. Glass and Hawk explode onto the scene, running. The mission is to get to the boat. It is strange that Glass needs to keep Hawk so protected. Now it is apparent that the attack is by Natives and Hawk himself is a Native. This world is far too complex for such simple racism.

Captain Henry is unable to save the men under his protection; he is lost, drowning in uncertainty. The water rises as they make for the boats. The endless war cry rings louder, the arrows more frequent, the breathing heavier, dominating over the other sounds. It is important to note here that Glass leads his son to safety, yet remains behind him at all times. The perfect metaphor for the leader needed in postnormal times.

The Revenant, directed by Alejandro Gonzáles Iñárritu, Screenplay by Mark L Smith and Alejandro Gonzáles Iñárritu, Twentieth Century Fox: Los Angeles, 2015.

The story here is essentially a father's guide to postnormal times. The film is unclear as to the biological certainty of Glass being Hawk's father, one could take the opinion that Glass is merely an adoptive guardian to Hawk, yet this does not detract from his dedication to the youngster's well-being. Glass's role as a father is interestingly complicated. Hawk's face is scarred from burns whose receipt is slowly reviewed throughout. The simple metaphor is that Glass, like the misguided political view of America, is carrying the beaten uncivilised world into posterity. Glass cannot foresee a light at the end of the tunnel in this journey. He is just trying to get them to the safety of a nearby fort. He is coerced into being the father of this group of white men who look to only him to save them from the ever present possibility of another attack by the Arikara tribe. Hawk is Pawnee, a more peaceful, and thus unfortunately a dying tribe. Glass, not persuaded by a White Man's Burden, is attempting to save the Pawnee culture, one which he himself has adopted. The quest has a high outlook towards failure, and even upon reaching the fort, what then? Glass must embrace the uncertainty of postnormal times, attempting to not prolong ignorance, for ignorance proves to be fatal.

Fitzgerald, likewise, is a sort of father. Let us call him the father of ignorance and Postnormal Lag. Fitzgerald takes the young Bridger (Will Poulter) as his son, corrupting him with the old paradigms that are slowly crumbling at the end of an epoch. Fitzgerald sees all Natives, be they Arikara or Pawnee, as savages. He recognises labour not as a becoming of humanity, but a simple means to money, the only chance man has for wielding power over his destiny. His philosophy is every man for himself, that suffering is completely unnecessary, and that lying is justifiable. All of these will collapse in the face of uncertainty. Bridger, desperately in need of navigation, freezes during the Arikara attack. He latches onto Fitzgerald and falls subject to the sins of this involuntary father. Bridger is then tied to Fitzgerald's crimes and his world view. Bridger must love thy father and refuse to accept the breaking paradigm Fitzgerald is faced with, that will sink both of them in the depths of ignorance.

Captain Henry is the false father. This is the father that we demand our governments and various subscribed organisations to be. The tragedy being that they are at the mercy of experts and public opinions, both subject to the damning fate of chaos and inevitable contradictions. Henry cannot save his children, his men. His faith in his own leadership and dedication to the military system cannot allow him to undo what has occurred. He is faced with the same problem of the false fathers in the real world. Governments and organisations have a real challenge in accepting change, for it admits fault in their system and exposes the fragility of their holding of power. Chief of the Arikara provides a sort of antithesis to Captain Henry. He is motivated, and thus his tribe, to find his daughter. He remains true to his identity but embraces the advantages of the white man's guns and horses. He even goes through the trouble of learning their language. His defiance of ignorance provides a potential for all the false fathers as they face tomorrow's uncertainty.

This film is a story of the convergence of these various fatherly techniques and gives us an interesting experiment in postnormal times. This convergence is wrought with confrontation, the most noticeable being that of Glass with the Grizzly Father.

My own father's view of bears is greatly influenced by his Cold War life. The bear was the ever-wandering ball of furry power in the forest. The Soviets. The Reds. May the democracy eagle kill the communist bear. In my own life time, bears have gone from pacified cartoon to force of nature. I grew up with Winnie the Pooh, Yogi Bear, and Baloo. All of them playful, dim-witted, and generally harmless. Theodore Roosevelt's dream of the friendly bear realised. They were natural beings, something to be saved along with the rainforests and abused pets. Then came Werner Herzog's *Grizzly Man* (2005). This documentary was fuelled by the spirit of saving nature and respecting its beauty, but taught us a valuable lesson. Nature is wild and we walk in its territory, are bound by its rules. America has no lions or tigers. The bear is the king of the American jungle. So why not let it be the natural father in Iñárritu's art?

Glass scouts ahead, looking for a path through the uncertainty before the men he has been chosen to lead. His breath is wild, that of a natural beast, ever watchful. Then we hear a strange noise, followed closely by a ruffling in the foliage. Two young bear cubs are at play. Glass freezes. He knows something that is far from uncertainty and the audience also knows what is to come next. For when there are children at play, a parent is never far. Based on the size of Glass's rifle, it will be hard for him not to be perceived as a threat. Again the camera takes us on a three hundred and sixty degree move. My eyes desperately tear apart all of the empirical data. Where is it? And then we hear it, a shrill, yet bellowed growl. Glass freezes. We are not the masters of the world as we once thought. Then the trees hurry to get out of the bear's way as it approaches. Once its view sees Glass, the defensive attack comes. The attack is two phases of agony, strain, and destruction of the body. It literally appears to be the classic man-versus-nature conflict. But this film is not about man versus nature. Battle always has an objective, a gain. Neither man nor nature gain from this battle. Instead this is a film that watches man conflict within man himself. As man corrupts nature, it devises a way to destroy him. Nature retains a position in the background, yet remains an active force, a character of sorts. Nature is the unchanged because it is in constant flux.

The tragedy of this film is that the conflict is amongst fathers. Like a father-son picnic, the winner of this competition is not dependent on who loves the most, who has the most innate fatherly prowess, or some other sense of the romanticised parental bond. It is mostly dependent on blind, dumb luck. Neither Glass, Fitzgerald, Henry, the Arikara Chief, nor the Bear are heroes in this story. They are also not anti-heroes of each other. Their conflict is superfluous and entirely accidental. These characters only converge due to the ignorance they all bear and in their fashion of approaching the uncertain future. Had the Arikara Chief's daughter not been kidnapped, their attacks would not have been so vicious. Had Fitzgerald not been the victim (or perhaps survivor) of an attempted scalping, his ignorance would not have ran so rampant. These major ignorance-fuelled actions propel the narrative; indeed, they are the original impulse of the story. In postnormal times, the heroes (or the close approximation of such) are not characters challenged to overcome a conflict that tests their being. Instead, these characters are faced with certain destruction, a force that we are the antagonist against. In *The Revenant* this is encapsulated in the concept of breath.

A vision of Glass's wife speaks to him during a dream. She says: 'When there is a storm. And you stand in front of a tree. If you look at its branches, you swear it will fall. But if you watch the trunk, you will see its stability.' The wind and breath are these invisible forces that appear to have minds of their own. They are the continuity of time in postnormal times. While they contribute to wonderful sound mixing in the film, they give us a hint at the truth at play in the film. Breath has often been important to theology. For instance, Yahweh, the Hebrew word for God, is also the phonetic approximation of a breath. The Sufis say 'Huwa, Huwa' — the breath that spells 'He is He'. God breathed life into Adam. In the singing of Judaism and Christianity, and *zikr* (remembrance of God) in Islam, God is praised in the supernatural utterance. In this film, as in reality, it is life or death. This utterance is a force, the contra to the Earth's wind. A resistance. Ignorance on the other hand is a corrupted breath, a force that plunges the agent into deeper uncertainty and probable annihilation in postnormal times.

The film makes a point of revenge. It would be hard for the viewer to make a case that this is a revenge story. Yes, revenge is sought out. Yes, from certain perspectives it is obtained. But this is not a revenge story. Rather, this is the deconstruction of the concept of revenge. Revenge presupposes justice and morality. In other stories, revenge is taunted as a hollow victory. Here revenge is looked at through a higher lens. Various characters refer to revenge being that of God and God alone. This reference brings to light Gandhi's quote of the blinding result of an eye for an eye justice. In the end, it is just a balancing of debits and credits, not between humans, but in general for the Earth. Wind versus breath.

One of the closing images of the film leaves us with running water charging through a tundra landscape, but now a massive blood stain dements the water's bank. A stark image. Hauntingly impermanent. For wind, water, and a fresh snow can return it to the beauty at the film's start. These are the stakes of postnormal times. The old concepts make less and less sense in practice. The sand castles that have been constructed for protection from the almighty wind are being revealed for their true natures. A deeper thought must be taken into the breaths we take. No amount of three hundred and sixty degree camera pans can reveal the whole truth. The truth is not simply empirical, but requires the second degree of reflection. Ignorant breaths will be defeated by nature's wind.

As the audience exits the theatre, back into the cold, uncertain world of winter, now recognisant of our breaths in a deeply subconscious way, we (whether we are aware or not) are challenged. How will we make our breaths?

TIGHTROPE WALKERS

Samia Rahman

Recently, I came across a photo essay in *The Calvert Journal*. A stunning array of earthy and breath-taking images brought alive the vanishing art of tightrope-walking in the mountain villages of Dagestan. The celebrated tradition had once flourished in this isolated region in the Caucasus but is dying out with the passing of time as younger generations are drawn away from the remote and rugged landscape to seek new lives in big cities. Some venture as far as Moscow, lured by the promise of opportunities otherwise unimaginable in this harsh terrain dominated by nature's unforgiving force.

Alisa Ganieva is not a tightrope-walker, but is similarly gifted with a rare talent to suspend disbelief and traverse gaping chasms. Brought up in the capital of Dagestan, Makhachkala, Ganieva mines intimate knowledge of her homeland. She combines this with the sophistication of a wordsmith who confesses to identifying firmly with Russian culture, while acknowledging the rich traditions of her Avar Dagestani roots. Young, educated and urban, she completed her higher education in Moscow, where she continues to live and work as a literary critic and journalist. It is from this objective distance that she conveys the stark reality of life in the Caucasus in her well-crafted work *The Mountain and the Wall*, the first Dagestani novel to be translated and published in English. Although this is destined to be the book that catapults Ganieva onto the international literary scene, she is in fact already an established writer, impressive for someone yet to enter her third decade. Her first published title, *Salam, Dalgat!*, won the Debut Prize in 2009. With a flair for literary playfulness, she chose to write under the pseudonym Gulla Khirachev. Amusingly, Dagestani literary circles immediately guessed that this was not a real name as 'Gulla' translates into 'bullet' in Avar. Subsequent frenetic guesswork and speculation as to the true identity of this lauded new writer ensued. However, the 'guess who' game neglected the possibility that the mystery author could actually be female. It was not until Ganieva stepped forward to accept her award that it become apparent that this was written by a woman, much to the literati's great surprise. *Salam Dalgat!* is considered a thoroughly masculine novel with an authentic male (dare I say, misogynistic) voice. The gritty, almost vulgar dialogue and keen observations that enable the reader to glimpse everyday life on the streets of Makhachkala through the eyes of the male protagonist, Dalgat, offer a clue as to why Ganieva opted to write under a *nom de plume*. Social convention in Dagestan deems it unbecoming for a female to be wandering male-dominated spaces in public, engaging in casual banter with men, whether familiar or strangers. In a nod to the constraints of society and with an expectancy of the discussion that the unveiling of her identity would entail, Ganieva managed to orchestrate a perfect storm that was in itself a social commentary on the machismo that characterises Dagestani society as well as the rise of religious conformism.

Persisting with the themes that permeate her first novel, *The Mountain and the Wall* sees a progression in the maturity of Ganieva's technical style. Emotions override sense as she lavishly employs magical realism to access a deeper understanding of reality. The plot revolves around a rumour that has gripped the Dagestani capital. A wall is to be constructed along the northern border with Russia. The wall is never seen, confirmed or denied, but symbolises the fractious relationship between Moscow and its Caucasian cousins. As Ganieva is no doubt aware, residents of the Caucasus who uproot and move to Russia suffer appalling discrimination, restrictive red tape and outright hostility. The region is perceived in Russia to be a hot-bed of Islamist violence and backwardness. It serves the central government's agenda to depict Dagestan as being in thrall to Islamic extremism, which, it is speculated by the Dagestanis in the novel, to be the reason for the wall's construction. The book's sometimes homogenous depiction of those who identify as Salafi, does little to problematise this view, lumping all the 'beards' together as one entity. Walls symbolise not just annexation but the barriers between individuals and ethnic groups: everyone is in a panic about something that is talked about with great certainty and fear, yet appears to be without evidence. Donald Trump advocates building a wall to keep out Mexicans. East European countries fence off their borders to stop desperate refugees from entering the

Schengen area in Europe. Israel continues to strangle the Gaza strip with its wall as well as other physical and trade barriers. So Ganieva's wall is a timely political construct and yet the preponderance of hierarchies and binaries belies a profound uneasiness in locating the centre of power in Dagestan, whether cultural, political or religious.

Over thirty ethnic groups, each with their own language, reside here. In echoes of Dostoevsky, Ganieva employs multitudinous raucous voices drowning each other out and talking over one another as testimony to the competing scramble for recognition and sovereignty that exists. For the reader unfamiliar with the socio-demographic make-up of Dagestan it can

Alisa Ganieva, *The Mountain and The Wall*, translated from the Russian by Carol Apollonio, Introduction by Ronald Meyer, Deep Vellum Publishing, Dallas, 2015.

be a bewildering read. Add the frequent use of un-translated Avar and Arabic terms and colloquialisms and *The Mountain and the Wall* becomes a slightly stuttering exercise that reads a bit like a semi-ethnographic study. It does, however, engage the uninitiated as we accompany our protagonist Shamil, a young journalist lurched out of a state of apathy to seek out the truth amid the wild conjecture. He navigates us through the rumours as all around him there is anarchy, with religious extremists seizing on the chaos and obsessing over the morality of people instead of offering pragmatic governance. In a personal sting, his fiancé, Madina, coolly jilts him for one of the 'beards' and starts to don the hijab, to the horror of her family.

What bothers Madina is the truth and justice she was promised is never realised. Instead, she is awoken regularly by the sounds of gun fire, the red glow of burning homes, and the screams of victims. She is happy to support violent action as long as it is directed towards the security forces and corrupt officials. She knits socks and sweaters for the Jihadis. Indeed, she 'was prepared to share everything she had with the *umma*'. But things changed quickly. First, her uncle is murdered by the *mujahideen* 'for some incautious remark'. Then, more and more family and friends get killed. 'What is going on,' she would ask her husband. 'Filth everywhere, there's no running water or electricity, and they're out persecuting perfectly innocent people.' Madina's disillusionment reflects Ganieva's own commentary on the hypocrisy and empty rhetoric of the religious militants as the promised utopia degenerates into dystopian chaos.

Madina, like the other female characters that we beguilingly glimpse but never meet in any depth, is viewed within the prism of a deeply misogynistic community. Religious fervour offers no protection to this searing treatment of women but even the secular Shamil is by no means innocent. His friends mercilessly objectify Amina and Zaira, two seemingly naive girls who are soon out of their depth, and ultimately, Shamil is not a hero.

It is apparent that Salafi intoxication in her homeland is deeply troubling for Ganieva, whose sympathy lies with the Sufi-inspired traditions of an imagined peaceful past. There is only a hint at the complexity of this romanticism. After all, Dagestani society was no less misogynistic and its leaders no less corrupt prior to the appearance of Salafi Islamism. Yet Shamil can only attain a semblance of clarity when he escapes the city to the mountain villages. It is deep within this mountain area that the novel's captivating dream sequence appears. On the mythological Holiday Mountain, the reader is offered a connection to a past where the people lived in harmony with nature. Nature has bestowed much of Dagestan with a forbidding yet beautiful landscape, one that has proved crucial in the country's historical highs and lows. Indeed, the country has no less than thirteen festivals a year, celebrating the cycles of nature – such as the winter solstice, festival of Mountain Skills, and the agricultural festival of First Farrow – as well as heroic deeds of history.

It is not without consequence that, nestled on the south-western shores of the Caspian Sea, Makhachkala was built as a fortress city, isolated by its breath-taking mountains and valleys punctuated by wistful waterfalls. The idyll belies the reality of a Muslim population standing at the cusp of modernity as competing forces of national government, imported Wahhabi influences and capitalism vie to replace the ebbing post-Soviet socialist experience. Ganieva grapples with these factors with varying degrees of success but, then, she is not an experienced tightrope walker. Artist Taus Makhacheva, the granddaughter of renowned national poet of Dagestan, the late Rasul Gamzatov, must have had Ganieva in mind when creating her latest video installation *Tightrope*. She features accomplished tightrope-walker Rasul Abakarov traversing the deep fissure of a canyon in the mountain region. In place of a traditional pole to maintain his balance, he carries in his hands works of art created by well-known twentieth century Dagestani artists. The camera follows silently as the art travels perilously over the abyss, impossibly safe in the hands of a man steeped in centuries of tradition. He embodies immeasurable hours of practise and dedication to perfect a skill in which he and his ancestors take great pride. But there is a vulnerability that cannot be fully negated. A triumph of the cultural past emerging out of the post-communist enclave to embrace a rapidly evolving present with a future that looks increasingly uncertain. Perhaps Ganieva is yet to fully perfect the tightrope of her own work. I think she is already almost there.

THE SEA, THE SEA

Rabia Barkatulla

The sea of my young self is calm. Yet, the purpose of depicting the sea in art and literature, it seems to me, has always been to illustrate its destructive power. As I devour the cultural gifts nature inspires, I find it endlessly evokes Turner's interpretation of slavery boats, or the pedestal for mighty ships from the Dutch golden age flexing their naval power. Only recently have the overflowing boats of migrants adrift on top of the sea surface fleeing conflicts from the Middle East forced me to avert my gaze. These images of the sea have entered the subconscious narrative of animosity towards Muslim immigrants, and I cannot help but feel uncomfortable. Perception of the sea is transformed. I ask myself if it can ever be reclaimed.

This is a question that also preoccupies the artist Hajra Waheed. What light could she, known for addressing cultural identity formation in relation to political history, popular imagination and the impact of colonial power, throw on the question? A mixed-media artist and 2014 winner of the Victor Martyn Lynch-Staunton Award, she generates existential questions imbued with complexities. The opening chapter of her visual novel, which exhibited in London in Spring 2016, encapsulates this talent perfectly. Waheed is no stranger to tackling intricate issues on high-profile platforms. Her work is well received internationally and she has featured prominently in numerous permanent collections including the Museum of Modern Art in New York, the British Museum in London, the Burger Collection in Zurich and the Devi Art Foundation in New Delhi. Born in Canada, she travelled to New York to study before returning to the country of her birth. Her previous works oscillate between loss and identity, including one that, for me, continues to resonate: the *Anouchian Passport Portrait Series (2010–)*. An ongoing project, this study in charcoal of

Lebanese men and women is taken from photographs of the Tripoli-based Armenian photographer Antranik Anouchian and held by Beirut's Arab Image Foundation. Waheed's series *The Missed* (2012) is also pertinent, comprising subjects devoid of identities. What we see before us are forgotten people, and the viewer is invited to write the story behind the image. It is hardly surprising, therefore, that she has been described as creating an 'index of the unidentifiable'.

'Sea Change', a body of work carefully constructed over five years, is described as a visual novel. I was unfamiliar with the genre, but a little research established that it is an emerging style. Originating in Japan where it is now prevalent, was borne from anime, the Japanese hand-drawn or computer animations. Consisting of non-linear branching storylines, a visual novel is often narrated from the first person perspective of one of the leading characters. I expect to witness an utterly unfamiliar concept but am intrigued to find that it has stylistic similarities to the neo-classical revival of Islamic Arabic prosimetric literature, the *Maqamah*. Widely believed to have been invented by the tenth century Persian author Badi al-Zaman al-Hamadhani, the *Maqamah* encompasses flourishes of poetic flamboyance interspersed with Arabic rhymed prose known as *Saj*. This wordplay is echoed by Waheed and I am greeted to a sight of slides, poetry, paintings and illustrations that spread out to fill the gallery space, comprising an arresting display of visual stimulus.

Tucked away on a corner plot in London's Earl's Court, the cultural space, The Mosaic Rooms, in which the opening chapter of 'Sea Change' is recreated, proves an intimate and fitting setting, perpetuating the themes that abound. The gallery is part of the A M Qattan Foundation's expansion of its Culture and Arts Programme, an initiative that has been welcomed by many Muslim artists in the UK, enthused by the organisation's aim to foster critical thinking and honour the rights of freedom of thought and creed. Mosaic Rooms first opened its doors in 2008 as a cultural centre located in West London, providing a platform for innovative and accomplished individuals destined to transform the artistic landscape of Arab communities. In this age of intense negativity surrounding the Arab world and its diaspora, Mosaic Rooms endeavours to showcase the rich cultural heritage that is so obscured, with the view that culture plays a vital role in facilitating cross-cultural dialogue and cohesion.

Hajra Waheed, 'Sea Change – Chapter 1: Character 1, In the
Rough', The Mosaic Rooms, London, 11 March – 21 May 2016

The premise for the first chapter of Waheed's visual novel is highly
original. It is with some skill that she enables the audience to visually
accompany her on a journey of exploration in the quest for quartz crystals
buried in sea rock. Quartz is renowned by advocates of alternative health
remedies for possessing healing properties and it seems this is not
insignificant. One of the most abundant minerals in the lithosphere of the
Earth, quartz is also closely associated with spirituality. It is expanses of
salt water across which numerous travellers have and will continue to risk
their lives in the hope of a better future. They are destined to be missed
and to become missing. To become fragmented. Waheed elevates such
symbolism without descending into cliché.

But you have to look closely to appreciate the nuances at work. There is
considerable depth in the detail. Just as the framed transfer paper obscures
blue hues and images of mountains on one wall, there is a struggle to see
how the threads weave the overall narrative together. I turn my head: on
the opposite wall, there are twenty-five framed drawings of gems in a
symmetrical square, in geometric detail entitled 'Gem Studies'. Another
set of frames depict step-by-step instructive diagrams of making an
origami boat. The beauty of the gem diagrams references the original
interaction with the sea around the Arabian Peninsula: that of pearl diving.
Dubai pearls formed the bedrock of the economy of the region before the
1930s. A dangerous and skilful art, pearl divers would visit oyster beds and
often be forced to shelter from storms on islets of the Gulf during their
arduous and protracted sojourns. Dubai is synonymous with naked, vulgar
capitalism, conjuring up an ideal that is as far removed from nature's
beauty as is possible. Pearl diving is a reminder that this region once had
humble traditions that are lost in the shadows of skyscrapers and man-
made theme parks. The gems are a window onto a lost past.

I cannot escape the sense that what we are being asked to question is
gently confusing, but here, the artist informs me, is the grand intention
behind the 'story': where is the space for intimacy in our modern visual
culture? She explains that her intention is to direct us towards individual

stories within the larger, disjointed and almost fractured rendering of a subject like the sea. The show, she concedes, is necessary to re-imagining our natural landscape, 'I believe that in order to change our engagement with the world, we must be able to re-imagine it – not expect it to stay the same every time we have a glance. This is important in my work.'

Waheed is anti-reductionist. In the current mass-media portrayal of the sea as simply the set piece, the backdrop for the drowning of unwanted refugees, this exhibition has real engagement: charming gouache paintings examine the surface of the water mounted on brass and wood against the deep blue wall, which serve to transport the viewer; cut-out images of steam rising from steam boats and sepia-tinged old postcards focus our attention on history and distance; Polaroids are mounted on twice-punched yellowing notebook paper, giving the impression of deep study. There is an engulfing big picture that holds intricate details of symmetry and sadness. Refrains from poetry, as if lost from a letter in a bottle, litter the walls. Lines such as 'Forgive the confrontations with life's jagged edges' punctuate the photographs of the sea and coast nestled on blue-green faded paper. Old, typewritten text is inked underneath. The overall effect is nostalgic. In the classic style of Waheed, there are no crashing, dramatic and arresting moments, rather a searching familiarity pervades the exhibition.

It is poignant that around the time I visit the exhibition our modern culture of visual saturation saw Pope Francis join Instagram in an effort to package his holiness' brand image. Dramatic moments engulf his feed because the public has a disinclination to look closely at appearance. Contemporary artists such as Helen Sear work with the idea that 'arresting' images have become something of a trope. Her photography is a re-education into the post-industrial markings of human and synthetic marks on nature. It is where birdsong meets chainsaws. Hajra Waheed is similarly preoccupied with this disinclination, but has an altogether different approach. The sea is the protagonist here, boldly presented front and centre, not a backdrop to anyone or anything. She blends together human and natural elements. We are enticed to become lost in the mystery of the sea, but just enough to allow anyone studying the alternating pieces to project their own fears and contradictions on to its silent surface.

These human and natural elements are epitomised by the metaphysical properties of quartz crystals as Waheed strikes a balance with the scientific components of this mineral. Quartz crystals emit an unfaltering vibration and are considered highly accurate timekeeping devices, favoured even by the likes of NASA during space missions. Nature offers its very own instrument upon which the most sophisticated and complex technological innovations continue to be dependent. Quartz crystal is also an unrivalled conductor of heat, light and ultraviolet rays and is regularly utilised in the deployment of light through bends and across angles. It is with this in mind that visitors to the exhibition will immediately be struck by the dominant work of the main room. 'Studies from co-ordinates' seamlessly negotiates the cutting edge of scientific and technological breakthrough revealing that, at its core, man's progress relies entirely on nature's mercy. From a distance, I can see images of the moon. Walking towards the display, the lower set of drawings looks like the horizon. I refocus, and the whole group becomes clear: you are working your way up from the panoramic sea, and a closer look reveals the xylene transfer depicts clouds, mountains and the surf, captured in black and white in a circle that resembles a heavenly body. The other-worldliness is not lost on anyone who walks past it, as they are slowly made uncomfortable with their first assumptions.

The sea, as Waheed is careful to point out, requires re-framing. It has, she points out, no borders or divisions, so powerful is it that we are all, whether we like it or not, an integral part of it. The sea is perfect for exploration, both metaphorically and narratively, and with earnest navigation, its treasures can be successfully located deep within its and our own depths.

ET CETERA

ON THE GREEN, GREEN GRASS OF HOME

Merryl Wyn Davies

The bards and singers of Wales have always extolled the country's landscape of mountains hills, valleys and rivers. This land of my fathers (the opening of the official national anthem) is both 'wild Wales' and by popular appropriation 'the green green grass of home'. Wild or benign in myth and legend as well as real history this land is imbued with particular meaning: *hiraeth,* an untranslatable condition compounded of endless yearning, loving and longing, presence and absence that underpins one's relationship to home and transmutes it into a moral, even some say 'religious' landscape. To the Welsh our land is always old and little and oh so meaningful because it is history in every sense of the word and this history is an ever present witness to the belonging of this people to this place. The clouds of witness, all who have gone before, are ever with us and this being Wales they frequently shower and deluge us not only with rain but also with moral judgement. We are forever conscious of what Dylan Thomas dubbed the 'Thou shalt not on the wall' the fashion for prominent display of censorious moral texts as cautionary reminder to the populace of the certainty that their every activity is observed and known and therefore they better be as good as they should. The landscape too is witness. It records what we are and have done and urges us to remember and learn from our misdeeds – but do we? Or is this land I love acquiring the forgetting that is becoming the norm of the unfolding global relationship to the natural world?

It is an old stereotype, but one not lacking in abundant foundation, that any gathering of Welsh people will at some point burst into song. The repertoire of song extolling Wales, the Welshness we feel and its deep rooted connection to the beauty of our land is extensive. Contemporary bard of the people Max Boyce has summed up this national musical reflex: 'And we were singing hymns and arias/Land of My fathers/*A hed a nos*' (all through the night), and so we do if given the chance. The hymns and arias are taken from the standard repertoire of every male voice or ladies choir that every village town and institution in Wales used, by traditional obligation, to produce in abundance. There was keeping a welcome in the hillsides, which were of course resounding with the deeds of heroes who would not yield. They would by operatic aria speed your journey or by the rivers of Babylon sit you down to mourn the loss of home as precursor to kissing away each hour of *hiraeth* because it is *hiraeth* that is encoded in each and every note they sing. The old dispensation of the choir meets modern usurpation in the popularity among all classes of Welsh singers, formal or merely overly lubricated, of the Tom Jones classic 'The Green Green Grass of Home'. This pop ballad is appropriated to national service despite having nothing whatsoever to do with Wales – except being popularised by our Tom. It takes its place alongside its companion piece, the other great Jones classic, 'Delilah' – well if you think about it, which is not really necessary, the lyrics of the one explain those of the other, and since both are about bad behaviour meeting just deserts so you cannot deny how well they fit the moral landscape of the Thou Shalt Not variety which may be the real secret of their popular adoption.

How can I better explain the circularity and connectivity, the ever present relevance of *hiraeth* and its meaning? Well take the latest and freshest example. During one of my recent stalkings through Facebook I was confronted by some photos posted by a friend. In one a man alone, 'eagle eyed' like 'some stout Cortes silent on a peak in Darien' surveys the very image of wild Wales. He stands, legs akimbo, perched on a treeless bracken covered hilltop with the distant backdrop of the Black Mountains hazily in view. The picture bore the single identifier Gwenddwr. I looked. My heart leapt and my mind raced on.

In the mythologically historical and possibly real annals of Wales, Gwenddwr was the seat of Brychan, the sixth century king of Brecheiniog, a region of the modern day county of Powys, part of the great underpopulated centre of Wales. Brychan may or may not have been sainted but among his extensive progeny saints abound. The family business was not merely rule over territory, the business of politics, but also the spreading of faith, education and good works. Among the sons and daughters aplenty spawned by Brychan, twenty-four of each according to some accounts even more according to others, was Tudful (or Tydfil both pronounced the same: Tidville, the spelling being largely irrelevant though vaguely politicised according to nationalist predilection). On her way to a meeting with her father after one of her missions spreading the faith Tudful (I concede to the archaic preference) was martyred by unspecified pagans, marauding land gobbling Saxons or even, it is quietly rumoured, local Welsh (shame on them!). Tudful is one of the bone fide saints of Brychn's brood. The place where the enormity of her demise took place was named in memory of the deed and the sainted woman who is also remembered for her passionate love of education: Merthyr Tydfil it became. And that is the very place where I was born and have returned to reside. Indeed Tydfil's Well, said to mark the infamous spot of her martyrdom, is just a short walk from every front door of every house in which I have ever resided in Merthyr Tydfil. It used to be in the forecourt of the Post Office and the quaint dwellings that once housed the essential duties of communication are currently being redeveloped, rescued from dereliction.

My connection to Gwenddwr does not end with Tudful. Gwenddwr is the location on the marriage certificate of one set of my maternal great grandparents. Rebecca Mason married John Price in Court Gwenddwr in 1888. They lived, according to the census in Maesmynis, not so much a place as a locality. It is a secluded tucked away glorious valley, exactly hills resounding and green green grass abounding, which from his elevated vantage point must be part of the panorama my friend surveys in the Facebook photo. Having married the couple speedily decamped for the cosmopolitan environs of Merthyr Tydfil. There they had seven children the youngest of whom was my grandmother, Beatrice Maud, our Maudie *Fach* (little Maudie) my Nan, she who articulated the rules of the universe that had to be obeyed without need to resort to admonitory text on the wall – one look from her gentle and quiet indulgent yet indomitable eye was sufficient to make the point.

I will admit that until recently the full significance of this circle of connection was a mystery to me. I knew only the vague talk that Rebecca Mason and John Price had run away from the family farms to come to Merthyr. Having fathered seven children John Price, famed for his ability to plait horses' manes for grand occasions and my Nan's for ditto, died leaving Rebecca to raise her brood by dint of hard work. When my grandparents arrived Merthyr Tydfil was still bustling but no long the preeminent industrial hub it had been a generation or two earlier. This birthplace of Britain's Industrial Revolution had for a time been the largest producer of iron and steel in the world. It saw the first steam engine to run on rails and went on to make the rails on which much of the world's railways ran. Henry Bessemer, who developed the first industrial process for the mass production of steel, worked there pioneering his process that came to be known after his name. Widow Lucy Thomas looking for outlets beyond the ironworks opened the export of anthracite coal that made the fame and fortune of the South Wales coalfield and powered the steam age. Merthyr also led the fight for human dignity and democratic suffrage from the Chartist movement for expanded democracy, to the secret ballot, to electing the first Labour Member of Parliament, Kier Hardie. You may gasp at my claims for my home town. Its history is largely secluded from the annals of English history books. It acquires occasional passing reference in more modern history books thanks only to the efforts of local boys made professors of history thanks to the passion for education inherent in their birthplace (pace St Tydfil!). It gets overlooked not because its achievements are mythic and legendary in the sense of being imagined and exaggerated but rather because much of it was lived in the Welsh language, a closed book to English historians; and because it was at times too controversial to be opened to general view, a Chartist insurrection that held a major economic centre for an entire week and was put down only by military assault is never good news for any public and because as the Encyclopaedia Britannia so memorably used to say 'For Wales see England' — marginality is and long has been with us even when we were central to our own story.

My great grandparents were part of that long drift of population by which Wales colonised itself. This demographic shift is what left the centre of the country largely devoid of population, except for sheep. Three quarters of the population of Wales today live in the valleys that run north-south in the south eastern quarter of the country comprising what used to be Glamorgan and Gwent. My forebears moved no more than approximately thirty miles from Maesmynis to Merthyr and in that small move shifted into another universe. From a sheltered and secluded valley they emerged to enter another kind of wild Wales. They lost themselves among the inhabitants of the furnaces, residents of the bleak and blackened environs of the ironworks that ran cheek by jowl with coal mines and ironstone quarries. The nearest ironworks to John and Rebecca's dwelling was just up the road from Tydfil's Well. The great Cyfarthfa Works, once the world's largest producer. Like all the other iron works it spewed out flame and fume twenty-four hours a day every day of the year, illuminating the night sky and spraying its smut over everything in the vicinity making the urge of cleanliness that is next to Godliness and inseparable from Welshness an unending round of constant war on futility.

From upland farms in the bracing air and green and golden valleys came the people of Wales to the brimstone fumes and fires of blast furnaces and the groaning dark and dangerous underground of the coal mines. Is it any wonder they brought *hiraeth* with them? Exiled in these dark places of yearning and heartbreak they rebuilt a culture of poetry and song, a chapel culture that inscribed a new moral landscape with longing for social justice and strove to make it so. The sense and feeling of their belonging acquired continuity of meaning, its agenda and application changed with the difference in the landscape that now enclosed them. And yet what so few who do not know the valleys of industrial Wales where degradation was and is an ever present moral threat fail to appreciate is that the green green grass was not absent from this environment of hard labour. Above the row on row of terraced housing perching on hillsides above narrow valley floors with their rivers turned to murk there remain higher hillsides leading to the *hafods*, the summer pastures, where sheep roamed free, and amble yet. When I was young 'winter, the old drover' regularly would send mountain ponies and sheep to topple the bins in every back lane. Every spring we would take a walk up some narrow lane and emerge onto a windswept bracken clad upland to breathe fresh air and blow away the cobwebs of the town. The absence that people exiled from their ancestral farmlands craved was present and part of who we became.

The people of furnace and pit worked to make a living as the world changed and worked to change the world in which they lived. But what did they sing? They sang of their land and their belonging and reflected on the change in their physical and moral landscape. They sang of this 'old land of my fathers' (*Mae hen wlad fy nhadau*) 'so dear to me' (*yn annwyl i mi*) which in the words of our national anthem is paradise to its poets. *Paradwys a bardd*, the paradise of the poets and the beauties in every valley and cliff that are the proofs of paradise are referred to in the second verse of the anthem, which we don't sing. What people ever know the second and subsequent verses of national anthems? The first verse, which is sung at every opportunity, gives mention to warriors and patriots, those our imagination is left to conjure from myth and legend or even real history, who spilled their blood for freedom. The third verse, seldom if ever sung, recalls the enemies who trampled the country underfoot and references treasonous acts that, as is so often the case, assisted the process. The chorus, which is invariably sung with gusto asserts our loyalty to this land (*pleidiol wyf i'm gwlad*) for all the reasons mentioned so far and ends with the heartfelt crescendo (*O bydded i'r hen iaith barhau*) may the old language – the Welsh tongue the vast majority of us do not speak – endure. For all the Anglicisation of Wales that was the legacy of industrial globalisation and determined English policy the anomaly, if that is the word I am searching for, is that Welsh people only know their national anthem in the old language, Welsh, like many of the songs they sing about their love of homeland. So one might say that in part the poet's plea has not gone unheeded – all that we know of the language is how the meaning of home can be euologised. And when we want to express what home and beauty mean to us we turn reflexively to the old language whether we understand it or not.

The Welsh national anthem was written in 1856 by Evan James and his son James of Pontypridd. It is essentially a reworking of ideas first articulated by Taliesin the ultimate and part legendary sixth century Welsh bard. According to legend Taliesin was King Arthur's bard. In his *Destiny of the Britons* he wrote: 'Their Lord they shall praise / Their language they shall keep / Their land they shall lose / Except wild Wales.' *Hiraeth* is that sense of being steeped in antiquity, the continuity of history and the permanent presence of a meaningful past that makes this old (*hen*) land of *my* fathers – there's belonging for you.

So what is 'wild Wales' and what is the connection to the green green grass of home? Being pedantic, even in the sixth century the landscape of Wales was shaped by human hands. We speak of the natural world but nature has been doing the bidding of human husbandry for millennia. Whether animals roam free or the earth is tilled, how humans made their living has left indelible marks on the land. Of course, it is always possible Taliesin was reflecting on how the weather, of which we have a great deal in Wales, interacts with the landscape. What does anyone know of the wild until they have struggled up or down hill and vale in horizontal rain! And the rain is not just simply horizontal. In proximity to persons it slants curves upwards working its way beneath waterproof cover of every kind to ensure total saturation to the bone – now there's wild for you. I suspect, however, that what was wild about Wales in Taliesin's vision of destiny is that it would remain beyond the bounds of marauding colonisation, that it would be free to make itself according to its own dictates, not tamed and domesticated to the power of others.

Wales: the land of quiet farming outposts dispersed around green and golden fields and hills where sheep would safely graze, where people formed fervent yet quietist dissenting communities to praise their Lord, who was no earthly potentate but an Eternal Ruler was another time of our history. When the novelist Daniel Defoe visited my valley he noted only a leafy wooded place 'through which a pleasant river runs, the Taff.' It was said that at the time a squirrel could go from south to north along the valley without setting foot on the ground. This age of sylvan amplitude gave way to a moral landscape and people forged by fire and fume and dark who tasted the peril and suffered the turmoil of a global industrialised world. My valley was despoiled. The green green grass turned grey, each autumn the bracken rusted as our iron never did and new hills grew to reshape the landscape. The white waste of the furnaces and the black waste of the mines made small mountains of their own. The trees diminished and disappeared, leaving the bare bones of hillsides sparse and spare. And yet the poet could search for and find the Taliesin's old connections in their new destiny even as they dug for coal in the permanent dark of the mine.

Huw Menai, his bardic name, was born in North Wales and came to
Merthyr Tydfil to work as a miner. I love his poem 'Pieces of Coal':

> Pieces of coal, hewn from the deeps of earth,
> Here in my hand, spectra of lights retain;
> Crystal on crystal knit, back in its birth —
> Sun meeting sun again.
>
> Shall I, when finished with this worldly pain —
> When of the sleep of death I am partaker —
> Shall I ascend from earth, a soul again,
> To meet my Maker?

To one that knows coal it is an amazingly tactile material. Years of setting
the coal fires before the arrival of central heating in my valley, let alone my
household, gave me an appreciation of the spectral lights that flash and
sheen upon the surface of black anthracite coal. I knew and loved the idea
of the poem before I discovered Huw Menai had lived locally. Should I be
surprised? Once upon a time in Wales all roads led to Merthyr. Then the
blight industry put upon the landscape became the blight that economic
collapse put upon the people. Cyfarthfa Works closed as iron and steel
making migrated to the coasts where its decline merely stalled a while. The
mines were in turmoil. In Merthyr, once the hub and centre of industrial
growth, the Depression years of the 1930s brought a British record of 78%
adult male unemployment. All that had been made with such effort left no
legacy of riches for those who toiled to generate the wealth. The moral
peril of the industrial landscape of which poets warned had come to pass.
As Idris Davies asked 'what is man the coal should be so careless of him/
And what is coal that so much blood should be upon it?'

There is *hiraeth* in every aspect of this story. For now that industry has
come and gone and come and gone again from my valley among my
generation there is a longing for a past that though wild and perilous was
proud and purposeful. You see, now the trees are coming back to
recolonise my valley. Every year more of the manmade hills are being
stripped away and their passing marked by freshly laid and ever so green
green grass. But hope and aspiration are drained from the people. The new

generations of young people feel themselves irrelevant to the onward march of the wider world. Globalisation has moved on. Now it is only the people who are left behind as the slagheaps of industrial futility – redundant. The moral peril of industrialism in all the wildness it spread created space to construct a world of praise, a vision of destiny beyond the limitations and perils of industrialism. It found language in poem and song that seem to have less and less hold and place in a tenable future. We have trees and glorious landscape but only *hiraeth* for the dignity of being constructive in our belonging to this land. As they sing about the green green grass of home in faux country and western accents young people in Merthyr are losing their sense of history, forgetting what they have never known. The clouds of witness are becoming ever mistier as they lose touch with the very concept that there might be ways to hope and work for bettering their life chances. If the Welshness of Wales is a sense of living in a moral landscape there is a growing perception that among the burgeoning beauty of our natural world we have flunked the test of the moral worth of our system of operating community. We are threatened with breaking the connection with our past as *hiraeth* hardens into genuine loss.

There once was Wales and it had such natural beauty. Now there is natural beauty but where will Wales be? What will the young people sing when they grow old? There is no moral purpose in under- and un-employment; only bitterness and the putting up of false barriers that generate new hates from the bitterness of exclusion. Not just in Wales are these the fears that come to haunt the landscape. Destiny beware.

ZIAUDDIN SARDAR'S TWELVE POSTNORMAL PLAGUES

I don't know about you. But I feel a bit unnatural. It has become rather unnatural to be an ordinary, caring, socially conscious human being. We ordinary everyday folk, who take for granted good, wholesome things such as community, tradition, looking after nature and each other, now find ourselves in postnormal times, where what we regarded as normal has evaporated and nothing seems to make sense. It is a period of contradictions, complexity and chaotic behaviour that brings us face to face with multiple, interconnected threats. The spirit of the age, *espiritu del tiempo*, is characterised by uncertainty, rapid change, insane technology, awesome scientific power, upheaval and deep, deep ignorance. It is a time when most developments are likely to lead to ruin, if not entirely over the edge of the abyss. So here are my twelve postnormal plagues, some already with us, some anticipated as lurking over the horizon, for you to contemplate.

1. Endless Progress

We must have growth, we must have progress, goes the mantra. And growth has to be perpetual, and progress has to be endless. That progress has become meaningless and gone mad is clearly illustrated by the patented systems for shaving one's facial furniture. The straight old fashioned razor that our ancestors used was first replaced by the safety razor. That certainly made shaving less hazardous. But it was soon replaced with single blade disposable razors. Then we had twin blade razors, and after that twin blades with lubricating strips. That was progress. But I would have stopped before the lubricating strip, which is horrible sticky stuff that makes getting a close shave harder rather than easier. After all, trees do not go on growing; they stop once they have reached homeostasis. But progress must progress – so we moved on to three blades, four blades and five blade systems – with gel protectors, lube strips, wobbly heads, and names like killer robots: Protector 3, Quattro Titanium, Fusion ProShield ProGlide/ Flexball, and Hydro Five Groomer. Soon, there will be more blades on a multiple blade razor system than the Ottoman army. Followed, quite naturally, by the Zombie Apocalypse, where, as we learn from 'The Walking Dead' and 'World War Z' everyone uses the old cut-throat razor without bothering to shave.

2. Corporate Greed

To call it corporate greed makes it sound like individual culpability, the failure of individuals within the system to exercise probity. It might run amok but such falling from the grace of prudential care and acceptable practice is just people being less than perfect. True, in some sense it is always people being less than perfect. However, ignore at your peril the fact that corporate licence is constructed and constrained to positively induce people to be bad – and that is the real plague that ails us. The requirement of corporate duty puts the pursuit of gain before, above and beyond any balancing of public duty, responsibility to community, society, nature or planet. Corporations exist to make money for select groups of investors – all else is mere PR and window dressing and therein lies the pestilential problem. The all else – how they treat their workers, how they share the beneficial bounty of profitability, what they sacrifice to ensure profitability, the impacts they have on community, society and planet – are the very things that determine the nature of civilisation, the refinement of moral values and ethics of organised existence. When all else is not part of corporate accountability and conceived as integral to how one does business, licenced greed and debauchery of community and planet is the way the world works. These corrupt institutions are blights on the face of humanity – for greed is insatiable, greed will deny, and greed will have you in chains to its rationale – end of story.

3. Privatisation

Privatisation is the impulse to transmute communal responsibility into sectional special interest, the giving over of public duty to private gain. This plague infects society with a Pontius Pilate hand washing. No longer is the duty of care for others a collective task, a cause to which we are all beholden and therefore all should be held to account to ensure the services, provision and resources necessary are provided for all. Privatisation means its someone else's job and what they do will be done because that's how they make their money. Folly? No something far more pernicious than folly to think that public need can be married to private greed and all will be well. Public duty privatised must generate profit first to exist whatever that means for services provided. Regulation, oversight, public scrutiny are nice ideas in ideal worlds but once Pontius' hands are wet a large measure of forgetting is normal.

4. Infectious Connectivity

That urge to grab your mobile even when there are no notifications; the desire to refresh your social media feed immediately after you have looked it over; a few sleepless nights spent consoled by a familiar screen. We do not fully understand the ways in which new technologies impact our all-too-human bodies, especially our brains, and the meteoric rise of smartphones and social media signals the advent of infectious connectivity, which is both a cause and effect of hyper-connective living. This plague has its extremes. There are those who believe that electromagnetic radiation, which emanates from all electronics, makes them sick, which has led some to live completely off the grid. For most, infectious connectivity is a means to navigate life in the modern world, but questions remain as to how this plague will affect future generations, particularly for those who grow up fully normalised to being connected anytime, anywhere, instantaneously.

5. Identity Theft

There is an instant price for all that connectivity. In the days of old, thieves would burgle your home, steal your property and valuables. But at least they did not have access to your personal and intimate information. But nowadays all our personal information is online and criminals have ways of accessing it. So now they steal your identity – that is, your very Self. Suddenly, you cease to be what you are and someone else is you – who is swiftly and happily emptying your bank account, applying for credit and mortgage in your name, taking over your house, and moving in with your spouse.

6. Packaging

The stuff you buy online comes in boxes, and boxes insides boxes, with cardboard wrapping to product the minuscule product inside, long, squiggly pieces of paper between boxes, and a generous supply of foam that is designed to stick to anything and everything. Getting the product out of the box is only part of the challenge. The real trial begins when you finally reach the desired object, which is often shrouded in military-grade indestructible plastic. You would be lucky to break through the plastic without doing yourself an injury. Then, of course, you have to get rid of all the packaging waste and you realise that it is actually worth more than the worthless object you bought online. Look at a bottle of a branded perfume and weep: the packaging and the bottle is worth more than the foul smelling liquid inside. Soon, we will need several planets as storage space for all the waste we produce.

7. Robocalls

The phone rings. You answer. It's a computerised auto-dialler delivering a pre-recorded message. Have you recently had an accident that was not your fault, are you about to retire and looking for an annuity, are you an illegal immigrant about to be deported: we have good news for you. In Britain, robocalls are usually made by pestiferous folks such as lawyers trying to make a quick buck from mis-sold payment protection insurance (PPI). But in Canada they have been used to misdirect voters to the wrong polling booth. In America political battles are fought through robocalls. During the 2008 election, John McCain used recorded robo messages to communicate Republican positions on various issues; Barack Obama, upset at McCain's robocalls, answered with a series of his own robocalls. Then, there are those vile automated answering services. Every self-loathing business has one. You ring to sort out an urgent problem, and a machine asks you to press 1 if you want this, or press 2 if you want that, or press 3 if you want the other... and, when you have eventually passed numerous hurdles, asks you to wait: 'Thank you for waiting. Your call is important to us. I'm sorry, but all of our operators are busy at the moment, but please stay on the line. Your call will be answered shortly'. While you wait and wait, your ears are pierced with what some tone-deaf person considers to be music. Just when you are about to run out of patience, there is a moment of relief: the music stops. And you think you are about to hear a human voice. No chance. 'Thank you for waiting. Your call is important to us...'. Finally, you are told to log on to a website. And to add insult to injury, the machine calls you back and insist that you provide feedback on their 'award winning service'. In the end, automated answering machines and robocalls leave you only with suicidal thoughts, and homicidal tendencies.

8. Selfies

Everyone is taking a selfie. It's the ultimate ego trip: the Self and the Ego dissolve into one in a selfie. If you can't find a suitable famous person or a 'celebrity' then you have to ensure that you have the right location, the right background and the right angle. No sooner has the selfie been taken, it has to be uploaded – to some contraption like Instagram, Facebook or Twitter – and shared with the world. Demented souls lacking self-confidence the world over spend, on average, five hours every week snapping themselves. Some have even killed themselves trying to get the right background and the right angle: standing on the edge of a cliff, posing on a track in front of a speeding train, posturing with a loaded gun. Selfie deaths are now said to be more common than shark attacks. There is even a Wikipedia page documenting selfie deaths.

9. All is for Rent

Having trouble paying your bills? Rent out a room on Airbnb. Still not making ends meet? Turn your car into an Uber at night and over weekends. If your struggles continue, rummage for something or make an item to sell on eBay or Etsy. Or, if you have one, you can sell your womb as a surrogate mother. Those not so equipped could sell their sperm, of course. It all began as nice, innocent idylls of a sharing economy, an alternative to a world ruled by greedy corporations. After the dream comes the nightmare. The rental, everything for sale, economy is now at such plague proportions that the only real answer is to start selling oneself. Accommodatingly, science will soon be offering the prospect of selling off oneself bit by bit, from slices of genetic information to slices of tissue and organs. The idyll has collapsed because building enterprises that serve, provide valuable service to, make things people want and need rather than merely stimulating desire for more things has gone the way of the dodo. To live in the economic dispensation of today and tomorrow we need ever more cash or credit generated by providing income to some financial corporation. To be a person in the estimation of much of society we need to consume – that is, accumulate – ever more things. The only way to keep pace is to rent or sell whatever we can at every opportunity. Why? In case you have not noticed the very concept of a job with a living wage, secure from robotisation, globalisation or privatisation and with a secure pensionable retirement is at one with the dodo aforementioned. In this world where everything is for sale or rent, nothing of real value remains.

10. Genetic Insects

First we had genetically modified (GM) food. Now here come GM insects. Insert a gene that determines the biology and behaviour into an insect and transform it into a transgenic creature which can make it fluorescent, or unable to reproduce, or resistant to particular pathogens, or whatever you like. The standard argument suggests they will be used to rid us of insect-borne diseases, such as malaria, replace nasty insects with less harmful ones, and generally improve the lot of human kind. But what if the GM insects establish another insect species, or develop strategies to select far more virulent pathogens, or the newly introduced gene transfers into another species? What effects will the GM insects have on human health, environment and ecosystems? What would they do to good old nature? Answers on an old-fashioned postcard, please.

11. DNA Editing

After insects, GM human beings. We now have the capability to edit your genes. There are things called TALENS, tiny molecular scissors that can cut and fix a broken gene in a cell. There is a highly accurate method of identifying precise positions on the DNA molecule called Crispr (pronounced crisper) which, with the help of an enzyme called CAs9, can be used to cut the double helix strands and replace them with synthetic DNA. The technology, we are told, will cure many genetic diseases such as sickle cell anemia and cystic fibrosis. No doubt it will. But then progress will take its course, and we will be editing all sorts of genes to produce all sorts of people. They are already producing 'milky white' babies in India. When it comes to eugenics, we have a strong track record, with some of our most prestigious universities leading the way. Harvard University's involvement with eugenics goes back to the nineteenth century when Charles William Eliot was the President. He was also the Vice President of the First International Eugenics Congress in 1912; and helped to organise the First National Conference on Race Betterment in Battle Creek, Michigan, in 1914. European universities have not been far behind. Given the emergence of the far right in Europe, the omens for DNA editing are not good.

12. AI

They already provide you with news, perform your chores, organise your life, put the baby to sleep, and sing you lullabies. It is not just computer language that computers now speak — they speak all languages. There's Apple's Siri, Amazon's Alexa, Facebook's M, Microsoft's Cortana, and Google's mobile search app. You can fall in love with their soft and silky voice just like the protagonist's of Spike Jonze's 2013 movie, *Her*. Soon, artificial intelligence will bore more deeply into your life and take over your work and employment, your emotional and sexual lives, dreams and desires, and watch 'every breath you take'. And not all AI will be as pleasant as Siri. Notice that it took just 15 hours for Microsoft's artificially intelligent chatbot, Tay, to turn racist and sexist. There could even be an AI that just doesn't like certain people — say left-leaning do-gooders, people of colour, or those nasty Muslims. Killer AI robots could do much more than just give you a close shave. No wonder, that august brain known as Stephen Hawking has declared that 'the development of full artificial intelligence could spell the end of the human race'. All these postnormal developments have one goal: to make human beings redundant — except, of course, the greedy corporations who will inherit the Earth. Everything will be terrifyingly convenient; and you will be good for nothing. In fact, you will be privatised, digitised, and controlled by some AI. Meanwhile, do you need to dry those tears of despair? Well, there's an app for that!

CITATIONS

Introduction: Out in the Open
by Jeremy Henzell-Thomas

Quotations from the Qur'an are based (with occasional alterations) mainly on the English translations in *The Message of the Qur'an* by Muhammad Asad (The Book Foundation, Bath, 2004; original edition, Dar Al-Andalus, Gibraltar, 1980) and *The Study Qur'an*, ed. Seyyed Hossein Nasr (HarperCollins, 2015).

On the outreach work of the British Mountaineering Council in facilitating greater participation in outdoor pursuits by members of ethnic minority communities, see, for example, www.thebmc.co.uk/mountain-muslims-bmc-holds-outreach-conference-in-birmingham, and bloominhealth.org.uk/2014/03/31/bmc-equity-symposium-2014-breaking-barriers/.

I have referred in this introduction to several of my own essays, articles and talks on Nature, including 'Walking in Nature: A Call to the Heart', *emel* Magazine, November 2006; 'The Festival of the Sacrifice: Surrendering One's Whole Being to God', *emel* Magazine, November 2009; 'British and Muslim: Holding Values to Account through Reciprocal Engagement', *Arches Quarterly*, Spring, 2011, 30-4; 'Spirituality and the Outdoors', keynote address, British Mountaineering Council Equity Symposium, Haworth, 30 March 2014 (posted on https://rumiscircle.com/2014/04/23/spirituality-and-the-outdoors/), and the Epilogue to *The Cosmic Script: Sacred Geometry and the Science of Arabic Penmanship*, by Ahmed Moustafa and Stefan Sperl (Thames and Hudson, London, 2014), 626-659.

The term 'Nature Deficit Disorder' was coined by Richard Louv in his book *Last Child in the Woods*, *Saving our Children from Nature Deficit Disorder*

(Algonquin Books, Chapel Hill, North Carolina, 2005; paperback edition 2010). *See* http://richardlouv.com/books/last-child/ See also Richard Louv, *The Nature Principle: Reconnecting with Life in a Virtual Age (Algonquin Books, Chapel Hill, North Carolina, 2011).* On the long-term benefits of adventure programmes, see Roland S. Barth, *Learning by Heart.* (Jossey-Bass, San Francisco, 2001), 50.

Research on how short-sightedness is reaching epidemic proportions was reported in the journal *Nature* in an article on 18 March 2015 entitled 'The Myopia Boom' and can be accessed at http://www.nature.com/news/the-myopia-boom-1.17120. For the OECD report on comparative time spent on homework, see D. Salinas, *Does Homework Perpetuate Inequities in Education?* (2014), accessed at http://www.keepeek.com/Digital-Asset-Management/oecd/education/does-homework-perpetuate-inequities-in-education_5jxrhqhtx2xt-en#page1. The report entitled *Play in Balance* (conducted by Persil) on the lack of time spent outdoors by children in the UK, and based on a survey of 12,000 parents around the world, was publicised in *The Times* on March 26, 2016 and discussed on the 'Learning Through Landscapes' website at http://www.ltl.org.uk/news/article.php?item=308.

Nick Robinson's apology for repeating the phrase 'of Muslim appearance' can be accessed at www.bbc.co.uk/news/uk-politics-22637048 and www.theguardian.com/media/2013/may/23/woolwich-attack-bbc-nick-robinson-muslim.

On Islamic principles of animal welfare, see Ruth Helen Corbet, '*Tayyib*: British Muslim Piety and the Welfare of Animals for Food.' *Muslims in the UK and Europe I*, ed. Yasir Suleiman (Centre of Islamic Studies, University of Cambridge, 2015), 67–75. On ritual slaughter on the occasion of Eid al-Adha, see Richard C. Foltz, 'Is Vegetarianism Un-Islamic?', *Studies in Contemporary Islam* 3 (2001), accessed at www.islamicconcern.com/isvegetarianismunislamic.asp, and Shahid 'Ali Muttaqi, 'The Sacrifice of Eid al Adha: An Islamic perspective against animal sacrifice', accessed at www.islamicconcern.com/sacrifice01.asp

Nafeez Mosaddeq Ahmed's views on the sanctity of the natural order are adapted from his 'Radical Political Dynamics of the Prophetic Model: Toward a Public Theology of Social Activism and Political Inclusion in Secular, Liberal Societies', a working paper prepared for *Contextualising Islam in Britain II*, Symposium 3 – 'Political Participation and Community', Prince Alwaleed Bin Talal Centre of Islamic Studies, University of Cambridge, 12th February 2011.

Visions of Man and Nature by James E. Montgomery

For the translations of The Story of Ḥayy ibn Yaqẓān, see: L.E. Goodman, *Ibn Tufayl's Hayy ibnYaqzān: A Philosophical Tale* (Chicago: Chicago University Press, 2003); and *Medieval Islamic Philosophical Texts*, trans. Muhammad Ali al-Khalidi (Cambridge: Cambridge University Press, 2005), pp. 99-154 (this version does not include Ibn Ṭufayl's introduction to his fable). For studies: S.K. Hawi, *Naturalism and Mysticism: A Philosophic Study of Ibn Ṭufayl's Ḥayy ibn Yaqẓān* (Leiden: Brill, 1994); L.I. Conrad (ed.), *The World of Ibn Ṭufayl: Interdisciplinary Perspectives on Ḥayy ibn Yaqẓān* (Leiden: Brill, 1996); A.W. Hughes, *The Texture of the Divine. Imagination in Medieval Islamic and Jewish Thought* (Bloomington, IN: Indiana University Press, 2004), pp. 13-81; Avner Ben-Zaken, *Reading Ḥayy Ibn-Yaqẓān. A Cross-Cultural History of Autodidacticism* (Baltimore, MA: Johns Hopkins University Press, 2011). The work by the Brethren of Purity is translated as *The Case of the Animals versus Man before the King of the Jinn: An Arabic Critical Edition and English Translation of Epistle 22*, ed. and trans. L. E. Goodman and R. McGregor (Oxford: Oxford University Press, 2009). For studies on their work, see G. de Callataÿ, *Ikhwan al-safa': A Brotherhood of Idealists on the Fringe of Orthodox Islam* (Oxford: Oxford University Press, 2005); N. El-Bizri (ed.), *Epistles of the Brethren of Purity: The Ikhwān al-Ṣafā' and their 'Rasā'il: An Introduction* (Oxford: Oxford University Press, 2008); my reading of this epistle is indebted to L. E. Goodman's 'Introduction,' in *The Case of the Animals versus Man*, pp. 1-55.

The quotations from the Brethren of Purity are from Goodman, p30, 40, 42; and from the Arabic edition pp. 278-279, 4, 42-43 – unless otherwise indicated, all translations are my own. The translation of the Qur'an 14:14-

16 is from Goodman and McGregor on p. 104, note 21. The Sarra Tlili quotes are taken from her *Animals in the Qur'an* (Cambridge: Cambridge University Press, 2012), pp. ix, 253, 252, 3, x and 256.

For a translation of the al-Shanfarā's poem, see Alan Jones, *Early Arabic Poetry: Select Poems* (Reading: Ithaca Press, 2011), pp. 157-266; see also: Suzanne P. Stetkevych, *The Mute Immortals Speak: Pre-Islamic Poetry and the Poetics of Ritual* (Ithaca, NY: Cornell University Press, 1993).

On al-Jahiz, see Ch. Pellat, *The Life and Works of Jāḥiẓ* (London: Routledge and Kegan Paul, 1967), pp. 130-185; Geert Jan van Gelder, *Classical Arabic Literature: A Library of Arabic Literature Anthology* (New York: New York University Press, 2012), pp. 179-194 ('Al-Jāḥiẓ on Flies and Other Things'); James E. Montgomery, *Al-Jāḥiẓ: In Praise of Books* (Edinburgh: Edinburgh University Press, 2013); Rebecca Stott, *Darwin's Ghosts. In Search of the First Evolutionists* (London: Bloomsbury, 2012), pp. 41-60 ('The Worshipful Curioisty of Jahiz'); Saʿīd Ḥ. Manṣūr's excellent *The World-View of al-Jāḥiẓ in Kitāb al-Hayawān* (Alexandria: Dar al-Maʿaref, 1977), pp. 301-304. In this section of my article I have followed al-Jāḥiẓ's compositional practice of recycling and paraphrasing an earlier work, my Preface to *Al-Jāḥiẓ: In Praise of* Books, pp. 3-20. The quotes form al-Jahiz are from: Al-Jāḥiẓ, *Kitāb al-Hayawān*, ed. ʿAbd al-Salām Muḥammad Hārūn, (Cairo: Maṭbaʿat Muṣṭafā al-Bābī al-Ḥalabī wa-Awlādihi, 1937-1947) volume III, pp. 274-277, 228-229; and volume V, p. 286.

On J.M. Coetzee, see his *The Lives of Animals* (Princeton, NJ: Princeton University Press, 1999), *Elizabeth Costello. Eight Lessons* (London: Vintage, 2004); and *Slow Man* (London: Secker and Warburg, 2005); and Stanley Cavell et all, *Philosophy and Animal Life* (New York: Columbia University Press, 2008).

On Abū Nuwās, see *Dīwān Abī Nuwās al-Ḥasan ibn Hāniʾ*, edited by Ewald Wagner (Wiesbaden: Franz Steiner, 1972), volume II, p. 324; and J.E. Montgomery, 'Horse, Hawk and Cheetah: Three Poems of Abū Nuwās,' published in the February 2015 edition of the online journal *Cordite Poetry Review*: www.cordite.org.au.

Investigating God, Investigating Nature
by Laura Hassan

The following secondary sources are cited: Stephen Gould, 'Nonoverlapping magisteria'. *Natural history* 106, no. 2 (1997): 16-22; Toshihiko Izutsu, *God and Man in the Koran*, (Salem, N.H.: Ayer Co. Publishers, 1987): 127-8; Fazlur Rahman, *Major Themes of the Qur'an* (Chicago: University of Chicago Press, 1980; repr. 2009): 54; Josh A. Reeves, 'The field of science and religion as natural philosophy'. *Theology and Science* 6, no. 4 (2008): 411; Thomas Kuhn, *The Structure of Scientific Revolutions*, (Chicago: University of Chicago Press, 1970, 2nd edition, with postscript): 35-42; and Seyyed Hossein Nasr, 'Islam and the problem of modern science'. *Islam & Science* 8, no. 1 (2010): 72 and 63.

The theological sources cited are: 'Abd al-Raḥīm ibn Muḥammad Ibn al-Khayyāṭ, *Kitāb al-Intiṣār wa-al-radd 'alā Ibn al-Rawandī al-mulḥid*. (Cairo: Dār al-kutub al-maṣriyya, 1965): 34-36, 39, 50 and 7; 'Abd al-Jabbār ibn Aḥmad ibn 'Abd al-Jabbār al-'Asadābādī, *Sharḥ al-uṣūl al-khamsa* (Cairo: Maktaba al-wahba, 1996): 216, 224 and 92; Al-Ḥasan b. Aḥmad Ibn Mattawayh, *Al-Tadhkira fī aḥkām al-jawāhir wa-l-a'rāḍ*, ed. D. Gimaret. 2 vols. (Cairo: Inṣtitut Français d'Archéologie Orientale, 2009): vol 1: 1; Abū Rashīd al-Nīsābūrī, *al-Masā'il fī al-khilāf bayn al-baṣriyyīn wa'l-baghdādiyyīn.* (Tripoli: Ma'had al-Inmā al-'Arabī, 1979): 28; Imām al-ḥaramayn al-Juwaynī, *Al-Shāmil fī uṣūl al-dīn*, ed. A. al-Nashshar. (Alexandria: Munsha'āt al-Ma'ārif, 1969): 142-205, 455-489 and 448-450; Avicenna, *The Physics of The Healing: A Parallel English-Arabic Text*, 2 vols., trans. Jon McGinnis. (Provo, UT: Brigham Young University Press 2009): Book 6, Chapters 10-12, and *The Metaphysics of The Healing: A Parallel English-Arabic Text*, trans. Michael E. Marmura (Provo, UT: Brigham Young University Press 2004): Book 10, Chapters 1-5.

Other works have been referenced: Josef Van Ess, '60 years after: Shlomo Pines's Beiträge and half a century of research on atomism and Islamic theology'. Proceedings from the Shlomo Pines memorial lectures. Israel Academy of Sciences and Humanities, vol 8, number 2 (2002); A. I. Sabra, 'Kalam atomism as an alternative philosophy to Hellenizing Falsafa' in

James E. Montgomery, ed. *Arabic Theology, Arabic Philosophy: From the Many to the One* (Leuven: Peeters Publishers, 2006); Dimitri Gutas, 'The heritage of Avicenna: the golden age of Arabic philosophy, 1000 – ca.1350', in: J. Jansses and D. De Smet, eds. *Avicenna and His Heritage. Acts of the International Colloquium* (Leuven: Leuven University Press, 2002); Ayman Shihadeh, 'From al-Ghazālī to al-Rāzī: 6th/12th century developments in Muslim philosophical theology'. Arabic Sciences and Philosophy: a Historical Journal vol 15(1) (2005): 141–179; Heidrun Eichner, 'Dissolving the Unity of Metaphysics: from Fakhr al-Din al-Rāzī to Mullā Sadrā al-Shīrāzī'. Medioevo 32 (2007), 139–98; and John H Brooke, *Science and Religion: Some Historical Perspectives* (Cambridge: Cambridge University Press, 1991, Reprinted 2014).

Geopoetics Call by Mohammed Hashas

The quotation from Seyyed Hussein Nasr is from *Man and Nature: The Spiritual Crisis of Modern Man* (1968; London and Boston: Mandala Unwin Paperbacks, 1990) p. 18; the first citation of Taha Abderrahmane is from 'A Global Ethic: Its Scope and Limits', Abu Dhabi, Tabah Paper Series, 1: June 2008, pp. 4-27, and the second against Descartes from his *rūḥu al-ḥadātha: nahwa al-ta'sis li ḥadātha islāmiyya* [*The Spirit of Modernity: An Introduction to Founding an Islamic Modernity*] (Casablanca and Beirut: al-markaz ath-thaqāfī al-'arabī, 2006) p. 44- 45; the piece of Jasser Auda is 'COP21 is not going to work!', retrieved on 20 December 2015, at: http://www.jasserauda.net/en/read/articles/461-cop21-is-not-going-to-work.html

Kenneth White's French titles are quoted here in English, and the translations are mine. White's citations of *Le Plateau de l'albatros: introduction à la géopoétique* are from this edition (Paris: Grasset, 1994) p. 13; 11-12; 31; *Geopoetics: Place, Culture, World* (Edinburgh: Alba Editions, 2003) p. 7-8; 11; 33; 31; *The Wanderer and His Charts — Exploring the Fields of Vagrant Thought and Vagabond Beauty* (Edinburgh: Polygon, 2004) p. 232-234; 243; 245; 236-238. White's 'Pathways to an Open World,' is found in Khalid Hajji, ed., *Islam and the West — For a Better Word* (Beirut: Arab Scientific Publishers, 2007) p. 34-38. The blurbs of *Le Figaro* and *The Sunday Times* are from his book *House of Tides* (Edinburgh: Polygon, 2000); *Une Stratégie paradoxale, essais de résistance culturelle* (Bordeaux : Presses universitaires de Bordeaux, 1998) p. 210; 164-5; *On Scottish Ground – Selected Essays* (Edinburgh: Polygon, 1998) p. 33; 67; 58-59 and 173; 59; *Une Apocalypse tranquille* (Paris: Grasset, 1985) p. 31; *Open World – The Collected Poems 1960-2000* (Edinburgh: Polygon, 2003) p. xxvi; 170; 127; 156; 213. Emmanuel Dall'Aglio, *Kenneth White: du nomadisme à la géopoétique* (Centre Départemental de Documentation Pédagogique de l'EURE: n.h., 1997) p. 13. Reference to *Terre de diamond* is cited in Pierre Jamet, *Le Local et le global dans l'œuvre de Kenneth White* (Paris: L'Harmattan, 2002) p. 185; *L'Esprit nomade* (Paris: Grasset, 1987) p. 244; *La Figure du dehors* (Paris: Grasset, 1982) p. 15; *Across the Territories* (Edinburgh: Polygon, 2004). Among White's main texts on the Orient there is *Le Visage du vent d'est* (1980), *Scènes d'un monde flottant* (1983), and *The Wild Swans* (1990); it is also present in his narratives: *Les Limbes incandescent*, trad., Patrick Mayoux (1976), and *Lettres de Gourgounel,* trad., Gil et Marie Jouanard (1979).

Other quotations are from: Tony McManus, *The Radical Field: Kenneth White and Geopoetics* (Dingwall: Sandstone Press, 2007) p. 40; Olivier Delbard, *Les Lieux de Kenneth White: paysage, pensée, poétique* (Paris: L'Harmattan, 1999) p. 26 ; Michèle Duclos, ed. *Le Poète cosmographe: vers un nouvel espace culturel –* entretiens (Bordeaux: Presses Universitaires de Bordeaux, 1987) p. 19; Duclos, 'Chemins transdisciplinaire de la géopoetique,' in Laurent Margantin, ed. *Kenneth White et la géopoetique* (Paris: L'Harmattan, 2006) p. 193 ; and George Amar, 'White Seminar,' in Michèle Duclos, *Le Monde ouvert de Kenneth White* (Bordeaux : Presses Universitaires de Bordeaux, 1995) 242.

Vicegerency and Nature by Munjed M. Murad

English translations of Qur'anic verses are taken from *The Study Quran: A New Translation and Commentary*, ed. S. H. Nasr et al., (HarperOne, San Francisco, 2015).

The quotation about Pontifical Man is from Seyyed Hossein Nasr, *Knowledge and the Sacred* (State University of New York Press, Albany, 1989), 161. For literature on Nasr's perspective on the environmental crisis, see Seyyed Hossein Nasr, *Religion and the Order of Nature* (Oxford University Press, Oxford, 1996); Seyyed Hossein Nasr, *Man and Nature: The Spiritual Crisis of Modern Man* (ABC International Group, Inc., Chicago, 1997). For a thorough introduction to the topic, see Tarik M. Quadir, *Traditional Islamic Environmentalism: The Vision of Seyyed Hossein Nasr* (University Press of America, Lanham, 2013).

The translation of the *ḥadīth qudsī* of the Hidden Treasure is taken from William C. Chittick, *The Sufi Path of Knowledge: Ibn al-'Arabi's Metaphysics of Imagination* (State University of New York Press, Albany, 1989), 391, n14. I use a lesser-known version of the *ḥadīth* because it is what Ibn al-'Arabī uses in his *Futūḥāt al-makiyyah* (Meccan Openings). For a translation of the more popular version, see p. 66 of *The Sufi Path of Knowledge*. The reference to the first chapter of *The Ringstones of Wisdom* as being structured by this *ḥadīth* is taken from James W. Morris, *Divine Calling, Human Response — Scripture and Realization in The Meccan Illuminations*, Part 1 (Journal of the Muhyiddin Ibn 'Arabi Society, Vol. 53, 2013), 5, n7. Available at http://www.ibnarabisociety.org/articles/divine-calling-human-response.html (Accessed March 2, 2016).

All translations of Ibn al-'Arabī's *Fuṣuṣ al-ḥikam* are from *The Ringstones of Wisdom (Fuṣūṣ al-ḥikam)*, trans. Caner Dagli (Great Books of the Islamic World Series, Chicago, 2004) and slightly modified wherever it seemed to me appropriate. Page references are: 3 (modified), 6 (modified), 6, 14 (modified; italics are mine), 6 (modified), 3 (modified; italics are mine), 3 (italics are mine), 7, 13, 8, 14 (modified), 6, 4-5 (modified), 14 (modified), 6 (modified; italics are mine), 6 (modified), 15. Referenced pagination has been organised in order of appearance of the translations.

For more on the Latin etymological note, see E.A. Andrews, William Freund, Charlton T. Lewis, and Charles Short, *A Latin Dictionary Founded on Andrews' Edition of Freund's Latin Dictionary* (Clarendon Press, Oxford, 1969), 702.

The reference to the Perfect Human Being as 'the Face of God in His creatures' has been taken from the introduction to 'Abd Al-Karīm Al-Jīlī, *Universal Man,* extracts translated with commentary by Titus Burckhardt, and translated from the French by Angela Culme-Seymour (Beshara Publications, Roxborough, 1995). I have slightly modified the English translation.

Chittick's analysis of Jāmī's explanation, starting with 'This 'two-pronged' self-disclosure' has been taken from William C. Chittick, *In Search of the Lost Heart: Explorations in Islamic Thought,* ed. Mohammed Rustom, Atif Khalil, and Kazuyo Murata (State University of New York Press, Albany, 2012), 145. Also from the same work are Chittick's responses to 'What of the world before the arrival of humanity?' and his explanation of humanity in light of God and the world, taken from pages 151 and 149 respectively.

The quote offered in explanation of the possible interpretation of *khalīfah* as etymologically rooted in *khalafa* has been taken from Caner K. Dagli, commentary on Qur'an 2:30, in *The Study Qur'an: A New Translation and Commentary,* 21. For a Qur'anic verse on the selectiveness of vicegerency, see 24:55.

For more on the human being as the microcosm and the world as the macrocosm, as well as the concept of *al-insān al-kāmil,* see Toshihiko Izutsu, *Sufism and Taoism* (University of California Press, Berkeley and Los Angeles, 1984), 218–24, and William C. Chittick, *The Sufi Doctrine of Rūmī: Illustrated Edition* (World Wisdom, Bloomington, 2005), 49–54.

On the nature of the human being as both servant and lord, see Charles Le Gai Eaton, *Man* in *Islamic Spirituality I: Foundations,* ed. S. H. Nasr, vol. 19 of *World Spirituality: An Encyclopedic History of the Religious Quest* (The Crossroad Publishing Company, New York, 1991), 358–9.
The following is a translation of a pertinent work by Ibn 'Arabi: *The Tree of Being: An Ode to the Perfect Man* by Shaykh Tosun Bayrak al-Jerrahi al-Halveti (Archetype, Cambridge, 2005).

Palestine and (Human) Nature by Naomi Foyle

The Seventeen Principles of Environmental Justice are available at www. ejnet.org/ej/principles.html. Recent reports on the environmental impact of the Occupation can be accessed at: www.middleeastmonitor.com/ resources/fact-sheets/3541-the-environmental-impact-of-israeli-settlements-on-the-occupied-palestinian-territories, www.ps.boell.org/ en/2015/12/03/2014-war-gaza-strip-participatory environmental-impact-assessment and www.aljazeera.com/news/2015/10/water-crisis-deepens-gaza-strip-151006081548621.html. In his George Orwell Prize winning memoir *Palestinian Walks: Notes on a Vanishing Landscape* (Profile Books, 2010), Raja Shehadeh gives a personal account of the environmental destruction of the West Bank. James Lovelock and Jean Jouzel's views on global warming can be read at www.telegraph.co.uk/news/science/ science-news/10752606/We-should-give-up-trying-to-save-the-world-from-climate-change-says-James-Lovelock.html and www.alternet.org/ environment/leading-climatologist-says-its-not-too-late-solve-climate-change. In *Burning Country: Syrians in Revolution and War* (Pluto Press, London, 2016) Robin Yassin-Kassab and Leila Al-Shami give a detailed account of the development of Syria's democratic neighbourhood councils. More information on green movements within Islam, Judaism and Christianity can be found at: www.en.qantara.de/content/islamic-environmentalism-the-call-to-eco-jihad, http://www.biggreenjewish. com/home/about/ and www.operationnoah.org/articles/read-ash-wednesday-declaration/. The International Jewish Anti-Zionist Network (IJAN) campaigns for environmental justice in Israel: www.ijan.org/ category/projects-campaigns/stopthejnf/.

The short video 'Bearing Witness — Interpal's Women's Delegation to Lebanon' can be viewed at www.youtube.com/watch?v=q9_C7pUym0c. Fuller responses from my fellow convoy members Victoria Brittain and Yvonne Ridley can be read, respectively, at: www.middleeasteye.net/ columns/ixty-years-shame-palestinian-camps-lebanon-23044460 [sic]; and www.middleeastmonitor.com/.../as-in-life-so-too-in-death-there-s-no-peace-for-the-palestinians, www.middleeastmonitor.com/.../23990-are-we-on-the-verge-of-a-palestinian-exodus-to-europe, www middleeastmonitor.com/.../the-tragedy-of-ahmed-and-palestine-s-feralchildren. Insightful information on the rebuilding of Nahr El Bared camp can be found at www.opendemocracy.net/opensecurity/monika-halkort/ rebuilding-nahr-el-bared. To learn more about the life and tragic death of Vittorio Arrigoni (1975-2011), visit www.en.wikipedia.org/wiki/ Vittorio_Arrigoni. 'Four Hours in Chatila', Jean Genet's eyewitness account of the aftermath of the Sabra-Shatila massacre can be read in full at: www.radioislam.org/solus/JGchatilaEngl.html.

B'Tselem's statement on the extrajudicial killings of Palestinian youth since October is available at: www.btselem.org/press_releases/20151115 _letter_to_pm_on_extrajudicial_killings.

'My Eyes Here', Ahmad Alshyyh's short documentary on the impact of the IDF bombardments on a young blind mother in Gaza, can be viewed at www.youtube.com/watch?v=HQPuqCEzxXA.

The Palestine Museum of Natural History and The Palestine Institute of Biodiversity Research welcome volunteers and visitors; both projects can be explored online at www.palestinenature.org/. For a full bibliography of work by Mazin Qumsiyeh and to read his blog, which furnished the final quote of the essay ['Lebanon Encounter', 14.01.16], visit him at www. qumsiyeh.org and www.popular-resistance.blogspot.co.uk. *House of Stone: A Memoir of Home, Family, and a Lost Middle East* (Houghton Mifflin Harcourt, 2012) by the late Lebanese-American journalist Anthony Shadid, also invokes the pluralist Levant of the past. Marda Permaculture Farm accepts volunteers all year round; to find out more about the farm, visit www. mardafarm.com. To hear Murad Alkufash speaking about his work, watch 'Marda Permaculture Farm: Planting Seeds of Hope in the Occupied Territories' at www.youtube.com/watch?v=2H90W_O6H1s. Bill Mollison's *Permaculture: A Designers' Manual* (Tagari Publications, 1988) remains the definitive text on the subject. Ben Hattem investigated the wild boar crisis in the West Bank for Vice Magazine: http://www.vice. com/read/the-wild-boar-and-feces-epidemic-in-palestine. Background and official updates on the Boycott Divestment and Sanctions campaign can be found at the website of the Palestinian BDS National Committee: https://bdsmovement.net/.

In his eloquent and comprehensive essay 'Palestine, Postcolonialism and Pessoptimism: Palestine and Postcolonial Studies' (*Interventions*, Routledge, 2016) the late Bart Moore-Gilbert draws on a host of Palestinian, Israeli and other thinkers to persuasively critique the moribund two state solution and promote a progressive one state future for the region.

Wild in the Forest by Zeshan Akhter

On the history of Scottish forestry see, Mairi Stewart, *Voices of the Forest: A Social History of Scottish Forestry in the Twentieth Century* (John Donald Short Run Press, 2016). John Muir's thoughts on nature can be found in *The Wild Muir* by John Muir and Fiona King (Yosemite Conservancy, 2013). David Quammen's *The Song of the Dodo* is published by Ssimon and Schuster, 1997; and Elizabeth Kolbert's *The Sixth Extinction* is published Bloomsbury, London, 2014. The biodiversity quotes are from: P Leadley et al, *Biodiversity Scenarios. Projections of 21st Century Change in Biodiversity and Associated Ecosystem Services,* CBD Technical Series No 5, Secretariat of the Convention on Biological Diversity, Montreal, 2010.

'The Colonial Origins of Forestry in Britain' by K. Jan Oosthoek, 2007, can be accessed from: https://www.eh-resources.org/colonial-origins-scientific-forestry/ Useful other websites include:

Engaged Ecology: Seven Practices to Restore Our Harmony with Nature, http://www.kosmosjournal.org/article/engaged-ecology-seven-practices-to-restore-our-harmony-with-nature/
Forestry Commission: www.forestry.gov.uk/forestry/cmon-4uum6r

Forestry Commission Scotland, scotland.forestry.gov.uk/

John Muir, My First Summer in the Sierra (Boston: Houghton Mifflin, 1911)

Scottish Biodiversity Strategy: www.gov.scot/Publications/2013/06/5538

Scottish Natural Heritage, www.snh.gov.uk

Scottish Natural Heritage Commissioned Report No. 243, Review of Research into Links between Enjoyment and Understanding of the Natural Heritage www.snh.org.uk/pdfs/publications/commissioned_reports /243.pdf The Islamic Foundation for Ecology and Environmental Sciences (IFEES) www.ifees.org.uk/projects/

Go Slow by Lali Zaibun-Nisa

For various statistics on global health, see D.E. Bloom et al., *The Global Economic Burden of Noncommunicable Disease*s (World Economic Forum, Geneva, 2011); Ala Alwan et al., *Global Status Report on Noncommunicable Diseases 2010* (World Health Organisation, Geneva, 2011).

Michelle Funk et al., *Mental Health and Development: Targeting people with mental health conditions as a vulnerable group* (World Health Organisation, Geneva, 2010); and C. Naylor et al., *Long Term Conditions and Mental health – the cost of co-morbidities* (The King's Fund and Centre for Mental Health, London, 2012).

Both Richard Louv's quotations are from *The Nature Principle* (Algonquin Books, Chapel Hill, 2012), p11; and Carolyn Merchant quote is from her *The Death of Nature: Women, Ecology and the Scientific Revolution* (Harper Collins, San Francisco, 1990), p169. James Hillman's *The Soul's Code* is published by Bantam Books, New York, 1987.

Our Multiple Selves by Shanon Shah

For more information on attitudes towards sex and gender in the early modern Ottoman Empire and Qajar Iran, see Khaled El-Rouayheb. *Before Homosexuality in the Arab-Islamic World, 1500-1800*. Chicago: University of Chicago Press, 2009, Dror Ze'evi. *Producing Desire: Changing Sexual Discourses in the Ottoman Middle East, 1500-1900*. Los Angeles: University of California Press, 2006, and Afsaneh Najmabadi. *Women with Mustaches and Men without Beards: Gender and Sexual Anxieties of Iranian Modernity*. Berkeley: University of California Press, 2005.

For more on how the one-sex model was replaced by the two-sex model, see Thomas Laqueur. *Making Sex: Body and Gender from the Greeks to Freud*. London: Harvard University Press, 1990. Also see more about the five-sex model at Anne Fausto-Sterling. 'How Many Sexes Are There?' *The New York Times*, March 12, 1993, sec. Opinion. www.nytimes.com/1993/03/12/opinion/how-many-sexes-are-there.html.

A short discussion on the sexual habits of the Adélie penguins can be found at Robin McKie. '"Sexual Depravity" of Penguins That Antarctic Scientist Dared Not Reveal.' News. *The Guardian*, June 9, 2012. www.theguardian.com/world/2012/jun/09/sex-depravity-penguins-scott-antarctic.

A strong critique of Yusuf Al-Qaradawi's pronouncement on homosexuality is by Scott Kugle and Stephen Hunt. 'Masculinity, Homosexuality and the Defence of Islam: A Case Study of Yusuf Al-Qaradawi's Media Fatwa'. *Religion and Gender* 2, no. 2 (2012). Also of interest would be the chapter 'Man Becomes Woman: The Xanith as a Key to Gender Roles' in Unni Wikan. *Resonance: Beyond the Words*. Chicago: University of Chicago Press, 2012. And an exhaustive reference on LGBTQI terminology can be found at International Spectrum. 'LGBT Terms and Definitions'. *Spectrum Center, University of Michigan*, https://internationalspectrum.umich.edu/life/definitions.

For more on Cynthia Nixon's gay-by-choice comments, see Larkin, Mike, and Marissa Charles. 'Cynthia Nixon "Gay by Choice": Actress Seeks to Clarify Comments after Causing Outrage'. *Daily Mail*, January 31, 2012. http://www.dailymail.co.uk/tvshowbiz/article-2094099/Cynthia-Nixon-gay-choice-Actress-seeks-clarify-comments-causing-outrage.html and for more on bisexuality and biphobia see 'What Is Biphobia?' *The Bisexual Index*. http://www.bisexualindex.org.uk/index.php/biphobia.

On menstruation, childbirth and sexual relations among the Kaulong, see Henrietta Moore. 'The Cultural Constitution of Gender'. In *The Polity Reader in Gender Studies*, edited by Polity, 14–20. Cambridge: Polity Press, 2004.

On the influence of society on biology in relation to sex differences, see Lisa Wade. 'The New Science of Sex Difference'. *Sociology Compass* 7, no. 4 (2013): 278–93.

Islamic Gardens by Emma Clark

For more details on the principles and elements of Islamic gardens, see Emma Clark, *'Underneath Which Rivers Flow': The Symbolism of the Islamic Garden*, Prince of Wales Institute of Architecture, London, 1977.

The Seyyed Hossein Nasr quote is from an article in *Sacred Web: A Journal of Tradition and Modernity* 31, 2013; the Martin Lings quotes are from *Symbol and Archetype* (Quinta Essentia, London, 1991), p. viii; the quote from Charles Eastman is from *Living in Two Worlds, The American Indian Experience* (World Wisdom Books, Bloomington, Indiana, 2010), p. 77-78; the quote from Constance Villiers Stuart is from *Gardens of the Great Mughals* (Hardpress Publishing, New York, 2012, original, London, 1913), p.68; and, finally, the quote from Titus Burckhardt is from *Art of Islam, Language and Meaning* (World of Islam Festival Trust, London, 1976), p. 46.

See also: Vita Sackville-West, *Passenger to Teheran*, first published in 1926 and reissued by Collins and Brown, London, 1990; and Hasan Fathy, *Architecture for the Poor* (University of Chicago Press, 2000), new edition.

CONTRIBUTORS

Zeshan Akhter works for Scottish Natural Heritage ● **Rabia Barkatulla** is a freelance writer and an Arabic Language Specialist Data Executive for the British Library Digital Archive ● **Emma Clark**, a Senior Tutor on the Masters Programme at The Prince's School of Traditional Arts, London, is the author of two books on the Islamic Garden, most recently *The Art of the Islamic Garden* ● **Merryl Wyn Davies** is a writer and a documentary film maker ● **Daniel Dyer**, an author, illustrator, and publisher, is the co-director of Chickpea Press and founder member of Rumi Circle ● **Tommy Evans**, visual artist, producer and all-round polymath, is best known as a musician and spoken-word poet ● **Naomi Foyle**, a lecturer at Chichester University, is a science fiction writer ● **Mohammed Hashas**, a Postdoctoral Research Fellow in the Department of Political Science at LUISS Guido Carli University of Rome, is currently editing *Islam, State and Modernity: Mohamed Abed al-Jabri and the Future of the Arab World* ● **Laura Hassan** is focusing on her research on post-classical Ash'arī *kalām* for her PhD at the School of Oriental and African Studies, University of London ● **Jeremy Henzell-Thomas** is a Research Associate and former Visiting Fellow at the Centre of Islamic Studies, University of Cambridge ● **Aamer Hussein** is an internationally-renowned short story writer ● **Tam Hussein** is a writer and television producer ● **C. Scott Jordan** works at the Asian World Centre, Creighton University, Omaha, and is a Research Fellow of the Centre for Postnormal Policy and Futures Studies ● **James E. Montgomery** is Sir Thomas Adams's Professor of Arabic, University of Cambridge ● **Munjed M. Murad** is a doctoral student at Harvard Divinity School, with a focus on religion and nature ● **Samia Rahman** is Deputy Director of the Muslim Institute, London ● **Shanon Shah** has just obtained a PhD in Islam and sexuality from the Department of Theology and Religious Studies, King's College London ● **Paul Abdul Wadud Sutherland** is an award winning Sufi poet ● **Charles Upton** is a well-known poet and metaphysician ● **Michael Wolfe** is a writer and film producer, his books include *The Hadj: An American's Pilgrimage to Mecca* and *One Thousand Roads to Mecca* ● **Lali Zaibun-Nisa,** who works on sustainability projects, is currently writing a book about mental health and humanity's relationship to the natural world.